Fourteen Landing Zones

University of Iowa Press ᛃ Iowa City

FOURTEEN

APPROACHES TO VIETNAM WAR LITERATURE

LANDING

EDITED BY PHILIP K. JASON

ZONES

University of Iowa Press,
Iowa City 52242
Copyright © 1991 by
the University of Iowa
All rights reserved
Printed in the United States
of America
First edition, 1991

Design by Richard Hendel

Printed on acid-free paper

Library of Congress Cataloging-in-
Publication Data

Fourteen landing zones: approaches
to Vietnam war literature / edited
by Philip K. Jason.—1st ed.
    p.   cm.
  Includes bibliographical
references.
  ISBN 0-87745-314-4 (alk. paper),
ISBN 0-87745-315-2 (pbk.: alk.
paper)
  1. Vietnamese Conflict, 1961–
1975—Literature and the conflict.
2. American literature—20th century—History and criticism.
3. War stories, American—History
and criticism. 4. War poetry,
American—History and criticism.
I. Jason, Philip K., 1941– .
PS228.V5F68 1991   90-46585
810.9′358—dc20   CIP

Contents

⊃ ○ ○ ○ ○ ○ ○

Acknowledgments

○ ○ ○ ○ ○ ○ ○ ○ ○

James R. Aubrey's essay first appeared in *Conradiana* 22 (Summer 1990); Jacqueline E. Lawson's essay first appeared in the *Journal of American Culture* 12 (Fall 1989). These are reprinted with the permission of the respective journals. Each of the other essays makes its first appearance here.

Excerpts from the following poems are reprinted by permission of the authors. John Balaban's "After Our War" from *Blue Mountain* by John Balaban, published by Unicorn Press, copyright 1982 by John Balaban. D. F. Brown's "Bluto Addresses the Real," "When I Am 19 I Was a Medic," "I Was Dancing Alone in Binh Dinh Province," "Still Later There Were War Stories," and "Returning Fire" from *Returning Fire* by D. F. Brown, published by San Francisco State University Press, 1984; "The Other Half of Everything" from *Ironwood* 31/32 (1988). W. D. Ehrhart's "Time on Target," "The Invasion of Grenada," and "To Those Who Have Gone Home Tired" from *To Those Who Have Gone Home Tired* by W. D. Ehrhart, Thunder's Mouth Press, 1984; "Parade Rest" and "Why I Don't Mind Rocking Leela to Sleep" from *Winter Bells* by W. D. Ehrhart, published by Adastra Press, 1988. Stan Platke's "And Then There Were None" from *Winning Hearts and Minds* edited by Larry Rottman, Jan Barry, and Basil T. Pacquet, published by 1st Casualty Press and McGraw-Hill, 1972. Bruce Weigl's "Amnesia," "Burning Shit at An Khe," and "Monkey" from *Song of Napalm* by Bruce Weigl, published by Atlantic Monthly Press, copyright 1988 by Bruce Weigl.

Special thanks are due to the United States Naval Academy Research Council for its generous support of this project.

Introduction

○ ○ ○ ○ ○ ○ ○ ○

Philip K. Jason

There has always been a literature of war. The classical epics are among its early prototypes. In American literature, Whitman's *Drum-Taps*, Melville's *Battle-Pieces*, and Crane's *The Red Badge of Courage* form the nucleus of a significant literature of the Civil War—yet Whitman was the only major writer who put himself in some proximity to the horrors of battle. Melville was only a casual visitor, and Crane was born years after the war's close. From this beginning (though we could go back further), the war literature of American writers has been a mixture of testimony, commentary, and imaginative reconstruction. Though many more creative works about the Civil War were written, only these nineteenth-century visions of that war are read today—and Melville's just barely. The distant reconstructions of that past include Michael Shaara's Pulitzer Prize novel of 1974, *The Killer Angels*, which treats the battle of Gettysburg, and Stephen Vincent

Benét's verse narrative, *John Brown's Body*, winner of a Pulitzer in 1928.

America's best-known literary treatment of World War I is *A Farewell to Arms*, though Hemingway's service was primarily as a volunteer Red Cross ambulance driver. Somewhat less celebrated are John Dos Passos's *Three Soldiers* and E. E. Cummings's *The Enormous Room*. James Jones's *From Here to Eternity* and *The Thin Red Line* are among our classics of World War II, as are John Hersey's *A Bell for Adano, Hiroshima*, and *The Wall*. Alongside of Kurt Vonnegut's *Slaughterhouse-Five*, Irwin Shaw's *The Young Lions*, Norman Mailer's *The Naked and the Dead*, and Joseph Heller's *Catch-22* are the retrospective epic treatments by Herman Wouk (*The Winds of War* and *War and Remembrance*) as well as *The Caine Mutiny Court Martial* drama based on his earlier novel. Of more recent vintage is Marge Piercy's highly acclaimed *Gone to Soldiers* (1987). *M*A*S*H* is our major imaginative rendering of the Korean "conflict," though it is often imagined by the viewers of the television series as a work about Vietnam.

This short checklist of well-known literary responses to our earlier wars reminds us by its very brevity that the winnowing processes of popular and critical acclaim canonize only a small percentage of the imaginative works written on any subject. The rest are left to special-interest readers and scholars. How will the writings on the Vietnam War be filtered? Which will survive—and why? The critical enterprise now underway, to which the present volume is an addition, has begun to engage these questions.

Why is there such a rich literature about the Vietnam War, a war that for so many years no one wanted to hear about at all? How did that experience stir the nation and discover so many interpreters? There are no conclusive answers to such questions, though some suggestions may be offered.

In the two decades between the end of World War II and our military buildup in Vietnam, the American educational system reached out to embrace greater numbers. The proportion of young men and women who achieved a higher literacy (at the expense of a smaller elite no longer attaining the highest literacy) may account for the great number of significant literary responses to the Vietnam War.

Though we read much about the demography of the armed services during the war that describes the disproportionate sacrifice of the disadvantaged and the drop-outs, the number of enlistees (and even draftees) who had some college education was not insignificant, and the educational attainment of the young officer corps was high. Which is to say that many of those who went to Vietnam had the equipment to turn their experiences into literary documents. And many others would, upon return, gain the skills needed to shape and reshape their memories.

We should note as well that among its literary fashions the sixties ushered in a personal journalism that employed novelistic techniques. Norman Mailer's *The Armies of the Night* (1968) is a classic of this kind. Such a genre was ready-made for the memoirs of the war and for the many autobiographical novels—often memoirs in thin disguise. (Ironically, Mailer's *The Naked and the Dead*, published twenty years earlier, is a model for most of the "old-fashioned" realistic-naturalistic combat narratives of Vietnam. Mailer's own treatment of this war is trendily oblique; his 1967 *Why Are We in Vietnam* is a grotesque stateside adventure in macho bloodletting, thus, a study in American character.) The related genre of the nonfiction novel—Truman Capote's *In Cold Blood* (1966) and William Styron's *The Confessions of Nat Turner* (1967)—also influenced the literary climate in which the first writings about the Vietnam War were nourished. And one can hardly imagine the stylistic hijinks of Michael Herr's *Dispatches* without the earlier work of Tom Wolfe.

Aside from anything one might say about the magnitude of cultural upheaval caused by the war, the circumstances of literacy and literature in the United States during the war years help explain the great numbers of writings and the generic outlines of this body of work—a corpus that began to gain momentum in the late seventies and a decade later became a significant facet of American publishing. The growing commercial viability of Vietnam fiction allowed early works like Ward Just's *Stringer* (1974) to be brought out ten years later in paperback and introduced a new generation of readers to Graham Greene's classic, *The Quiet American* (1955).

In fact, many bookstores have "Vietnam" shelves. The "Vietnam: Ground Zero" series by Eric Helm, now approaching twenty titles (including *The Raid, Incident at Plei Soi, Cambodian Sanctuary*, and *Payback*), is representative of the mass-market success of Vietnam material. The developing "Wings over Nam" series by Cat Branigan lengthens the bandwagon. Indeed, every paperback house has its Vietnam titles, both fiction and nonfiction, both serious and escapist. There are even a couple of bookstores dedicated exclusively to Vietnam War publications, and a few college libraries have undertaken special collections of Vietnam material. New Vietnam-related works keep tumbling onto the bookstore shelves. In 1989, Lucian K. Truscott IV's *Army Blue*, John Amos's *The Medallion*, and Franklin Allen Leib's *The Fire Dream* were among the most conspicuous, while 1990 has brought Tim O'Brien's *The Things They Carried* and Gustav Hasford's *The Phantom Blooper*.

Of course, given the economics of publishing, it is easier to find a copy of James Webb's *Fields of Fire* than John Balaban's Lamont Prize poetry collection, *After Our War*. The same concern for the ledger that led Avon Books to drop W. D. Ehrhart's excellent poetry anthology, *Carrying the Darkness* (since reissued by Texas Tech Press), led Zebra Books to bring out a mass-market edition of his memoir, *Vietnam-Perkasie*, first published by a small press in North Carolina. Many titles receive a second life as they become the basis for films. Ron Kovic's *Born on the Fourth of July* is a recent (and worthy) beneficiary of this marketing system. And who can tell what motivated the Bantam hardback publication of Steve Mason's *Johnny's Song*, a collection of mediocre poems wrapped in the flag and destined for coffee tables?

A number of works about the war have earned and gained recognition, most notably Robert Stone's *Dog Soldiers*, Tim O'Brien's *Going after Cacciato*, Gloria Emerson's *Winners and Losers*, Larry Heinemann's *Paco's Story*, and Neil Sheehan's *A Bright Shining Lie*—all winners of National Book Awards. Pulitzer Prizes have been awarded to Sheehan's book and also to Frances FitzGerald's *Fire in the Lake*.

The battle among scholars and politicians who have tried to explain this war is a battle for our collective memory—for the "truth" that future generations will share about the reasons for, conduct of, and outcome of this conflict. Our novelists, playwrights, and poets are significant players in this engagement—few, if any, are above a political or moral vision, and many works are overtly propagandistic.

Certainly, the fact that the war was "witnessed" by the American public on television and, however tentatively, in movies does not escape the notice of the literary and dramatic artists who approach it. The constant allusions to John Wayne movies in Gustav Hasford's *The Short-Timers* and elsewhere, the Ozzie and Harriet game played by David Rabe in *Sticks and Bones* in which the television doesn't work and David's movie can't be seen, the concern with photographic and cinematic images in Stephen Wright's *Meditations in Green*, Emmett's obsession with "M*A*S*H" reruns in Bobbie Ann Mason's *In Country*, and Sgt. Krummel's comment in James Crumley's *One to Count Cadence* that the maimed Vietcong "flipped out of the tree like a Hollywood stunt man" (282) all remind us of the different planes of perception, intersecting and overlaying, through which the truths of the war are offered us. Indeed, some of the most significant literary art is reportage (Jonathan Schell's *The Real War* and Gloria Emerson's *Winners and Losers* come immediately to mind), and some of that is fundamentally concerned with the act of reporting, of representing, the war to the public. Thus, works like Michael Herr's *Dispatches* are, at one level, about the limits of perception and representation.

The works that will last, one must suppose, will be those that transcend the representation of a particular arena of military engagement. The more provocative stories that unfold in the literature of the Vietnam War are not simply or finally stories of armed conflict in a distant land. They are stories about American society as it evolved through the sixties and seventies. They are understandings, and sometimes underminings, of American myths. Many of the critical responses that follow are alert to the ways in which the literature confronts the myths of American innocence, American invulnerability, and American righteousness. In particular, Maria S. Bonn's "A Different World: The Vietnam Veteran Novel Comes Home" addresses the lost myth of an American homeland that could be depended on to nurture its returning soldiers.

Writing about the early collection of Vietnam War fiction, *Free Fire Zone* (1973), Jerry Griswold observed, "These writers have ceased to believe in the myth of an imperfectible America, and their stories are meant to make uncomfortable the complacent who do believe in it." He went on to note that these writers "can't be comfortable in their disbelief either" (540). The myth of a fair-minded, egalitarian America is threatened by literary reflections of an American society that tolerated and even fostered racism and sexism. Jacqueline E. Lawson's "'She's a Pretty Woman . . . for a Gook': The Misogyny of the Vietnam War" uncovers the tragedy of a sexist America in the memoirs of Vietnam War veterans. Though Lawson does not here treat the imaginative literature of the war, her approach is one that can be applied to a significant portion of the poetry, drama, and fiction. Katherine Kinney's "'Humping the Boonies': Sex, Combat, and the Female in Bobbie Ann Mason's *In Country*" provides a specific application of feminist reading that complements Lawson's overview. These essays are evidence of how much the feminist consciousness has to tell us about who we are.

The dominant literature of the war—whether autobiography or fiction, whether by veteran or not—is cast in the dominant genre of prose narrative. Lorrie Smith and Don Ringnalda question the effectiveness of narrative to contain or release the Vietnam experience. Smith's "Resistance and Revision in Poetry by Vietnam War Veterans" argues that lyric utterance best serves the social and personal purposes of the veteran writer. Ringnalda, in "Doing It Wrong Is Getting It Right: America's Vietnam War Drama," looks closely at the limits of the master narrative and maintains that the oblique approaches of the dramatists have been more significantly expressive of this war's central traits. Both essays survey the vision and technical invention of major voices in the maverick genres.

Does war narrative have its own traditions that are passed on from one generation of writers to the next? John Clark Pratt makes one set of connections in "Yossarian's Legacy: *Catch-22* and the Vietnam War," along the way defining a significant subgenre. Pratt's own novel, with its peculiar mixture of private, generic, and more broadly literary allusions, is the subject of James R. Aubrey's "Conradian Darkness in John Clark Pratt's *The Laotian Fragments*." Owen W. Gilman, Jr., in "Vietnam and John Winthrop's Vision of Community," asks which species of narrative is likely to have the most profound impact. He makes a case for the "typological" narrative, finding in the Puritan vision of Winthrop an unexpected but instructive model.

The Vietnam conflict happened over there, but it happened here as well. Many fought against the war, and many who fought in it also fought with themselves. These are the concerns of Jacqueline R. Smetak's "The (Hidden) Antiwar Activist in Vietnam War Fiction." Many veterans carried the war home, and all citizens lived in the shadows of its stateside reverberations. Matthew C. Stewart underscores the former situation in "Realism, Verisimilitude, and the Depiction of Vietnam Veterans in *In Country*." Stuart Ching, in "'A Hard Story to Tell': The Vietnam War in Joan Didion's *Democracy*," examines one literary work that illustrates the latter perspective. While this war was an American moment in Asia, it was first of all an Asian ordeal. In his "Darkness in the East: The Vietnam Novels of Takeshi Kaiko," an analysis of works by an important Japanese writer, Mark A. Heberle drives this realization home.

The human capacity for violence is nothing new, though the actors and victims change. What seems different in the literature of the Vietnam War is how directly and minutely atrocities are described and how conscious the writer (witness or perpetrator) is of the horror and of the moral implications of the event and of its record in language. In his "Line of Departure: The Atrocity in Vietnam War Literature," Cornelius A. Cronin demonstrates this awareness by contrasting Vietnam War narratives with a representative narrative of World War II. Kali Tal, on the other hand, doubts that traditional literary criticism can meaningfully explore what our traumatized participant-writers have created. In "Speaking the Language of Pain: Vietnam War Literature in the Context of a Literature of Trauma," Tal argues the limits of critical approaches that tend to the unraveling of metaphor. Insisting that the writings of veterans and those of nonveterans comprise radically separate categories, she begins the task of finding a new approach by linking the literature of Vietnam veterans to that of other survivor literatures, particularly the literature of the Holocaust and the literature of sexual abuse.

Along with the representative works treated in these essays are scores of others deserving of attention. The list, which I won't attempt to give, contains enormous variety. It includes David A. Willson's *REMF Diary*, a comic portrait of rear echelon service; Wayne Karlin's

Lost Armies, a haunting psychological thriller of the war's long aftermath of suffering; and the lyrical sequence *Fatal Light* by Richard
Currey (all 1988).

Though battlefield stories still dominate the body of Vietnam War
literature and thus the attention of critics, it is clear that the focus of
Vietnam War criticism is shifting as that of the literature itself has
shifted. The shift, among writers who were veterans of the war, follows their own experience from the war they fought to the war they
took home. Among both veteran and nonveteran writers, one movement is to a vision of larger perspective: works that integrate the
Vietnam War into a reading of the larger American story. Susan
Fromberg Schaeffer's novel, *Buffalo Afternoon* (1989), is one such effort. Walter MacDonald's collection of poems, *After the Fall of Saigon*
(1988), is another.

The history of criticism on Vietnam War literature is, of course, not
a very long one. The key titles are James C. Wilson's *Vietnam in Prose
and Film* (1982), Philip Beidler's *American Literature and the Experience of Vietnam* (1982), John Newman's annotated bibliography of
Vietnam War Literature (1982; 2d ed. 1988), John Hellmann's *American Myth and the Legacy of Vietnam* (1986), Timothy J. Lomperis's
"Reading the Wind": The Literature of the Vietnam War (1987), Thomas Myers's *Walking Point: American Narratives of Vietnam* (1988),
Susan Jeffords's *The Remasculinization of America: Gender and the
Vietnam War* (1989), and Sandra M. Wittman's *Writing about Viet-
nam: A Bibliography of the Literature of the Vietnam Conflict* (1989).
These titles, referred to by many of the essayists in the present collec-
tion, are only the beginning of what promises to be a provocative en-
gagement with the literature, with history itself, and with method-
ological problems. Collections of critical essays edited by William J.
Searle (*Search and Clear*, 1988), Jeffrey Walsh and James Aulich
(*Vietnam Images: War and Representation*, 1989), Stephen H. Knox
(*Vietnam Studies*, 1990), and Owen W. Gilman, Jr., and Lorrie Smith
(*America Rediscovered*, 1990) preceded the present volume.

This scholarship is serving the great interest in Vietnam studies of
all kinds that are proliferating at American colleges and universities.
That interest comes, in part, from the curiosity of those born about
1970 who are now in college, which is to say old enough to be fighting

in a war. The eighteen-year-olds who lived through the Tet Offensive are now entering middle age. The cadre of young officers (some of whom became authors) was four or five years older. They, and the larger group who came to majority during the 1965 to 1975 period, are the Vietnam Generation. *Vietnam Generation*, a quarterly journal, has become the major clearinghouse for interdisciplinary studies on the war's centrality to contemporary American culture. The first general anthology for classroom use, Nancy Anisfield's *Vietnam Anthology: American War Literature*, appeared in 1987. Robert M. Slabey's *America in Vietnam/Vietnam in America: Reading and Teaching the Vietnam War* was planned for release in 1990.

The academics' debate over how the war should be taught, which works should be canonical in Vietnam studies, and which works will find a place in the canon of American literature is obviously connected to the struggle for the national memory. While the discussion is often heated, few new fields of study have engaged so many scholars in cooperative endeavors. Unfortunately, there has been little encouragement from the most powerful professional organizations; scholars proposing panels for Modern Language Association meetings have experienced only limited success. The annual combined meeting of the American Culture Association and Popular Culture Association has become the major forum for scholarly discussion in this area, and many of the articles in this collection (as in those mentioned above) originated as papers delivered at ACA/PCA meetings.

For all of the activity in Vietnam War studies, more work needs to be done to discover and assess literature that provides both perspectives on the Vietnamese and Vietnamese perspectives. Literary representations of the Vietnamese range from racist slurs to outright admiration of these people as a skilled and valiant enemy to total disrespect for a seemingly inept ally. These valuations tend to be collective: generic. Few Vietnamese are seen up close. Typical figures are Kit Carson scouts (Vietcong turncoats working with American military units) and prostitutes. Among the few works that provide rich treatments of Vietnamese characters is David Halberstam's *One Very Hot Day* (1968). And, of course, we have yet to pay much attention to Vietnamese accounts of the war.

In the September/October 1989 issue of *Poets & Writers Magazine*,

Wendy Larsen, coauthor of *Shallow Graves: Two Women and Vietnam* (1986), took out an ad in which she announced that the title was out of print. She offered signed hardcover copies for ten dollars. A critical success (and even issued in paperback), this book told Americans more than we wanted to know about noncombatant life and about Vietnamese culture. It revealed, beyond Larsen's own experience in Vietnam, the outlook and life story of a Vietnamese woman, Tran Thi Nga, whom Larsen employed and then befriended. While critics rightly complain that the Vietnamese are largely missing from this body of literature, not many readers are prepared to accept their most significant appearances.

As a field of special study, the appraisal of war literature has had sporadic growth. Indeed, fields of literary study centered on the *subject matter* of the literature tend to be considered as marginal, transient, suspect endeavors. While literary criticism becomes more and more concerned with theory and methodology, the questions about what literary works *express* receive less and less attention and little respect. Scholars who are concerned with myth, paradigm, and genre are making valuable contributions to our understanding of Vietnam War literature. Indeed, the essays here make that apparent. Yet often these and other approaches seem designed to dignify a pursuit by mainstreaming it into an appropriately rarified critical channel. Some critics seem a bit nervous about the "humanities" approach to literature, which asks us to find in our study of artworks keys to understanding the human condition. Certainly it is what the literature of war tells us (*shows* us) that claims our attention and concern. Each of the essays in this collection shares that assumption.

Douglas Wapniak, the overeducated sergeant in Susan Fromberg Schaeffer's *Buffalo Afternoon*, is constantly asking questions, theorizing, and jotting things down in his notebook. An oddball to those around him, Wapniak has a sense of history. To all the other men, their LT is just "Lieutenant," but Wapniak wants to know his full name. When asked why, Wapniak replies:

"Some day this war's going to be important. People are going to study this war. Right now there might be complaints about it, but people are looking at it. This war won't go away. When people come back to look at it, when they see how important it was, what significance it had, they're going to want to know *names*. They're going to want to know who made it possible, because, believe me, Lieutenant, there's meaning in this war. Mankind's never going to be the same after this war. I don't know what it means yet. Nobody does, but it means something. We ought to sit down and talk about this. I've given it a lot of thought." (221–222)

With hindsight, Schaeffer has made her character prophetic. She has also anticipated the argument against her ambition. A man like Douglas Wapniak is prepared to test the authenticity of Vietnam War narratives. Is a nonparticipant and nonobserver, like Schaeffer, prepared to write one? Of what value, and to whom, is the test of authenticity? Is Lt. Howard Hollingshead's name the issue, or is it the "something" that the war means? If the latter, then we have to look for this meaning together in the recollections of the grunt and in the visions and insights of all those writers and thinkers who have dedicated their talents to the search.

During the Vietnam War, an LZ or landing zone was an area designated for helicopter set-downs to insert troops near suspected enemy forces. Often a small clearing in the jungle, the LZ—meant to be secure enough for the immediate purpose—was often vulnerable as the noise of the propellers signaled arrival. From the LZ, squads would fan out to accomplish their mission of interdiction or intelligence gathering. Each zone marked a stage of approach toward a defined objective. From these clearings, trails were discovered—or created—and followed cautiously to uncertain destinations.

WORKS CITED

Crumley, James. *One to Count Cadence*. 1969. New York: Vintage, 1987.
Griswold, Jerry. "Truth Is the First Casualty." *The Nation*, Nov. 19, 1973, 539–540.
Schaeffer, Susan Fromberg. *Buffalo Afternoon*. New York: Knopf, 1989.

Fourteen Landing Zones

A Different World

The Vietnam Veteran Novel

Comes Home

○ ○ ○ ○ ○ ○ ○ ○ ○ ○

Maria S. Bonn

In a letter included in Bob Greene's book, *Homecoming*, one veteran writes of his dislike of war movies and claims that the only good war film is *The Best Years of Our Lives*. When viewed in the post–Vietnam War era this film demonstrates a peculiar blend of shrewdness and naivete. Made by William Wyler in 1946, its shrewdness lies in its recognition that the world of the returning soldier is not all parades and kisses in Times Square—and it is undoubtedly this shrewdness that Bob Greene's correspondent is applauding. On the other hand, the film promises that, through love and understanding, veterans will be able to successfully reincorporate themselves into civilian life—a promise often unfulfilled for the Vietnam veteran.

The film follows three World War II veterans through their first several months back in their hometown of Boone City. It is an honest and foresightful treatment of the difficulties that these men find in readjusting to peacetime life. Although these soldiers do not return to a bright world, they do find a world where the darkness can still be chased away. The home fires, carefully and lovingly tended by several good women, can still penetrate the shadows cast by years of separation and war. Healing is still possible here—a healing that is private and familial. *The Best Years of Our Lives* works at contradicting the popular image of the returning hero's easy and successful assimilation into civilian life. At the same time it perpetuates an alternative image of the power of love to bring about that assimilation. Each of our heroes must assume the role of father, son, and husband. Only when they have successfully resolved their familial and romantic roles can they achieve readjustment.

The veterans returning from the Vietnam War in many ways underwent the difficulties represented in *The Best Years of Our Lives*, difficulties that have also begun to be represented in the literature of the Vietnam War. Veteran-authors Larry Heinemann and Philip Caputo have both written novels that represent the problems involved in the Vietnam veterans' attempts to reincorporate themselves into society. The protagonists of *Close Quarters*, *Paco's Story*, and *Indian Country* each confront a United States in which the mythic imagination of familial and patriotic love is no longer adequate for defining and confronting the war experience. Each of these three novels posits a different alternative for the veterans' responses to this shattering of their conception of their home society.

William J. Searle, in his essay "Walking Wounded: Vietnam War Novels of Return" succinctly summarizes many of the problems encountered by the Vietnam veteran. Searle reveals the prominence of the "sick vet" image in the press and entertainment media, a revelation that leads him to point out:

> Ambushed at home, returning combat soldiers, reminders of "dishonor and embarrassment" (Figley and Leventman xxviii), feared hostility and blame from their peers who did not fight in an "immoral" war and also suffered from lack of respect by veterans of earlier wars who blamed them for not winning a war against a military inferior. Norma Wikler notes that "never before had Americans returned so quietly and so unwelcomed" (103). While

many returning soldiers began to fear and even dislike civilians, many civilians in turn feared and disliked them as threats to domestic tranquility. (148)[1]

Lately there has been much discussion about our failure, as a country and as a culture, to do well by the Vietnam veteran. What is lacking from these discussions, and what we also need to understand, are the kinds of expectations that the veterans had of their return and the strategies of those soldiers for confronting the disappointment of those expectations. John Hellmann, in *American Myth and the Legacy of Vietnam*, ably illuminates the American "sense of mission" (Hellmann's phrase), its connection with the national myth of the frontier, and the role that myth played in American perceptions of Vietnam. He points out that "the prototypical myth features stalwart frontiersmen, entering the vast wilderness alone or in small bands, who draw on the virtues of nature while battling its savage denizens in order to make way for a settlement of yeomen farmers" (8). This myth, coupled with the sense that the United States was divinely appointed to spread and protect democracy, created an imaginative space which Vietnam could occupy in the American consciousness. Hellmann goes on to note that the popular myth was so powerful that "America had been able to hold on to the ideal of the 'middle landscape' of Jefferson's agrarian ideal and Franklin's small-businessman virtues long after the reality of technological progress had transformed America into a largely industrial landscape" (34). Hellmann is extremely persuasive in arguing the ability of the frontier myth to propel the United States and its soldiers into Southeast Asia. He is less concerned with showing the effects of this mythic vision of America upon the combat soldiers who become the frontiersmen of the Vietnam War. Indeed it has become almost a commonplace in the criticism of Vietnam War literature to assert that the movement into Vietnam was an extension of the frontier ideology. But we must also reckon with the power of the mythic space behind the frontier—the home that is left behind and that the soldier is fighting to bring forward. And it is that mythic space which shapes the veterans' expectations of their return from Vietnam.

Coming back from the time warp of the one-year tour of duty in Vietnam, many veterans discovered that the place they had looked to as home was a country only of the heart. Throughout the narratives of the Vietnam War—the fiction, the nonfiction, the letters—we find a collection of images of home that assumes mythic proportions. An American mythology of democracy and protection was at least part of the reason American soldiers were in Vietnam, and it is a kind of American mythology that comforts them in that alien country. The images of home that emerge from this literature are seen through a soft, golden filter and are a nostalgic representation of a rich and fertile land populated by close families and wonderful women.

In Tim O'Brien's celebrated Vietnam novel, *Going after Cacciato*, the protagonist—Paul Berlin—dreams of going home, a dream represented by a collection of images of an archetypal America:

> He would go home to Fort Dodge. He would. He would go home on a train, slowly, looking at the country as it passed, recognizing things, seeing how the country flattened and turned to corn, the silos painted white, and he would pay attention to details. At the depot, when the train stopped, he would brush off his uniform and be certain all the medals were in place, and he would step off boldly, boldly, and he would shake his father's hand and look him in the eye. "I did okay," he would say. "I won some medals." And his father would nod. And later, the next day perhaps, they would go out to where his father was building houses in the development west of town, and they'd walk through the unfinished rooms and his father would explain what would be where, how the wiring was arranged, the difficulties with the subcontractors and the plumbers, but how the houses would be strong and lasting, how it would take good materials and craftsmanship and care to build houses that would be strong and lasting. (68)

Paul's dream of returning home comforts him by promising a triumphant homecoming, but even more than that it confirms that Paul has been at war for a country worth fighting for. The United States that is represented by the cornfields, his father, and his father's buildings is a fertile, nurturing, and sheltering country.

In the letters home from Vietnam collected in Bernard Edelman's *Dear America* we also have a record of the kinds of pictures of home that soldiers created while stationed in Vietnam. One writer speaks longingly of his wife and children, "the smell of cut grass, the wind blowing over the lake and making the trees and grasses sway" (60). Another soldier writes to his mother of his desire to be with her, to eat roast beef, corn on the cob, mashed potatoes, and (he goes on to say) to "bow my head for the blessing, and look up and see my mother—pretty and smiling—searching for any way she can to make her son comfortable" (136). Yet another speaks of his need for his family and of his longing to be traveling and exploring the Pacific coast with them and then continues, "Letters from home are like Bibles: they tell of tales so distant from this reality that they demand a faith before one can actually believe them. Is there really such a beautiful place, and such a good life on that distant island, or is it a memory based on some childhood myth I was awed into believing?" (6).

The questions that this letter writer asks are incisive. They recognize that the picture of home the writer creates may be based more upon a mythic vision of what home should be than upon any actual experience of what home is. These idyllic memories of home center upon two important aspects of the popular myth—the individual's relationship to the family and to the land. Isolated in the hostile environment of Vietnam, where the very countryside around them seemed to be allied with the enemy, American soldiers found themselves dreaming of a loving family and a hospitable landscape. And when the veterans returned home they often found that those dreams did not correspond to any reality.

This disjunction is explored in Larry Heinemann's first novel, *Close Quarters*. Philip Dosier, the novel's central figure, has nearly mythic memories of home that are similar to those in the letters quoted above. His memories are particularly tied to his family and to his girlfriend, Jenny. In his first miserable days in country, he dwells on his recollections of going to a carnival with his father and of playing in the snow with his brothers, making dreamlike snow angels. Later on his memories center on Jenny "and her fine brown hair; whose skin smelled of Caswell Massey soap and borrowed perfume . . . who liked farm work because it was clean and honest work; who was just the right height in bare feet to dance with, and who loved to polka best of all" (185). Jenny's fondness for farm work connects the love of the woman and the love of the land for Philip. He also recalls their first love-making session, where again Jenny and the landscape around her merge into idyllic memory: "It rained at dusk, and we huddled under the crumbling eaves of the orchard shed, watching the May rain among the apple trees—the trees crowded thickly with white and pink blossoms" (186).

Philip Dosier's pleasant memories anticipate a homecoming that is actually uneasy and difficult. He finds himself unable to bear being with the family he loves. When he settles down to sleep in the bed he has longed for, he enters a nightmare world. Philip finds that he can only rest, covered by one thin blanket, on the floor. But *Close Quarters* ends on a note of some hope, a hope provided by the same strategies as those offered in *The Best Years of Our Lives*. Through love and the restitution of the familial order, Philip finds a means of reintegration. He achieves this by the development of two family relationships. First, he marries Jenny, a paragon of virtue who provides him with all the love, understanding, and fidelity that he needs. Second, he becomes a surrogate son to the parents of Quinn, his dead war buddy.

For much of the novel Quinn has served as a double for Philip; Quinn undergoes the same dehumanization and same increasing brutality and pushes that brutality into an even greater violence than Philip can express. Philip rotates out earlier than Quinn, and Quinn dies. We suspect that Quinn must die in order for Philip to begin to be free of the dark side of his self that Vietnam has brought to the surface, but Philip must also assume a sense of responsibility for the death that liberates him. He does this by visiting Quinn's parents and becoming intimate with them over the course of several years. By replacing Quinn as the son-returned-from-Vietnam, Philip reconstitutes the family and initiates his recovery.

But it must be stressed that the recovery is only partial and is equivocal. The motives for Philip's marriage to Jenny are somewhat dubious: "The first chance we had Jenny and I got married—me because I could not stand sleeping alone anymore; she because she did not know how else to help" (330). Furthermore, the novel does not end on an up beat; in the last line of the book Philip tells us of how he stood by Quinn's grave and "drew my hands out in the cold, making fists and letting go. 'Goddamn you Quinn'" (335). The power of love, which could conquer all in a 1946 film, here seems to help—but whether it can heal is still an open question.

In contrast to this at least partial recovery by means of the tried and true aegis of love, Heinemann's next novel presents a world in which there is no way to rediscover a governing sense of meaning for the returning veteran. Paco Sullivan, the protagonist of *Paco's Story* and sole survivor of a massacre at Fire Base Harriette, returns to the United States to wander through a world without familial or social connection. Like the veterans of *The Best Years of Our Lives*, Paco returns to Boone (a name no doubt chosen for its quality of Anywhere, USA), but this Boone has none of the possibilities that consoled the heroes of the film. Like Paco himself this world is physically and psychologically fragmented, shattered and fast falling apart.

The elements of love and family, which at least began Philip Dosier's reintegration into society, are striking here in their absence. There is no mention of Paco's family throughout the entire novel. Ernest Monroe, the diner owner who gives Paco work, has no family. Mr. Elliot, a local Russian immigrant, can communicate only with a dead wife. Betsy, who almost befriends Paco, lives alone on her parents' estate while the parents cruise around the world. There is one family, made up of the owners of Paco's boarding house, Earl and Myrna, and their niece Cathy, but Myrna's suspicion about Cathy's sex life comprises our entire view of family interaction.

Romantic love fares no better in *Paco's Story*. The narrative voice tells us that Paco has talked and slept with several women since returning home, but the talk seems valueless because the women only listen as a prerequisite to getting Paco into bed so they can look at his scars. Paco and Betsy have a near miss, when they both consider becoming lovers, but they never act upon this. Other than that there are three episodes in which Paco interacts with women: the brutal rape of a VC girl, the playing of a sadistic and futile sexual game with Cathy, and—the only successful sexual encounter—an absolutely anonymous episode where a nameless nurse stimulates Paco to orgasm in his hospital bed.

Although the chances for family and romantic love are bleak, the possibility for Paco to develop a redemptive connection with the land at first appears plausible. Chapter 4, "Paco Coming into Town," contains a long, rhapsodic description of the river that Paco crosses as he walks into Boone. But a closer look reveals that even if the river has a certain beauty, it is certainly not part of any agrarian ideal. The description of the river is inseparably linked with the bridge that crosses it—and that bridge is described in strictly mechanical and industrial terms. Paco views the river as it spills over a rock-and-concrete dam; a rainbow appears only to disappear into the ironwork of the underside of the bridge; even the sweet smell of rain is linked with the odor of well-soaked asphalt. The notion of any tie to the land for Paco is further refuted when he looks at the help-wanted advertisements and does not acknowledge the advertisement for work on a dairy farm, even though he has said earlier that he will do anything.

We are told all this by a narrator who speaks in the first person plural and who represents either the collective ghosts of the Harriette massacre (the identity that the voice asserts) or perhaps Paco's own projected conscience. The hallmark of this narrative voice is the recitation of lists. Everywhere in the book there are long and detailed lists. There is a two-page list of the passengers on the bus that brings Paco to Boone that reads like a litany of the disenfranchised. There is an exhaustive inventory of the contents of the Texas Lunch. The narrative voice enumerates the kinds of customers at a roadhouse and the kinds of restaurant menus. The last chapter, "Paco the Sneak," records all the different booby traps that Paco set in Vietnam.

These lists are all characterized by a lack of any organizational pattern. They are an attempt to hold together a fragmented world, but all the narrative voice can do is list the parts, not re-form them into any cohesive whole. The only episode in which these fractured parts are given an order is in the six-page detailing of Paco's dishwashing routine at the back sink of the Texas Lunch. This is the one point where Paco's life seems to be forming into an ordered existence. He has a job, a place to live, a good relationship with Ernest, and what seems like a harmless flirtation with Cathy. But this brief period is only a momentary stay against the chaos of Paco's life, and the rigid routine at the sink, like all the other lists, is presented as merely a failed attempt at holding off disintegration.

Paco himself remains a cipher throughout the book. We never learn how he responds to the horrors of his Vietnam experience or to the difficulties of his return, beyond what he says to another drifting vet, who asks him if he is bitter: "I've spent many a night brooding about that, rolling that around in my mouth, so to say, and yeah, I expect I'm as bitter as can be, more than tongue can tell most likely. But I'll tell you something else: I'm just glad to be here—isn't that what Thurman Munson says?" (163). But even here in his one confessional moment Paco does not truly express himself; instead he falls back upon another's cliché to voice his feelings. This encounter with another returned soldier is Paco's one real attempt to form a bond, but the attempt fails after their conversation in the Texas Lunch. Paco asks the drifter to stay around and talk more, but the vet replies he is moving on. For the most part Paco moves in and out of Boone as if he were never really there; he is a fragmented man in a fragmented world, adrift without connections and without the ability to make them.

Larry Heinemann's novels are flip sides of a coin. In *Close Quarters* we have a story of partial reintegration through a traditional mythos of romantic and familial love, while *Paco's Story* is a tale of ongoing disintegration in a world where there is an absence of any sort of governing mythology. In Philip Caputo's *Indian Country* we see a Vietnam veteran-protagonist working from disintegration to reintegration through the acceptance and creation of an alternative American mythology.

Indian Country opens with a long section about Chris Starkmann's childhood, his relationship to his father, and his close friendship with Boniface George St. Germaine (known as Bonnie George) which impels him to go to Vietnam. When the narrative present begins in part 2, Chris has been back from the war for over a decade and is in the process of becoming increasingly debilitated by the effects of post-traumatic stress disorder; he is paranoid, his natural reticence is turning into acute withdrawal, he is increasingly violent, and he is beginning to suffer from flashbacks. Through Chris's memories we learn of his initial homecoming from Vietnam and his inability to reestablish any meaningful ties with his family or community. He is unable to talk to his parents, he does not go to his own homecoming party, and he feels out of place at the college he attends for one semester. His Vietnam veteran status hurts his chances of getting a job in an already poor economy, and, as his uneasiness with mainstream American life increases, he decides to head for the remoteness and desolation of Michigan's Upper Peninsula, where he spent the summers of his childhood.

At the beginning of this section of the novel Chris has already tried the methods of readjustment that worked so well in *The Best Years of Our Lives* and worked partially in *Close Quarters*. He has married a strong, patient, and loving woman. He has become a father. But rather than the love of a good woman chasing away the effects of Vietnam, we see the effects of Vietnam beginning to chase away the good woman. The marriage has failed to reincorporate Chris into peacetime life, and now the marriage is falling apart.

Chris has also tried to relieve his uneasy psychological state by forming a close connection with the land. He has moved to the Upper Peninsula, bought forty acres of land, and now works for a logging company where one of his primary objectives is to save as many trees as possible. But this too is unsuccessful. His treasured plan to set up a nature preserve through his work fails, and since he is unable to save any trees he becomes just another part of a machine to rape the forest. He is also unable to divorce his relationship to the land from his Vietnam experience; he sets about turning his home and property into an armed fortress.

This unsuccessful relationship to the land mirrors Chris's unsuccessful relationship with his wife, June. Chris's choice of wife is reminiscent of Jenny in Heinemann's *Close Quarters* because June, like Jenny, has an intimate, sensual connection with the land. This connection is more explicitly spelled out than in Heinemann's book; the broad-hipped, generously proportioned June becomes an archetypal earth mother. As her marriage to Chris degenerates she becomes increasingly involved with the planting and nurturing of her garden, an involvement that reaches its apex when, in a sort of homegrown fertilization rite, she strips naked and masturbates in the freshly tilled soil of the garden. As Chris becomes increasingly impotent in his efforts to save the forest he loves he also becomes sexually impotent, without the ability or the desire to make love to his wife. He becomes complicit in the rape of the land and then almost destroys his marriage by forcefully sodomizing June—an act that takes place as a brutal storm destroys June's garden. This anal rape denies June's humanity and her potential to reconnect Chris to the land and to society.

Part of Chris's inability to maintain a successful marriage and to take control of his life is caused by his unresolved and angry relationship with his minister father, a strident peace activist who never forgave his son for enlisting for Vietnam. Thus we might at first assume that Chris remains a renegade from society because he has only accepted the responsibilities of husband and father and still needs to work through his role as son. Chris realizes his love for his father and his need for family reconciliation about halfway through the novel, but his father dies before Chris can speak with him, thus exacerbating Chris's psychological problems rather than mitigating them. Chris must then find other means for achieving reintegration.

Like Philip Dosier of *Close Quarters*, Chris finds these means by becoming a surrogate son who takes the place of a dead friend. Chris is literally responsible for the combat death of his friend Bonnie George, an Ojibwa Indian whom he has known since childhood. On the eve of his induction into the military, Bonnie George goes with Chris on a fishing expedition into the forests of the Upper Peninsula. Chris slips while fishing and almost drowns, but Bonnie George saves him. This incident causes Chris to reject his college draft deferral and enlist along with his friend and go to Vietnam. The two young men serve in the same company until Chris accidentally calls in the wrong coordinates for an air strike on the nearby enemy—the resulting napalm bombing kills Bonnie George, who is in a listening post just outside the perimeter. Thus Chris is burdened with the double guilt of killing a man who had once saved his life.

Before Chris realizes that in order to save himself he must resolve the guilt he feels for Bonnie George's death, he pushes himself to the very brink of self-destruction. He assaults his wife and almost kills her by setting a booby trap in their home. Dressed in his marine uniform he spends a day and a night patrolling the perimeter of his property, sleeping in a foxhole he has dug, and plotting suicide by laying his plans to goad the police into killing him. At this point he can only interpret his life according to the lessons he learned in Vietnam, and he goes to elaborate lengths to make his present life conform to patterns that he recognizes from the war. To heal himself he must learn new lessons from the present which will enable him to reinterpret his past.

In the final section of the novel, in order to make amends for Bonnie George's death, Chris decides he must seek out his friend's grandfather, Louis, the Ojibwa medicine man who raised Bonnie George. The redemptive capacity of Chris's quest to gain forgiveness from Louis is augmented by the fact that Louis was once a close friend of Chris's father and thus represents a means of confronting that unresolved relationship.

Chris and Louis meet at Louis's remote camp in the Hurons, where Louis has gone to fast and perform sacred rites that will invite Bonnie George's ghost to confer with him. Louis is concerned about having no heir to whom he can pass down his knowledge. At the climax of the ghost rites Chris appears from the woods. After a period of initial misunderstanding the two men come to realize that they fulfill a mutual need. Because of the language barrier they are not able to completely articulate this, but they do manage this exchange: "'There's a lot of things I know you don't,' the old man repeated. 'Like how to snare grouse?' 'Things like that.' 'Like life is a gift?' 'Things like that too'" (430). Chris discovers, through Louis, how to forgive himself, and Louis finds in Chris a spiritual heir. The spiritual reconciliation is carried out in Louis's dream in which he uses his Ojibwa healing arts to cleanse Chris's soul. The token of that reconciliation is Louis's offer to take Chris fishing—this act that once formed a bond between Chris and his father, Chris and Bonnie George, and Louis and Chris's father thus initiates and represents the newly constituted family.

To repeat, this re-creation of the family is similar to that which Philip Dosier enacts with Quinn's parents, although Caputo spends much more time elaborating upon the formation of this relationship. The bond forged between Chris and Louis is also significantly different from the bond between Philip and the Quinns because it is a relationship between a white man and a Native American. Throughout the novel, "Indian Country" is a double landscape. On the one hand it is the Vietnam soldier's slang term for the hostile Vietnamese landscape, on the other it is the backwoods of the Upper Peninsula, where Chris must find his peace. This double metaphor also reveals the twin sets of cultural guilt that Chris must come to terms with. He sees the ravages that his dominant culture has brought upon Louis's people—the ravages that have turned Bonnie George's mother into a "blanket ass," that have deprived Louis of friends and heirs in his old age, and that have caused the Ojibwa to ignore their own culture. The same imperialistic spirit that destroyed the Ojibwa also has ravaged the people of Vietnam. As a white man Chris is complicit in these ravages, and in the latter case he is complicit because of his physical presence in Vietnam. By reconciling with Louis rather than his own father, Chris finds a way out of the dominant American ideology and embraces an alternate mythology. Only when he has achieved this cultural and personal harmony can he successfully operate in his family and in society.

Of the three stories about veterans discussed here, Chris Starkmann's is probably the closest to a success story. Philip Dosier falls back upon an established means of reincorporating himself into the world, but those means are not quite adequate for the needs of the Vietnam veteran. Paco Sullivan can find no means at all for meeting those needs—for him the world has no answers. But Chris Starkmann finally has the ability to reconceive the blend of individual and societal reconciliation needed for readjustment after Vietnam. Through love and imagination he at last comes home.

NOTE

1. William Searle's parenthetical citations are to Charles R. Figley and Seymour Leventman, "Introduction: Estrangement and Victimization," and to Norma Wikler, "Hidden Injuries of War," both in *Strangers at Home: Vietnam Veterans since the War*, ed. Charles R. Figley and Seymour Leventman (New York: Praeger, 1980).

WORKS CITED

Caputo, Philip. *Indian Country*. 1987. Toronto: Bantam, 1988.
Edelman, Bernard, ed. *Dear America: Letters Home from Vietnam*. New York: Norton, 1985.

Heinemann, Larry. *Close Quarters*. 1977. New York: Penguin, 1986.
———. *Paco's Story*. 1986. New York: Penguin, 1987.
Hellmann, John. *American Myth and the Legacy of Vietnam*. New York: Columbia University Press, 1986.
O'Brien, Tim. *Going after Cacciato*. 1978. New York: Laurel-Dell, 1987.
Searle, William J. "Walking Wounded: Vietnam War Novels of Return." *Search and Clear: Critical Responses to Selected Literature and Films of the Vietnam War*. Ed. William J. Searle. Bowling Green, Ohio: Popular, 1988.

"She's a Pretty Woman . . . for a Gook"

The Misogyny of the Vietnam War

O O O O O O O O O O O O O

Jacqueline E. Lawson

On April 16, 1977, the body of Le My Hanh was discovered in a vacant apartment in a run-down housing complex in Queens, New York. The seventeen-year-old honors student had been bound, gagged with her own scarf, punched in the jaw, beaten "over and over," raped, sodomized, and finally strangled. Her body, trussed so tightly that it appeared "hogtied," was stuffed into a closet. Official cause of death: asphyxia by ligature strangulation. Homicide. Earlier that morning Louis Kahan, a thirty-year-old ex-marine and Vietnam veteran, confessed to the crime, informing police officers, "I did something wrong" (Bain 8). When asked to describe his victim Kahan replied, "I don't know. I just know she was Vietnamese" (10). According to his defense attorney, Kahan did what "he was trained to do. . . . Kill women. . . . So what was so difficult about doing this again . . . kill one more Vietnamese girl?" (202, 203). Louis Kahan was acquitted of the murder of Le My Hanh. He was found not guilty by reason of insanity, in the court's judgment, "by reason of the fact that he lacks substantial capacity to appreciate the wrongfulness of his conduct" (206).

The case of Le My Hanh and Louis Kahan is documented in *Aftershocks: A Tale of Two Victims*, David Haward Bain's attempt to recount, in reportorial fashion, the events leading up to the crime. It is Bain's contention that the rape-murder of Le My Hanh was the inevitable result of the war in Vietnam, that, in fact, the war had made a killer-rapist out of Louis Kahan. Kahan's actions can thus be satisfactorily explained as a clear case of posttraumatic stress disorder resulting from his 1966 tour of combat duty as an infantryman in Vietnam.

> Rape was an ever-present coercive force in field interrogations. By threat of forcible intercourse or sodomy, women could be persuaded to give information, if they had any. The procedure in the units to which Kahan was attached was to isolate a woman from the rest of her family and village. She would be tied up, threatened, and raped regardless of what she told her captors. . . . The men took turns as each occasion arose, thus reinforcing the credo that "they were all in it together"; they had all participated. There were no exceptions, and there were no objections. Kahan actively took part in the interrogations twice as a rapist; once he was able to perform; once he was not. (Bain 83)

One comes away from Bain's *Aftershocks* disposed to believe that the controlled mayhem which for eleven years defined U.S. military conduct in Southeast Asia created Louis Kahan, sex-killer. Accordingly, the war, in the form of misguided policies, the absence of any clear-cut strategy, and a failure of U.S. military might, assumes the personified aspect of "villain" while Kahan emerges as a pathetic "victim" demanding our sympathy and deserving our empathy, a twisted symbol of the waste and devastation that marked America's failure in Vietnam.

It has become standard practice for critics of the Vietnam War to anthropomorphize and isolate the war, to see "it" as the locus of evil and to blame "it" for the atrocities committed in "its" name. This comforting but reductive view ignores the very real links between sex and violence that exist in our culture, links which help make war possible. In his classic study of the soldier in World War II, J. Glenn Gray acknowledges the "curious affinities between love and war," noting, "there is enough of the rapist in every man to give him insight into the grossest manifestations of sexual passion . . . this kind of love is intimately associated with the impersonal violence of war" (66). More recent commentators on men in battle have used the Vietnam War to posit even more irreducible theories linking the male lust for combat with male sexual power, and, by extension, with misogyny. In seeking to explain "why men love war," author-veteran William Broyles, Jr., concedes that war is "a turn-on" for it "cloaks men in a costume that conceals the limits and inadequacies of their separate natures. It gives them an aura, a collective power, an almost animal force" (62).

Cultural critic Mark Gerzon makes even more explicit the ties that bind virility and violence; "one of the obvious links between the two," he allows, "is the emotion of fear . . . Only something as repugnant as being considered a woman or a faggot . . . is sufficiently terrifying that men are willing to die to avoid it. . . . This fear of our feminine side, the 'anima' in Jungian terms, seems inextricably involved in triggering our capacity for destructiveness." (40). In sum, war is the sine qua non of maleness, the agency of legitimized violence and the stronghold of undisputed male power where men are free to exercise/exorcise the thinly veiled fear of women that lurks beneath the surface of patriarchal culture.[1]

War does not create misogynists. Neither does "it" create rapists, racists, mass murderers, or criminals. A predisposition to misogyny, expressed explicitly though by no means exclusively in acts of violence against women, is built into the very fabric of American culture, finding its expression most often in peacetime. Violence against women is on the rise, and rape is the fastest growing crime in America. Between 1972 and 1976, the number of rapes in this country reportedly increased by 105 percent (Griffin 31); according to a recent estimate based on FBI statistics, a woman in America is raped every three minutes (Dworkin, *Pornography* 103).[2] Not only is rape the fastest growing of all major crimes, it is also the most underreported and the most difficult to prove. As Harvard law professor Susan Estrich points out in her *Yale Law Journal* study of rape and the law, "the law has done more than reflect the restrictive and sexist views of our society; it has legitimized and contributed to them" (1093).

Rape laws in this country have historically favored the perpetrator;

the burden of proof has rested squarely on the victim and, as a result, conviction rates for rapists are among the lowest of all criminal cases brought to trial. And incidents of rape, attempted rape, acquaintance rape, gang rape, and marital rape continue to burgeon. In three independent surveys of college students published in 1986, one in five women in each study reported being forced to engage in some type of sexual act by a known assailant; in an earlier study, 50 percent of female college students surveyed reported acts of "offensive male sexual aggression" during the previous year (Estrich 1165).[3] Not all men are rapists, of course, any more than all women are victims of rape. That all women fear rape—and that most men fail to realize the pervasiveness of this fear—may, however, suggest that the nature of gender relations in this country is more adversarial than we are willing to admit and that perhaps the solution to the growing problem of sexual violence has as much to do with narrowing the gap of understanding between men and women as with implementing social change.

It is important to remember that violence against women is not a cause but a symptom of misogyny and that rape is only one of the ways in which women are victimized by a culture that claims to abhor violence but can't seem to stop celebrating it: the degrading images of women purveyed through advertising, the media, commercial film, and pornography are some of the powerful cultural forces that conspire to make women targets of male violence. These are the same forces that help lead us into war, and they are the same forces that lead to violence against women in war. A culture that has given us Rambo, the A-Team, Terminator, RoboCop, and slasher films; a culture in which adult bookstores, video porn shops, and X-rated cinemas are as ubiquitous as the local 7-Eleven; a culture that regards sex and violence as entertainment, aggressiveness as a virtue, and women as objects to be leered at, peered at, commercialized, and commodified should not be surprised when its soldiers go off to war and commit atrocities against women. As Susan Griffin points out, "A culture that creates rape creates images of rape. These images pass on the ethos of rape, and they encourage rape" (63). Louis Kahan is not a victim of the vague abstraction popularly known as "the war in Vietnam." Rather, he is implicated in a much larger conspiracy that has its roots in the misogynistic attitudes valorized by American culture and legitimized by the values inherent in a patriarchal, mass-culture society.

For as long as there have been wars, there have been crimes against women in wartime—crimes which are not considered crimes—and in this respect, the Vietnam War is not unique.[4] What distinguishes the war in Vietnam from other wars is the number of atrocities committed against women (Vietnam was our longest war and involved more men) and the fact that these atrocities are copiously documented in the memoirs and oral histories produced by Vietnam veterans. These non-fiction narratives, the veterans' own accounts, are replete with misogynistic allusions to the women of Vietnam: acts of rape, gang rape, assaults on women, torture, mutilation, and murder crowd the pages of these texts, raising disturbing questions about this nation's combatants and the culture they sought to defend.

How do we explain the profusion of sexually explicit, at times heart-stoppingly graphic, accounts of these atrocities contained in the pages of the veterans' memoirs? Much of the brutality associated with the Vietnam War was undeniably racially motivated. While racism alone does not explain the high incidence of sexual atrocities perpetrated against Vietnamese women by American GIs, like misogyny, racism does have its basis in fear and, like misogyny, racism manifests itself in powerful assertions of superiority directed against an objectified, inferiorized other. But racism itself has misogynistic overtones, encoded in our culture and deployed through familiar images, like the guy in the bar—or the bully next door—who hurls racial epithets to prove that he's a "bigger man." The tendency to see women as scapegoats is likewise culturally derived, finding expression in boyhood taunts of "sissy," "wimp," and "fag." The need of some men to adopt a supermasculine persona may thus be compensatory, a means of blunting the fear of emasculation. This explains, in part, the overwhelmingly male fascination with super-macho figures like Rambo or his sixties' counterpart John Wayne; to be like Rambo or John Wayne is most assuredly *not* to be a sissy.[5]

This fear of emasculation is exploited most effectively by the military, whose job it is to turn "boys" into "men." Few forces in our society so openly encourage misogyny as the U.S. military, and military recruiting ads are among the most pernicious propaganda ploys in American culture. They play unabashedly on the fear of the feminine that is so much a part of the mythology of war, a mythology dependent on divisive stereotypes of male aggressiveness and female passivity, of heroism and cowardice, strength and weakness, manliness and womanliness. The male tendency to view women as objects of dread, instilled through the gender-defining process of boyhood and powerfully reinforced by cultural conditioning throughout the remainder of men's lives, is one of the coercive weapons used by the military to lure new recruits into the fold. A recent army recruiting ad is a case in point. A romantically tinted photograph shows a lone parachutist descending bravely into the clouds. Superimposed over the photo is a handwritten letter:

> Dear Dad,
>   Remember the time you told me that real courage is putting your fear aside and doing the job? I thought about that a lot this morning. You see, Dad, here in the Army, everything you taught me really means something.

The boldfaced logo, bottom right, completes the picture: "ARMY. BE ALL YOU CAN BE."[6]

Mom is nowhere mentioned in this advertisement. Presumably, the child doesn't learn lessons about "real courage" from mom. And "here in the Army," whatever lessons mom does teach "really mean nothing." Thus, in the traditional patriarchal paradigm, femininity is depicted as a negative value, a fact the military is quick to exploit.

Military slogans like "the marine corps builds men," "the Marine Corps is looking for a few good men," and "Army. Be all you can be" trade openly on male fear—the fear of emasculation, of becoming sissified, of losing one's manhood in front of other men, in short, the fear of becoming a woman. The army's latest ad campaign is no less anti-female than the familiar ads of twenty years ago. For many in the post-Korea pre-Vietnam era, the masculinist image held out by the marine's tough-minded sloganeering proved irresistible. Marine lieutenant Philip Caputo:

> I had another motive for volunteering, one that has pushed young men into armies ever since armies were invented: I needed to prove something—my courage, my toughness, my manhood, call it whatever you like. . . . it was . . . a matter of doing something

that would demonstrate . . . that I was a man after all, like the steely-eyed figure in the recruiting poster. THE MARINE CORPS BUILDS MEN was another slogan current at the time, and on November 28 [1960] I became one of its construction projects. (6, 7)

After six grueling weeks of basic training, Caputo graduated from the Marine Corps's elite Officer Training School. He endured this "ordeal of initiation" not so much from a desire to succeed as from a fear of failure, a fear of being tainted with "the virus of weakness." As he recalls, "nothing . . . could be as bad as having to return home and admit to my family that I had failed. It was not their criticism I dreaded, but the emasculating affection and understanding they would be sure to show me. I could hear my mother saying, 'That's all right, son. You didn't belong in the Marines but here with us. It's good to have you back' " (10). For Caputo, failure is equated with home, home is defined as mother, and mother is the source of "emasculating affection and understanding," the soothing presence who will celebrate his failure as a marine, thereby confirming his failure as a man. So long as young men are conditioned to define themselves through popular culture images of maleness—"steely-eyed" marines, John Wayne, Rambo—then the military will continue to mount successful recruiting campaigns aimed at depicting women as the enemy.[7]

Humiliating new recruits in basic training by calling them "pussies," "pansies," "ladies," and "faggots" actualizes the fear of emasculation, bringing it immediately to the surface. Ron Kovic and John Ketwig recall incidents from boot camp:

"Awright, ladies! . . . There are eighty of you, eighty young warm bodies, eighty sweet little ladies, eighty sweetpeas. . . . Grab your trousers!" shouted the sergeant. "These are trousers . . . not pants! Pants are for little girls! *Trousers* are for marines! Put your trousers on!" . . . THIS IS YOUR RIFLE LADIES I WANT YOU TO KNOW IT ALL EVERY PART OF IT! CAN'T YOU READ SWEETPEA? this is my rifle this is my gun this is for fighting this is for fun. (Kovic 76, 82, 89)

Sarge walked up to him, bent at the waist, and made an exaggerated inspection of the guy's naked privates. Satisfied, he rose,

and turned back to us. "He's got balls! . . . Long as he's got balls,
I can work with him! I'll make him a man. I'll make you all men!"
(Ketwig 24)

The fear of becoming a woman (of losing one's "balls") is one of the
indoctrinational weapons used by the military in preparing young men
for battle.[8] Trainees in boot camp are conditioned, by both culture and
the military, to see the enemy (and the enemy within, the Jungian
"anima") in misogynistic terms. It is telling that the epithets used to
terrify new recruits headed for Vietnam were not "dink," "slope," and
"gook" but "pussies," "ladies," and "faggots." Vietnam memoirist Tim
O'Brien vividly describes the emasculating rhetoric of boot camp:

> He said I was a pansy. . . . A couple of college pussies. . . . You're
> a pussy, huh? You afraid to be in the war, a goddamn pussy, a
> goddamn lezzie? You know what we do with pussies, huh? We fuck
> 'em. In the army we just fuck 'em and straighten 'em out. (54)

Killing an enemy in battle may thus also be an attempt to eradicate
the other, more fearsome enemy—the feminine. This was especially
true in the war in Vietnam where the Vietnamese came to be regarded
as weak, effeminate, devious, and wanton. The South Vietnamese soldiers in the ARVN were particular targets of American contempt, re-
viled by many GIs for their cowardice, passivity, feebleness, and ser-
vility—in short, their effeminacy. Veteran Jeff Needle:

> There is a large gap of feeling and understanding between the
> American soldier and the Vietnamese. . . . They don't respect the
> South Vietnamese soldier because they don't trust him while
> fighting alongside of him. They don't respect the Vietnamese
> people because they do our laundry, clean our buildings, fill our
> sandbags, polish our boots, wash our dishes, and women sacrifice
> their bodies. . . . The people whose freedom we're fighting for
> have become our servants. (Lifton 196)

The American perception of the Vietnamese male as womanly, a perception reinforced by his small stature, delicate features, and "effeminate" customs—in Vietnamese culture, male hand-holding and male
kissing are signs of respect—led to what psychiatrist Robert Lifton

has labeled "the gook syndrome," the transformation of the enemy into a scapegoat-victim.[9] The sight of Vietnamese men kissing, holding hands, and squatting fueled the Americans' homophobia, strengthening the belief that the Vietnamese were a weak and cowardly people and thus not worth fighting for. Veteran Charles R. Anderson:

> In addition, there was still another characteristic about the Vietnamese which completely repulsed the grunts. Asian peoples are much less inhibited than westerners about displaying their affection for friends of the same sex. Among Asians, holding hands or walking arm in arm in public does not arouse suspicions of homosexuality. The grunts, however, were shocked at such behavior. They needed to believe their allies and those whose freedom they were supposedly defending were better than "a bunch of queers." (208)

Dehumanizing—by feminizing—the enemy was crucial to the military's propaganda program, both in country and back in the States. Reducing the Vietnamese to mere "gooks"—something between a woman and an animal—helped bolster the morale of the troops in the field, who needed to believe that they were fighting an enemy they could handily beat. In the words of one veteran:

> The Vietnamese were generally looked upon as lesser beings. They were considered stupid, cowardly, small, ugly, poor, to be killed if you wanted to. I'm sure sexual attitudes toward the women went right along with this, and that rape occurred. Some soldiers had this attitude that they could go into a hamlet or village and take what they wanted and slap people around. Rape in Vietnam would have to be seen in the larger context of hatred and disrespect for the Vietnamese. (Beneke 92)[10]

For more than eleven years the United States occupied a country whose people it subjugated, whose culture it debauched, and whose lands it systematically plundered and destroyed. Rape is thus a fitting metaphor for America's military conduct in Southeast Asia. The very language of the war is sexually fraught, conjuring up images of forcible entry, of dominance and submission: "pacification," "engagement," "escalation," "de-escalation," "withdrawal," "free-fire zone," "troop strength," "firepower," "slick" (slang for helicopter), "R & R" (commonly known as "rape and ruin"), "humping the boonies," "search and destroy," "cherry" (an uninitiated soldier), "grunts," "point-man," and, finally, the favorite expletive of virtually every Vietnam participant, "fuck." The war in Vietnam begins to take on the character of a protracted and brutal act of sexual intercourse.

"Raping" Indochina through the use of incendiary, "bully boy" tactics like napalming, air strikes, search-and-destroy missions, and chemical warfare—frequently directed at civilian targets—was America's way of flexing its military muscle, an act of exhibitionism designed to reassure the world, allies and enemies alike, that the United States hadn't gone "soft." "Withdrawal" at this stage of the action was unthinkable. It becomes increasingly apparent after reading the veterans' accounts that an American loss in Vietnam—certainly to the high command and the majority of grunts in the field—was tantamount to being emasculated in the eyes of the world. Asserting America's manhood by "rolling over" the Vietnamese, North and South, was thus the means of flaunting our national virility. The bombing of North Vietnam, South Vietnam, Laos, and Cambodia was a swaggering display of U.S. economic and ideological potency—a global "bang"—designed to emasculate the North Vietnamese, while symbolically castrating the Soviet Union. John Ketwig:

> We had already dropped more tons of bombs on Vietnam than we had dropped on Hitler; more than twelve tons for every square mile in both North and South Vietnam . . . over one hundred pounds of explosive for every man, woman, and child in the Vietnams. Nixon talked of withdrawing troops, but we could see the bombers overhead every day. . . . There was only one way to win, and the United States always wins. . . . They get all the colonels and generals out of there, then drop the Big One and send a lot of letters to the parents. Wait for Hanoi to surrender. . . . Victory! Intimidate the world. (274, 275)

Xenophobia, institutionalized anti-Communism, and above all racism and misogyny are essential ingredients if the United States is to wage war successfully in a Third World region. All of these ingredients were present in the war in Vietnam, finding expression in one of the most familiar refrains of the war: "The only good gook is a dead gook." America's declared enemies in Vietnam were the Soviet-supplied North Vietnamese and Vietcong. But the confusion that marked the war—the absence of well-defined strategic boundaries, the importance placed on body counts and kill ratios by the high command, and the fact that to the untrained American eye, all Asians looked alike—created a situation that invited the most pernicious forms of racism, stereotyping, and misogyny. Lieutenant Michael Lee Lanning:

> One day I passed a young woman naked to the waist standing under a thatch awning. Using a small basin of water and a cloth, she was bathing. When she noticed me, she immediately turned her eyes, covered herself as much as possible with the cloth, and ran into the hut. I was much surprised at her embarrassment. . . . I never saw any modesty among the GIs. We went about as if we were around animals rather than human women and children. In our minds, it was they who were the barbarians, not we. (*The Only War We Had* 77)

The feminization of the Vietnamese also served to reassure Americans back home that the war would be won quickly or, as that became unlikely, simply won. Barry Zorthian, U.S. press relations, Saigon:

> LBJ or Congress or whatever, assumed it affected *the guy* in Des Moines, so Washington would react violently to a TV spot. TV is a headline service; it hardly lends itself to subtleties and nuances. What the hell are you going to show in a war where turf is not the benchmark? Rice growing on TV? Hearts and minds being seized? You show action. (Willenson 183, emphasis added)

The purpose of this "action," of course, was to humiliate North Vietnam, to bring Hanoi to its knees. This failing, America's young soldiers would bring Vietnam's women to theirs.

Raping a Vietnamese woman became a hallmark of the guerrilla phase of the war—the war fought on the ground by young American males intent on asserting their superiority, their potency, their manhood (and by extension, their country's) by terrorizing, torturing, and sexually abusing the women of Vietnam. The extent to which these practices were allowed, accepted, encouraged, and carried out—raping a woman in a combat zone is something a man "has" to do, "needs" to do, has a "right" to do—suggests how close to the surface misogynistic attitudes lie and how easily women are reduced and objectified when the rules of social engagement no longer apply. Mark Baker's *Nam*:

> You take a group of men and put them in a place where there are no round-eyed women. They are in an all-male environment. Let's face it. Nature is nature. There are women available. Those women are of another culture, another color, another society. You don't want a prostitute. You've got an M-16. What do you need to pay for a lady for? You go down to the village and take what you want. (206)

Rape is a part of war because rape is a part of male-centered culture. The devaluation of women that informs cultural codes, attitudes, and values leads ineluctably to the belief, expressed openly in wartime, that "taking" a woman is a man's natural entitlement, his natural right, perhaps even his natural obligation. Anderson:

> Hell, we figure we might be dead the next minute or day anyhow so what the fuck difference does it make what we do? What difference does it make if we shoot at farmers in their paddies or screw village girls or jerk an elder's beard or beat up a cowboy trying to steal the watches right off our arms? Who would give a shit? And even if they caught us what could they do that was any worse than shaving our heads and sending us to Nam? Ha, we're already here! (212)

Acculturated feelings of superiority, invincibility, and aggressiveness were intensified for young American males during the Vietnam War. Many veterans report being suffused with godlike feelings of male omnipotence, a super-machismo instilled by the military in basic training and reinforced by the "boys will be boys" attitude that prevailed in virtually every combat zone. Mark Baker's *Nam*:

> I had a sense of power. A sense of destruction. See, now, in the United States a person is babied. He's told what to do. You can't

carry a gun, unless you want to go to jail. . . . But in the Nam you realized that you had the power to take a life. You had the power to rape a woman and nobody could say nothing to you. That god-like feeling you had was in the field. It was like I was a god. I could take a life, I could screw a woman. I can beat somebody up and get away with it. It was a godlike feeling that a guy could express in the Nam. (190, 191)

Giving a young man a gun, and then ordering him to use it, is the state-sanctioned license to commit violence. That the gun takes on phallic properties scarcely needs to be elaborated. Mark Baker's *Nam*:

Being in that kind of environment, you give a guy a gun and strange things happen. A gun is power. To some people carrying a gun constantly was like having a permanent hard on. It was a pure sexual trip every time you got to pull the trigger. (206)

Veteran "JC":

During my second and third fights I was fucking excited, man; I mean erotically turned on, really fucking excited, wow, man. (Brende and Parson 48)

The male fear of the feminine, of woman's power to unsex man, is evidently so deep-seated and urgent a fear that the act of firing a weapon is imbued with the markers of sexual arousal and release. Firing a weapon that has become a surrogate penis is an act of sexual aggression: spontaneous, instinctive, and overpowering. Male sexual power, and the authority to use that power, vested in men by a patriarchal culture (including, but not confined to, institutions like the government and the military), was one of the conspiratorial forces behind the misogyny of the Vietnam War. Private First Class Reginald "Malik" Edwards, U.S. Marine Corps:

I mean we were crazy, but it's built into the culture. It's like institutionalized insanity. When you're in combat, you can do basically what you want as long as you don't get caught. You can get away with murder. And the beautiful thing about the military is there's always somebody that can serve up as a scapegoat. Like Calley. (Terry 16)

The 1968 massacre at My Lai, in which an estimated 450 to 500 South Vietnamese civilians, most of them women, were gunned down with automatic weapons by the members of Charlie Company, has come to epitomize *the* atrocity of the Vietnam War. My Lai was the most sensational, because most publicized, event of the war, numbering among its crimes rape, gang-rape, torture, and mutilation. That these sexual atrocities were not originally reported by the media but were only later publicized during the legal phase of the investigation is further evidence of how conspiratorial misogynistic attitudes are (Hallin 180).[11] Ronald L. Ridenhour, helicopter door gunner, 11th Brigade, flew over My Lai several days after the massacre. This is what he saw:

> The hamlet was completely desolate. There were no people around, no signs of life anywhere. [There was] . . . a woman, spread-eagled as if on display. She had an 11th Brigade patch between her legs—as if it were some type of display, some badge of honor. (Hersh 87)

The events at My Lai were atrocious, to be sure, but it is a mistake to view the massacre as an isolated incident; the fury unleashed on civilian women by the members of Charlie Company was remarkable only in the extent of the morning's savagery and not in the fact that the savagery occurred. My Lai participant John Smail, speaking about rape, commented: "That's an everyday affair. You can nail just about everybody on that—at least once. The guys are human, man" (Hersh 185).

Atrocities perpetrated against women in wartime are not aberrations if the propensity for misogyny is culturally induced. If the guys are "human"—socialized, acculturated—then rape *is* reduced to an "everyday affair."

I'd like to introduce you to some of "the guys." They'll tell you what they did, each day, every day, during the war in Vietnam.

Arthur E. "Gene" Woodley, Jr., Specialist 4, U.S. Army:

> When I seen women put to torture as having Coca-Cola bottles run up into their womb, I did nothing. When I heard this other team raped a woman and then rammed a M-16 in her vagina and

pulled the trigger, I said nothing. And when I seen this GI stomp on this fetus after this pregnant woman got killed in a ambush, I did nothin'. What could I do? (Terry 256)

Mark Baker's *Nam*:

"Come on back, it's the Bell Telephone Hour. We're wiring somebody up." . . . I'd go in and there'd be some poor woman or some old man, some kid even. . . . Often the person we were wiring up would be a young woman who was maybe comely. There were all kinds of sexual overtones to that. Domination. The misogyny of war is being denied women, and then having your only contact with women in some sort of subjugated positions. (214, 215)

Lieutenant Michael Lee Lanning:

My final night in Charlie Company was spent with the sergeants and officers in the NCO Club. . . . The party ended when one of the men grabbed a mini-skirted waitress and threw her on top of the table. He was almost successful in burying his head between her brown thighs before the club bouncers and MPs arrived. The club manager expressed concern that none of us around the table had tried to stop the activities and had, instead, only laughed at the girl's shrieks. McGinnis explained with a reasonably straight face that he thought it was part of the floor show. (*The Only War We Had* 241)

Veteran "X," 3rd Battalion, 5th Marines:

. . . his group liked to rip the clothes off women villagers as they walked by; another unit would slowly drive their jeeps close to women riding bicycles and grab them between the legs and hold them as the two vehicles were driven parallel. It was fun, the men said, to feel the women squirm and to hold them as long as possible. . . . During missions into villages, even routine searches for hidden weapons became wholesale grope sessions. (Bain 65)

Tim O'Brien, 3rd Platoon, Alpha Company:

Her face lay in the dirt. Flies were all over her. There was no shade. It was mid-afternoon of a hot day. The medic said he did not dare squirt morphine into her, it would kill her before the wound did. He tried to patch the holes, but she squirmed and twisted, rocked and swayed, never opening her eyes. She flickered in and out of consciousness. "She's a pretty woman, pretty for a gook. You don't see many pretty gooks, that's damn sure." "Yes. Trouble is, she's shot dead through the wrong place." A dozen GIs hovered over her. . . . "Fuckin'-aye, she's wasted." (115)

Lieutenant Michael Lee Lanning:

The VC pair, who had escaped pursuit for over a decade, had died without returning a shot. The bodies had been taken into Cam Tam for display in the public square. Before the villagers had filed by the bodies, the woman's black pajama bottom had been pulled down, fully exposing her privates to the viewers. (*A Company Commander's Journal* 21)

Private First Class John Ketwig, U.S. Army:

The girl was on her back now, and naked. Her bound wrists were over her head, held by a swarthy GI. . . . The girl's legs were held apart. A burly black stood over her, screaming. . . . "Cunt! Whore! You gonna die, oh, you gonna die bad, Mama-san! You gonna wear your cunt in your mouth, Mama-san!" . . . The huge hose was brought into the circle. The giant black, still raging, shook it in front of the girl's face. . . . She closed her eyes, shuddered a little. The tarnished brass nozzle was forced between her legs, forced against the resilient folds of flesh. Her eyes started open. A scream started from her throat, a sound unlike any other! Red and pink and brown and white and green, a torrent of mixed flesh and high-pressure steam knocked the intimate circle back. The white flood of water died away, the lifeless hose was discarded. (80)

Mark Baker's *Nam*:

Guys are taking turns screwing her. It was like an animal pack. "Hey, he's taking too long to screw her." Nobody was turning their back or nothing. We just stood on line and we screwed her. I was taking her body by force. Guys were standing over her with rifles, while I was screwing her. She says, "Why are you doing this to me? Why?" . . . Baby-san, she was crying. So a guy just put a rifle to her head and pulled the trigger just to put her out of the picture. . . . After we raped her, took her cherry from her, after we shot her in the head, you understand what I'm saying, we literally start stomping her body. . . . And everybody was laughing about it. . . . Then we start cutting the ears off. We cut her nose off. The captain says, "Who's going to get the ears? Who's going to get the nose? So-and-so's turn to get the ears." . . . We cut off one of her breasts and one guy got the breast. But the trophy was the ears. (211, 212)

Dwyte A. Brown, Radarman Second Class, U.S. Navy:

. . . mama sans be on the base cleanin' our shoes. I give her a dollar. But this guy says, "You ain't do it good enough." Maybe smack her. Or throw her daughter down, pull her clothes up, try to have sex with her. She just thirteen or fourteen. She there tryin' to sweep the floor. The mother was just too scared to say somethin'. And like they cleanin' up our showers while we takin' a shower. I see it's a woman. I'd keep my towel on me, right? This white guy didn't have nothin' on. He'd say, "Hey, Come here. Jump on this." He shake his dick at her. . . . Then he grabbed the little daughter. I say, "Hey, man. Why don't you leave the little girl alone? They just doin' their work." He say, "Aw, fuck it, man. We protectin' them. I'm over here savin' their life." (Terry 273)

Veteran "Daniel," U.S. Marines, 1967:

A Viet Cong woman had been wounded and was taken prisoner by a Navy corpsman and the following morning we heard the story that this Navy corpsman and one or two other soldiers had tried to rape her, and when she resisted they put their fingers in the wound in her back, and tried to probe into her lungs to get her to submit. . . . Vietnamese women were made into objects of fear and dread, and it was easy to feel angry at them. (Beneke 58–59)

Luther C. Benton III, HM2, U.S. Navy:

They had this young Vietnamese female, and they had her standing on a little tiny stool with three legs on it, like a milk stool. They had taken all her clothes off. She had her hands tied behind her. And there was this ROK Marine doin' the interrogating. . . . So what he did was he took a flare and he pushed it up in her body between her legs. Phosphorous flare. He stuck it up in her vagina, enough for it to stay there. And he lit the flare. It burned her legs. Then she just fell off the stool and flopped around. She moved around. And he just let the flare burn. . . . She was screamin'. You hear her outside the room. The scream. When she quit screamin'—when she quit screamin', I knew she was dead. (Terry 72–73)[12]

These, then, are "the guys." America's sons. We can deplore their actions. We can denounce the war in which these actions occurred. We can even reject the policies that led us into the mire of Vietnam and which threaten to lead us back into the mire in Central America. What we cannot do is vilify the war and make victims of the warriors—warriors like Louis Kahan. The war in Vietnam did not beat, rape, sodomize, and strangle Le My Hanh. He did. And so did we.

NOTES

1. While these scholars agree that a fear of the feminine underlies the male fascination with war and implicitly with misogyny, a fuller range of opinion exists. Radical feminist Andrea Dworkin argues for a "male supremacist," phallus-centered ideology as the prime mover of male power. Thus to Dworkin, male sexual power is reified through the penis and sexuality is always a violent act. She argues this position forcefully in *Pornography: Men Possessing Women* (see especially 13, 51–55) and more recently in *Intercourse*. Adrienne Rich likewise sees male sexual power as a "dehumanizing" and "corrosive" force which is "carried over from sex into war" ("Vietnam and Sexual Violence," in *On Lies, Secrets, and Silence* 108–116). In her important study of gender and war, *Women and War*, Jean Bethke Elshtain refutes the notion that violence is an exclusively male province, insisting on seeing war as a concatenation of cultural forces driven and legitimized by men and women. Elshtain's thesis, while indispensable in broadening the parameters of future discussions of war, does not address the question of misogyny. The range of opinion on the growing subject of men, women, and war will likely continue to widen.

2. The statistics on battered women are equally staggering. By Dworkin's calculations, a woman is battered in America every eighteen seconds. According to a more recent estimate, domestic violence occurs in one out of every

three American households, making spousal-partner abuse the number one cause of injury to women. In the past year, three to four million women took refuge in domestic violence shelters nationwide; in Michigan alone, over 17,000 women and children were forced to seek shelter from domestic violence in 1987. I am indebted to Patricia Briggs of the Michigan Coalition against Domestic Violence for providing this information.

3. As with all statistics, those on rape vary, though not as widely as one would expect. The data reported by Estrich, for example, based on figures from *National Crime Surveys and the Bureau of Justice Statistics* and covering the period 1973 to 1982, are consistent with those provided by Beneke (1, 2); Beneke's data cover roughly the same period as Estrich's and are derived largely from FBI statistics, *Uniform Crime Reports* (1980), and personal interviews with rape crisis professionals. See also Griffin (139–144) and Susan Brownmiller's groundbreaking study, *Against Our Will* (387–420). These scholars agree that the incidence of rape has climbed steadily, doubling over the last decade.

4. Brownmiller exhaustively traces the incidence of rape in wartime; as she points out, although rape carries a maximum penalty of death under Article 120 of the American Uniform Code of Military Justice, conviction rates for rapists in wartime are predictably low, with the number of courts-martial for rape lower in the Vietnam War than in previous wars. In *The "Uncensored War,"* Daniel C. Hallin underscores the dismissive attitude toward rape held both by military investigators and civilian researchers. In his analysis of attacks on Vietnamese civilians, Hallin states that while large-scale massacres like My Lai were "not a normal part of war," assaults on a smaller scale, such as individual acts of rape, "seem to have been more common," leaving the reader to conclude that rape is a "normal" part of war (151–153). In an accompanying chart documenting causes of civilian casualties between 1965 and 1973, including kidnapping, murder, destruction of homes, and abuse or torture of prisoners, rape is nowhere mentioned (153).

5. For a discussion of mass culture's influence on the images of manhood see Gerzon, chapters 1 and 2.

6. This ad has appeared in the February, March, April, and June 1988 issues of *Newsweek*, *Time*, and *People*.

7. As Elshtain notes, we are currently witnessing an increasing militarization of American culture: militarized breakfast cereals, toys, clothing, and commercially successful films like *Top Gun*, *Rambo*, and even the critically acclaimed *Platoon* glorify "the male identity called forth or made explicit by war . . . that of a *killer*, an unchained luster after blood" (199). Extolled by Hollywood and aggressively marketed by Madison Avenue, the combat-fatigued, weapon-toting he-man has become a culturally sanctioned icon, a mass-culture hero of the Reaganized eighties whose bellicose—and unmistakably virile—image reinforces the equation of male (sexual) power with vio-

lence and, implicitly, with patriotism—witness the recent adulation of Oliver North. In selling the image of the marauding soldier as hero we are, in fact, openly selling male violence, a retrograde phenomenon reminiscent of the John Wayne shoot-'em-up, blow-'em-up attitudes of the fifties and early sixties. The correlation between the proliferation of bellicose images of masculinity and the rise in violent crimes against women is not, I think, coincidental, and may be an additional manifestation of the masculinist backlash against the women's movement; in an era when women have entered a number of hitherto all-male strongholds, combat remains the exclusive domain of the American male, an arena where men are still indisputably "men."

8. For a more detailed analysis of the altering effect of boot camp on the masculine identity see Jacqueline E. Lawson, "'Old Kids': The Adolescent Experience in the Nonfiction Narratives of the Vietnam War," in *Search and Clear*. The threat of emasculation with which drill instructors routinely terrorized Vietnam-era recruits was paradoxically more than mere rhetoric. As a number of veterans have attested, a wound to the genitals was the most feared wound in the Vietnam War—and the one most likely to be inflicted by the mines and booby traps planted by the Vietcong and the NVA, in particular the fearsome "Bouncing Betty" mine, designed to explode waist-high. As Michael Lanning notes, a wounded soldier's invariable first question to the medic was not "Am I going to make it, doc?" but rather "Do I still have my balls?" (*The Only War We Had* 71). For the damage inflicted on the human torso by stepping on a land mine see Glasser (57–59). One of the most moving passages on the mines in Vietnam is in Tim O'Brien's eloquent memoir, *If I Die in a Combat Zone* (125–130). See also Baker (276) and Caputo (272, 273).

9. In *Home from the War* (197–216), Lifton equates the racial stereotyping of the Vietnamese with the "psychic numbing" of American soldiers, a condition in which the blurring of racial distinctions came to serve as a combat survival mechanism, a way for soldiers to distance themselves from the brutality of war. One problem with Lifton's analysis is that he also sees "the gook syndrome" as a means of justifying atrocities since, as he states, psychic numbing "meant ceasing to feel the humanity of the Vietnamese and, at some level, cooperating in their victimization" (203). He goes on to suggest that avoiding "the gook syndrome" was virtually impossible for soldiers in Vietnam owing to peer pressure and the pervasiveness of the syndrome, a fact corroborated in the veterans' memoirs. See, for example, Anderson (207); Lanning, *The Only War We Had* (56) and *A Company Commander's Journal* (30); Santoli (144–145, 157–158); Terry (94); Baker (185–217); Beneke (58–59); O'Brien (52); Bain (63–69); and Caputo (254–255).

10. The attitude expressed here, that rape in Vietnam must be seen "in the larger context" of the war, is common among veterans. The refusal to see Vietnamese women as victims of *sexual* violence, the failure to acknowledge

complicity in their victimization, and the denial that rape in wartime is a crime are precisely the attitudes that led to atrocities in Vietnam. Commenting on this passage, a sexual assault counselor for the Alameda County Victim Assistance Program points out that the Vietnam veteran's refusal to see the rape victim as human is *"exactly* what happens when a rapist rapes a woman in America" (Beneke 160).

11. Seymour Hersh's Pulitzer Prize–winning *My Lai 4* was the first source to detail the sexual atrocities committed at My Lai, yet his investigative study did not appear until nearly two years after the incident occurred. Following the publicity generated by Hersh's account, press reports of the massacre proliferated. See, for example, "Calley Takes the Stand," *Life* (March 5, 1971); Joseph Goldstein et al., "The My Lai Massacre and Its Cover-Up: Beyond the Reach of Law?" in *The Peers Commission Report*; Richard Hammer, "My Lai: Did American Troops Attack the Wrong Place?" *Look* (February 10, 1970); "Interviews with My Lai Veterans," Laser Film Corp., 1970; Lt. Gen. W. R. Peers, *The My Lai Inquiry.* In January 1971, members of Vietnam Veterans Against the War convened the Winter Soldier investigation in Detroit, a public forum designed to publicize military policies that led to atrocities in Vietnam; transcripts were subsequently published in *The Winter Soldier Investigation.* James Reston's *Sherman's March and Vietnam* discusses the crimes of My Lai and the Winter Soldier investigation in the larger historical context of wartime atrocities. The confusion surrounding the events at My Lai—the extent of the savagery, the number of participants and casualties, and the fact that the hamlet itself was misidentified—continues to plague educators and researchers. For an incisive analysis of the problems encountered in teaching this aspect of the war, see David M. Berman's "Every Vietnamese was a Gook: My Lai, Vietnam, and American Education," in *Theory and Research in Social Education.* I am thankful to Berman for calling a number of these sources to my attention.

12. We are reminded in the preceding passages of William Broyles's statement that war gives men an "aura, a collective power, an almost animal force." I would suggest that it is American culture that endows men with the power to commit the acts described here, a power that is indeed "collective" and one which only we as a society can redress.

WORKS CITED

Anderson, Charles R. *The Grunts.* 1976. New York: Berkley, 1987.

Bain, David Haward. *Aftershocks: A Tale of Two Victims.* 1980. New York: Penguin, 1986.

Baker, Mark. *Nam: The Vietnam War in the Words of the Men and Women Who Fought There.* 1981. New York: Quill, 1982.

Beneke, Timothy. *Men on Rape*. New York: St. Martin's, 1982.

Berman, David M. "'Every Vietnamese Was a Gook': My Lai, Vietnam, and American Education." *Theory and Research in Social Education* 2 (Spring 1988): 141–159.

Brende, Joel Osler, and Erwin Randolph Parson. *Vietnam Veterans: The Road to Recovery*. 1985. New York: Signet-NAL, 1986.

Brownmiller, Susan. *Against Our Will: Men, Women and Rape*. 1975. New York: Bantam, 1986.

Broyles, William, Jr. "Why Men Love War." *Esquire*, Nov. 1984, 55–65.

Caputo, Philip. *A Rumor of War*. 1977. New York: Ballantine, 1978.

Dworkin, Andrea. *Intercourse*. New York: Free Press, 1987.

———. *Pornography: Men Possessing Women*. 1979. New York: Perigree-Putnam, 1981.

Elshtain, Jean Bethke. *Women and War*. New York: Basic, 1987.

Estrich, Susan. "Rape." *Yale Law Journal* 95 (May 1986): 1087–1184.

Gerzon, Mark. *A Choice of Heroes: The Changing Face of American Manhood*. Boston: Houghton, 1982.

Glasser, Ronald J. *365 Days*. 1971. New York: Braziller, 1980.

Goldstein, Joseph, Burke Marshall, and Jack Schwartz. "The My Lai Massacre and Its Cover-Up: Beyond the Reach of Law?" *The Peers Commission Report with a Supplement and Introductory Essay on the Limits of Law*. New York: Free Press, 1976.

Gray, J. Glenn. *The Warriors: Reflections on Men in Battle*. 1959. New York: Harper, 1970.

Griffin, Susan. *Rape: The Politics of Consciousness*. 1979. San Francisco: Harper, 1986.

Hallin, Daniel C. *The "Uncensored War": The Media and Vietnam*. New York: Oxford University Press, 1986.

Hersh, Seymour M. *My Lai 4: A Report on the Massacre and Its Aftermath*. New York: Random, 1970.

Ketwig, John. *. . . and a Hard Rain Fell: A GI's True Story of the War in Vietnam*. New York: Pocket, 1985.

Kovic, Ron. *Born on the Fourth of July*. 1976. New York: Pocket, 1977.

Lanning, Michael Lee. *The Only War We Had: A Platoon Leader's Journal of Vietnam*. New York: Ivy-Ballantine, 1987.

———. *Vietnam, 1969–1970: A Company Commander's Journal*. New York: Ivy-Ballantine, 1988.

Lawson, Jacqueline E. "'Old Kids': The Adolescent Experience in the Nonfiction Narratives of the Vietnam War." *Search and Clear: Critical Responses to Selected Literature and Films of the Vietnam War*. Ed. William J. Searle. Bowling Green, Ohio: Popular, 1988.

Lifton, Robert Jay. *Home from the War: Vietnam Veterans, neither Victims nor Executioners*. 1973. New York: Basic, 1985.

O'Brien, Tim. *If I Die in a Combat Zone, Box Me Up and Ship Me Home.* 1973. New York: Dell, 1979.

Peers, Lt. Gen. W. R. *The My Lai Inquiry.* New York: Norton, 1979.

Reston, James, Jr. *Sherman's March and Vietnam.* New York: Macmillan, 1984.

Rich, Adrienne. *On Lies, Secrets, and Silence: Selected Prose 1966–1978.* New York: Norton, 1979.

Santoli, Al. *Everything We Had: An Oral History of the Vietnam War by Thirty-Three American Soldiers Who Fought It.* New York: Ballantine, 1981.

Terry, Wallace. *Bloods: An Oral History of the Vietnam War by Black Veterans.* New York: Random, 1984.

Vietnam Veterans Against the War. *The Winter Soldier Investigation: An Inquiry into American War Crimes.* Boston: Beacon, 1972.

Willenson, Kim, ed. *The Bad War: An Oral History of the Vietnam War.* New York: New American, 1987.

"Humping the Boonies"

Sex, Combat, and the Female in

Bobbie Ann Mason's *In Country*

○ ○ ○ ○ ○ ○ ○ ○ ○ ○ ○ ○ ○ ○ ○

Katherine Kinney

Sex and war are the oldest of metaphorical bedfellows. Since World War II, writers of war literature have become increasingly explicit in using the language and imagery of sexuality to define their emotional and moral relationships to war. In the final chapter of *The Great War and Modern Memory*, Paul Fussell celebrates Thomas Pynchon's portrayal of the masochistic desire with which veterans will relive their combat experiences. Fussell argues that in *Gravity's Rainbow*, "for almost the first time the ritual of military memory is freed from all puritan lexical constraint and allowed to take place with a full appropriate obscenity" through Pynchon's use of "the style of classic English pornographic fiction" (328, 330). The literature of the Vietnam War was and is being written during a period marked in Fussell's words by "the virtual disappearance . . . of the concept of prohibitive obscenity, a concept which has acted as a censor on earlier memories of 'war' " (334).

For women writing about the Vietnam War, this sexualizing of the experience of war has offered an apparent entrée into the male domain of combat. Sex offers itself as a potential common ground of experience for women writers and their female characters seeking an imaginative identification with soldiers. But the use of sex as a metaphor for war, especially to encode its "full appropriate obscenity," most often demands the objectification of women, as the female becomes the subjective battlefield on which the "ritual of military memory" is enacted. This subjective battlefield may become literalized through the violence of rape or it can construct the female in more nostalgic, although still oppositional, terms.

Michael Herr's *Dispatches* has been especially influential in establishing the language of Vietnam War literature, a language suffused with sexual entendre. Herr invokes sexual metaphors directly to express to the reader the inexpressible feeling of what it's like to be in battle. "Under fire . . . the space you'd seen a second ago between subject and object wasn't there anymore, it banged shut in a fast wash of adrenalin" (66). Sex is an obvious and powerful metaphor for this overwhelming feeling of subjectivity. After a firefight, Herr writes:

> . . . you couldn't recall any of it, except to know that it was like something you had felt once before. It remained obscure for a long time, but after enough times the memory took shape and substance and finally revealed itself one afternoon during the breaking off of a firefight. It was the feeling you'd had when you were much, much younger and undressing a girl for the first time. (144)

It is worth noting that the objective distance between self and other which Herr claims collapses under fire is reconstituted in memory. The objectification of the emotional experience of combat is absolute in the second passage. It is unquestionably the awe-inspiring experience of a male self (Herr and the reader collapsed in the use of the second person—"you") witnessing the unveiling of the mysterious female other. The female and war, sex and death are linked as objects of the desire to get as close as one can to the unknown and unknowable. In "The

Laugh of the Medusa," Hélène Cixous writes, "Men say there are two unrepresentable things, death and the feminine sex" (255).

Bobbie Ann Mason's *In Country* is a novel explicitly about a woman trying to comprehend an experience which "men say" she by definition of her gender cannot understand. Her Uncle Emmett, a Vietnam veteran, tells her "women weren't over there. . . . So they can't really understand" (107), hermetically sealing the war from her interrogation. Sam Hughes is a war baby, conceived during the one month of marriage before her father, Dwayne, was sent to Vietnam and born a month after he returned in a body bag. The Vietnam War is her literal inheritance, and at the age of eighteen she comes forth to claim it. At her high school graduation the commencement speaker turns Sam's mind to the war with his talk of "keeping the country strong." But Sam's attempts to learn about the war are continually frustrated by people who won't talk and history books that can't tell her what she wants to know—what it was like to be there. The Vietnam War is like the blank piece of paper she actually receives in lieu of a diploma—until she can fill in the imaginative space occupied by her father and the war, her education will remain incomplete.

Because Sam cannot actually experience the Vietnam War directly, her investigation is by necessity at the level of metaphor and simile. As Judith Stiehm has noted, "For many Americans, especially women, combat is not so much an abstract idea as it is fiction" (Huston, "Tales of War" 274). Fiction tells us what combat is like—and the first thing Vietnam fiction usually tells us is that it's not like books or, more often, the movies. The power and pervasiveness of sexual metaphors lie not only in their invocation of emotional intensity, of experience beyond words, but in their oppositional quality. The status of sexual discourse as controlled, suppressed, censored, and obscene expresses both the horror and desire of an experience (whether sex or combat) which overturns romantic preconceptions (whether of moonlit summer evenings or John Wayne landing at Iwo Jima).

But the quest of Sam Hughes to learn what Vietnam was like challenges the universality assumed by both Herr and Fussell of fictions constructed through sexual metaphor. Suppose Sam Hughes turned, as many do, to Michael Herr to find out what combat was like and discovered it was the feeling she had "undressing a girl for the first time." War literature becomes a male plot which reconstitutes war as the domain of male activity enacted upon female passivity. As Nancy Huston has stated, "War imitates narrative imitates war" ("Tales of War" 273). Again and again, when Sam asks about the war she is told, "Don't think about it," "It doesn't concern you," "Hush"—enforcing upon her the passive female role of war narrative.

At one point Sam attempts to enact the most traditional female role in the fiction of war as sex—sleeping with a soldier. The mutual sexual attraction between Sam and the veteran Tom seems to offer Sam an intimacy which could break down the barriers to understanding that others insist stand in her way. Leaving the veterans' dance with Tom, "she felt she was doing something intensely daring, like following the soldier on point" (124). Her imagination keeps invoking comparisons with Vietnam—orange lights are like napalm, the patchwork quilt on Tom's bed stands in contrast to a soldier's poncho. Sam's imagination is continually able to animate her surroundings with likenesses of Vietnam, but she has no basis for judging their appropriateness. A relationship with Tom might be able to give her that standard of judgment. This is not to say that Sam's interest in Tom is intellectual; her desire is fueled by her developing sense of her own sexuality as well.

But when Tom proves to be impotent, a psychological wound secretly carried from Vietnam, sex becomes yet another symbol of the way in which the experience of war seems to irrevocably divide men and women. Impotence, like the war, is something Sam can't talk about; Tom's embarrassment tongue-ties her, in the same way the veterans' silence seems to her to reflect their feeling that Vietnam was "something personal and embarrassing" (67). But as is typical of Mason's treatment of the relationship between women and war, and of gender difference in general, the hardening of this division becomes further motivation to seek unity. Whereas Sam was originally drawn to Tom in her desire to understand the war, she now feels an even greater need to achieve such understanding in the hope that it will allow her to get closer, through sex or language, to Tom.

The most obvious source for Mason's Tom is Hemingway's Jake Barnes. As Sandra Gilbert has argued, the modernist literature that emerged from World War I describes again and again the wounded, symbolically if not literally emasculated man who returns from the war to confront women empowered, set free by the social dislocations wrought by the Great War. Male rage against the war turns against the female who apparently reaps its benefits. Hemingway's Brett Ash-ley becomes in Gilbert's words "a kind of monstrous anti-fertility god-dess to whose powers the impotent bodies of men had ceaselessly been offered up" (444). While many feminist critics have challenged Gilbert's contention that women actually did feel empowered by the destruction of men and masculinity in the war, her reading of *The Sun Also Rises* is a useful counterpoint to understanding Mason's purposes in rewrit-ing this plot (see Marcus 295–296).

Although Sam feels frustrated to the point of tears when confronted with Tom's impotence and especially his silence, it is true that the Vietnam War is in one sense a source of empowerment for her. It is the death of her father that gives her life the qualities she prizes most highly. Sam's grandmother says to her,

> "I keep thinking about Dwayne and how everybody's life is differ-ent without him. If he had lived, he'd have a house down the road with Irene, and you would have grown up there, Sam, and I'd have knowed you a lot better, sugar. And you'd have some broth-ers and sisters."
>
> Sam shudders at the idea of growing up on a farm, doing chores, never getting to go to town. (13)

Sam clutches at the idea that her father might have resisted such a traditional role, as her Uncle Emmett has done, but at her grandpar-ents' farm she pictures her father there, "discussing blue mold and whether to take risks on wheat prices" just like her grandfather. The legacy demands in turn that her mother "wouldn't have gone to Lex-ington" and that Sam herself would by now be "jiggling a baby on her knee" (195). It is probably only her father's death that allows her to break with traditions she sees as stultifying.

But if Sam's life was affected by her father's death, apparently for the good, that does not make her responsible or vampiric. Mason avoids the extreme logic of the oppositions Gilbert describes between men and women, combat and home, impotence and power, which in-evitably define the female as the enemy. In *The Sun Also Rises*, Jake's impotence is the ground zero of the novel's construction, an irreduc-ible, unavoidable, biological fact that structures all of the novel's events and relationships. Manhood for Hemingway has a singular, apparently biological and thus "natural" definition. In *In Country*, Tom's impotence is not presented as a problem absolutely beyond solution. Tom describes for Sam the little salt-water pump that could be implanted allowing him to simulate an erection. And while cost and fear seem likely to stand in the way of such a move, the possibility of healing his wound remains. For Jake Barnes, Brett Ashley's desire is salt rubbed into his wound. For Tom, Sam's desire, while it cannot heal him directly ("I thought" he tells her, "it would be different with you. . . . "), might just motivate him to seek new possibilities (128).

While rejecting the possibility that women may learn about war through a simple enactment of its sexual metaphor, Mason further interrogates the connection between sex, combat, and the female by digging at the roots of gender constructions—the apparently irreducible, even biological point of difference: men fight wars and women have babies. When Sam's friend Dawn becomes pregnant, questions of gender and sexuality are thrown into crisis for Sam. Sex with her boyfriend becomes an image of invasion: "A billion wiggle-tailed creatures with Lonnie Malone's name on them shot through her" (104). Tom's impotency seems for a moment positive in comparison: "Maybe it was just as well that Tom couldn't make it with Sam. Sex ruined people's lives" (158). But out of this very female fear of unwanted or uncontrollable pregnancy, Sam moves a step closer toward feeling the emotional truth of a soldier in the jungle: "Since Dawn got pregnant, Sam had been feeling that if she didn't watch her step, her whole life could be ruined by some mischance, some stupid surprise, like sniper fire" (184). In *Dispatches*, Herr says that what he really needed in Vietnam was "some generous spontaneous gift for accepting surprises" (12).

In her treatment of the metaphorical relationship between childbearing and going to war, Mason demonstrates the ambiguities and ambivalence of gender difference as a series of collapsing and reforming social constructions. When Dawn becomes pregnant, she is faced with a choice not unlike that which sent Sam's father off to war eighteen years before. Girls don't go to war and boys don't get pregnant, but each event constitutes a rite of passage in which children become adults by conforming to culturally prescribed roles, be it as soldier or wife and mother. At this level, however, while childbearing and combat are both liminal experiences which involve the crossing of boundaries, these boundaries are still mutually exclusive, enforcing the basic gender distinction that women nurture and men kill (see Elshtain 222–223). When Sam urges Dawn to have an abortion, this difference too collapses. Out in the swamp Sam thinks, "Soldiers murdered babies. But women did too. They ripped their unborn babies out of themselves and flushed them away, squirming and bloody" (215). The more conventional Dawn won't consider abortion; her own mother died soon after Dawn was born, a pregnancy that destroyed her health. Dawn feels compelled to bear this child even at personal sacrifice. Dawn's reaction to the word abortion, "I'll pretend I didn't hear that" (141), parallels Sam's grandmother's reaction when Sam asks her if she could go back in time, would she tell her son not to go to Vietnam. Mamaw exclaims, "Oh, Sam. . . . People don't have choices like that" (197). For Dawn and Mamaw personal pain does not become the grounds for challenging the social order; having babies and going to war remain natural facts beyond question.

Dawn and Sam call themselves the "baddest girls in Hopewell," each growing up wild in one-parent households. The deaths of Dawn's mother from childbirth and Sam's father in war are culturally parallel—in ancient Greece these were the only deaths that earned the inscription of one's name on a tombstone. Sam, unlike Dawn, uses her socially marginal position as a "bad girl" to rebel against the cultural constructions of childbirth and war, female and male. Mason makes it abundantly clear that childbearing is as much a cultural as a biological process. Sam's mother, Irene, has two babies seventeen years apart. She was proud of Sam, a "bottle baby," and of Heather because she is "naturally" breast fed. Fashions change even in mothering. Sam doubly rejects this heritage of gender roles by advocating abortion, and thus rejecting compulsory motherhood, and by her insistent desire to learn what war was like, further rejecting the limits placed on female experience and understanding.

Sam's rebellious sexuality and desire for knowledge of the war merge in the novel's most profoundly ambiguous and troubling image: dead babies. After her first mild flirtation with Tom and learning of Dawn's pregnancy,

> . . . Sam dreamed she and Tom Hudson had a baby. In the evening, the baby had to be pureed in a food processor and kept in the freezer. It was the color of candied sweet potatoes. In the

morning, when it thawed out, it was a baby again. In the dream, this was a happy arrangement, and no questions were asked. But then the dream woke her up, its horror rushing through her. (83)

Here the relationship between war and childbirth takes on the mythic dimension William Broyles describes in "Why Men Love War":

> The love of war stems from the union, deep in the core of our being, between sex and destruction, beauty and horror, love and death. War may be the only way in which most men touch the mythic domains of our soul. It is, for men, at some terrible level the closest thing to what childbirth is for women: the initiation into the power of life and death. (61–62)

Sam's dream also unites the oppositions Broyles names: "sex and destruction, beauty and horror, love and death." The common ground between childbearing and war becomes the terrible mutability of the human body, which can be destroyed and reconstituted in endless cycles of birth and death. Sam herself is the miracle baby who replaced Dwayne, although not a perfect likeness—"Everybody expected a boy, of course, but we loved you just the same," her grandfather tells her (199). But the idea of literally taking his place, living on the farm, jiggling yet another baby on her knee, repulses her. Her father's combat diary reveals his purpose in war: "Unreal thought. A baby. My own flesh and blood" (204). "It's all for [Irene] and the baby, or else why are we here?" (202). Sam's gestation becomes the social and cultural justification of historical cycles of violence and death.

Sam's peevish jealousy of her mother's new baby further feeds her morbid imagination:

> The baby was like a growth that had come loose, Sam thought—like a scab or a wart—and Irene carried it around with her in fascination, unable to part with it. Monkeys carried dead babies around like that. A friend of Emmett's knew a lot of dead-baby jokes, but Sam couldn't remember any she had heard. In Vietnam, mothers had carried their dead babies around with them until they began to rot. (164)

Here Sam's initial horror at the mutations of the female body in pregnancy gives way to a more profound appreciation of motherhood's truly ambivalent nature. Nancy Chodorow has theorized what most people know from experience—in a society in which mothers are the primary care givers, they will be the child's first source of disappointment as well as nurturance (83–86). And as the extreme case of war makes vivid, mothers have no supernatural power to sustain the lives of their children—a truth Sam's own mother actively denies, snatching the *Newsweek* cover shot of the morbid Vietnamese madonna from Sam's hands and burning it. Such monstrous truths are further suppressed by the cheap catharsis of dead-baby jokes which are told on the local college radio station along with quadriplegic jokes. Here the horrors of war are diffused and distanced, given expression without ever having to confront their origin or meaning. One wonders if Vietnam did in fact give rise to the popularity of dead-baby jokes.

By going to Cawood's Pond, Sam seeks to confront as directly as she can her relationship to her father's experience. Her trip to the swamp is both a running away from and a running toward her knowledge of her father, of war, and of herself. In Dwayne's notebook, which her grandmother hands her like a diploma, she finds the uncomfortable truth: her father at his most horrible is also the most like herself. The apparently dehumanized soldier who can so casually and dispassionately describe his interest in the rotting corpse of a "dead gook," its special smell, a friend taking a tooth for luck, is for the first time really her father, an individual who has bequeathed to Sam his own morbid curiosity. By reenacting a soldier's experience, she paradoxically hopes that by trespassing directly on the male domain of combat she will discover that she is different from her father and by extension all men.

Her attempt to "hump the boonies" is doomed to failure as an effort to transcend gender difference, as the sexual suggestion of the term itself implies. Once again, however, the result is paradoxical. Although she is forced to acknowledge that "this nature preserve in a protected corner of Kentucky wasn't like Vietnam at all" (214), when morning comes and she hears footsteps approaching, she is filled with the very real fear of a woman alone in an isolated place—the threat of rape. Even in her fear, Sam recognizes the irony, "What an idiotic thing to happen, she thought—to face the terror of the jungle and then meet a rapist" (217). But although the threat of rape reinforces once again that she is a woman, and therefore not a soldier, these moments of waiting in fear are the closest she will get to knowing what it was like to stand watch against an unknown and unseen enemy. In her comic efforts to fashion a weapon out of a can of smoked oysters, she again proves to be her father's daughter, displaying the same ingenuity Dwayne shows in his comments about how he could use a cigarette as a weapon if surprised by the enemy.

The intruder is not, of course, a rapist but Emmett. The fear, anger, and relief Emmett feels finding Sam all right lead him to tell her one war story, in which only Emmett survives a mine blast and hides from an NVA patrol under the dead bodies of his friends. Sam watches in awe as Emmett breaks down: "Emmett's sorrow was full blown, as though it had grown over the years into something monstrous and fantastic" (224). At the pond, Emmett gives birth to his sorrow; as they leave, "from the back he looked like an old peasant woman hugging a baby" (226). Mason's use of combat and childbirth as reciprocal metaphors reveals the equally ambivalent qualities of both states. If motherhood is not wholly nurturant, combat is not simply destructive. The experience of combat is largely felt as defensive, motivated by the practically maternal feeling of what J. Glenn Gray called in *The Warriors* "preservative love"—the soldier's desire to protect those immediately around him (83). Emmett's pain defines not only the horror of smelling and tasting death and being too afraid to move, but the guilt of having failed to protect those who continued to protect him even in death.

In the novel's closing scene, the simultaneous existence of difference and sameness is revealed when Sam finds her own name engraved on the Vietnam Veterans' Memorial. This reconciliation is earned not by denying the differences of age and gender which separate Sam from the Sam Hughes who died in Vietnam, but by Mason's insistent illustration that self and other, male and female are not static, absolute terms but multiple, interactive constructions which can aid as well as hinder imaginative identification. What Sam finally learns about Vietnam is that "she is just beginning to understand. And she will never really know what happened to all these men in the war" (240). Knowledge becomes a process, not a prize, and when she acknowledges this her emotions are so powerful that "it feels like giving birth to this wall"

(240). In this revisionary image the daughter gives birth to the father, the future to the past, the living to the dead—but the relationship between destruction and regeneration is no longer horrific because the fictional spell of its "naturalness"—the assumption that "men will fight wars as long as women have babies"—is broken (Huston, "The Matrix of War" 119).

WORKS CITED

Broyles, William, Jr. "Why Men Love War." *Esquire*, Nov. 1984, 55–65.

Chodorow, Nancy. *The Reproduction of Mothering: Psychoanalysis and the Sociology of Gender*. Berkeley: University of California Press, 1978.

Cixous, Hélène. "The Laugh of the Medusa." *New French Feminisms*. Ed. Elaine Marks and Isabelle de Courtivron. New York: Schocken, 1981.

Elshtain, Jean Bethke. *Women and War*. New York: Basic, 1987.

Fussell, Paul. *The Great War and Modern Memory*. New York: Oxford University Press, 1977.

Gilbert, Sandra M. "Soldier's Heart: Literary Men, Literary Women, and the Great War." *Signs* 8 (1983): 422–450.

Gray, J. Glenn. *The Warriors: Reflections on Men in Battle*. New York: Harper, 1970.

Herr, Michael. *Dispatches*. 1977. New York: Avon, 1978.

Huston, Nancy. "Tales of War and Tears of Women." *Women's Studies International Forum* 5 (1982): 271–282.

———. "The Matrix of War: Mothers and Heroes." *The Female Body in Western Culture*. Ed. Susan Rubin Suleiman. Cambridge: Harvard University Press, 1986.

Marcus, Jane. "Corpus/Corps/Corpse: Writing the Body in/at War." Afterword. *Not So Quiet . . . Stepdaughter of War*. Helen Zenna Smith. New York: Feminist Press, 1989.

Mason, Bobbie Ann. *In Country*. New York: Harper, 1985.

Resistance and Revision in

Poetry by Vietnam War Veterans

O O O O O O O O O O O O O O

Lorrie Smith

For ten years after American troops withdrew from Indochina, we willed our longest war out of memory. Though we no longer forget the Vietnam War, we still have trouble looking at it head-on or accepting full and collective responsibility for its consequences. Our remembering is often simplistic, overburdened with whatever emotional or ideological baggage we still carry. Moreover, understanding the war's significance is harder than ever because of the media blitz which has helped jog but also clog our memories. Popular perceptions of Vietnam have coalesced around patriarchal, patriotic myths which Hollywood, the mainstream media, and the political establishment work hard to reinforce. Few popular treatments of the war examine its political contexts or interrogate the cultural forces that allowed us to wage an immoral war for over a decade.[1]

In opposition to popular treatments of the Vietnam War stands an astounding body of poetry by witnesses who live with its nightmares. Inherently more subversive than narrative, poetry is well suited for a literary project that seeks to disrupt and reimagine cultural myths and values rather than reproduce the status quo. Good poems threaten the social order and offer, in the words of Hélène Cixous, "the very *possibility of change*, the space that can serve as a springboard for subversive thought, the precursory movement of a transformation of social and cultural structures" (245). Though poetry occupies a tenuous position in the canon of Vietnam literature and though the audience for poetry in America is an endangered species, marginality has actually been a source of strength and power for poets of the Vietnam War. Until very recently, veterans themselves were responsible for the grass-roots work of writing, circulating, editing, publishing, anthologizing, and critiquing their own work; hence the poetry has never strayed far from the immediate experience and memory of the war. Moreover, poetry remains free of the mass-market vortex which swallows almost all other forms of expression in America. For the poet who hopes to effect change, the periphery can become the site of a truly subversive art that disrupts the cultural and political mainstream but speaks directly to the concerns of common people—a conundrum, to be sure, but one with far-reaching implications for the future of American poetry.

In many ways, veterans of the Vietnam War share a similar position with women and ethnic minorities: mute, invisible, objectified by the dominant culture, blamed for circumstances which in fact have victimized them. Writers in this position necessarily find an authentic voice by resisting the cultural codes that define them as other, and they necessarily challenge prevailing literary norms. The work of veterans can be seen, then, as part of a larger movement energizing American poetry over the past twenty-five years. Speaking from the cultural and literary margins, Vietnam veteran poets have contributed to an insurrection against the academic center in American poetry, which suffers from what Steven Kowit, editor of *The Maverick Poets*, calls a "debilitating preference for the tepid, mannered and opaque" (2). The "dominant mode" in contemporary poetry, according to Charles Altieri, relies on craft and professional decorum and is built around modest epiphanies which attempt to salvage the remnants of a "shattered heritage" of romanticism through "claims to visionary presence" (35). At its worst, this effort produces triviality and solipsism. For *Parnassus* editor Herbert Leibowitz, "what is in short supply is experience not tied to the apron strings of the academy, where so many poets have hung out their shingles" (6). The one thing Vietnam veterans bring to their poems, and ultimately to the academy, is experience outside the writing workshop. Though these writers, like women and people of color, are now gaining entry to the academic poetry establishment, they change and challenge it in crucial ways. Most important, writing by Vietnam veterans helps revitalize the strained relations between poetry and politics in America.

Traditionally, poetic "making"—poesis—has been aligned with the magic of metamorphosis. Such transformation is implicitly political, though the American critical establishment has always been wary of admitting it. In "Responsibilities of the Poet," Robert Pinsky argues that poetry is effective only when it resists and changes the culture's perception of a subject:

> In some way, before an artist can see a subject—foreign policy, or any other subject—the artist must transform it: answer the received cultural imagination of the subject with something utterly different. . . . Society depends on the poet to witness something, and yet the poet can discover that thing only by looking away from what society has learned to see poetically. (9–12)

Poets, therefore, must be responsive to the community as well as to poetry itself. In the dialogue between the poet and the community, Pinsky says, "The vision and rhetoric of a poem spring from a prior resistance to what the culture has given." Thus, all poetry is implicitly, if not overtly, political:

> The act of judgment prior to the vision of any poem is a social judgment. It always embodies . . . a resistance or transformation of communal values. . . . The poet's first social responsibility, to continue the art, can be filled only through the second, opposed responsibility to change the terms of the art as given—and it is given socially, which is to say politically. (19)

In the dialogue between poets and their art, war poets have actually had little to answer to (and little to guide them). While fiction writers must place themselves within a long and weighty tradition in their efforts to write about war, poets have virtually had to invent their own tradition. Few really good eyewitness war poems have been circulated and anthologized in America: some battlefield elegies by Whitman, a few poems by Randall Jarrell, William Meredith, James Dickey, and Richard Eberhart.[2] Along with a marginal position in the culture and the canon, this lack of literary precedent has assured poets of the war a good deal of freedom to work outside or up against the bounds of received ideas and language. Now that there is a large body of Vietnam War poetry and a clearly emerging canon, the challenge may be to keep the war unpoetic. How poets contend with the dangers of writing too well or too poetically about the war may end up being an important measure of their success.

A poet writing about the Vietnam War is thus necessarily political—not because war is a political topic but because it comes laden with "communal values" which the poet-witness must judge, resist, and revise if the art is to be kept alive and true. These values are not only embedded in the circumstances surrounding the war itself but now reside in the ways our culture remembers and represents the war. "What the culture has given" about the war in Indochina is an evasion of collective responsibility; an unwillingness to make moral and political judgments rather than analyses of the war's strategic failures; an inability to deal honestly with American loss, guilt, and confusion; and a refusal to apologize or make reparations for Vietnamese suffering.

Not surprisingly, Vietnam veterans have carried these darker truths of the war for us, while the culture-at-large congratulates itself for learning lessons which are in fact simplistic and often contradictory: we have regained our national confidence (Rambo's cartoon assertion that we can go back to Vietnam and reclaim our power is eerily paralleled in Reagan's show of muscle in Grenada); we have given Vietnam veterans the overdue honor they deserve (we build memorials yet ignore the alarming number of veterans who have committed suicide, who are homeless, and who suffer the effects of posttraumatic stress disorder and dioxin poisoning); we know better than to intervene in the affairs of Third World countries (yet the government finds increasingly ingenious and illegal ways to fund counterinsurgent mercenaries like the Contras and military dictatorships like El Salvador); we teach our children that war is hell (yet GI Joe is alive and well and

Platoon shapes a whole generation's perceptions of Vietnam's moral wilderness by glorifying its hero's trials and apotheosis). The path of least resistance has been to gloss over such contradictions by subsuming Vietnam into the grandiose, heroic, or redemptive narrative patterns of earlier wars. In even the most sophisticated antiwar fiction and films the soldier is glorified, the premises of American foreign policy go unexamined, and the deeper political and cultural structures that assume war is natural and America is invincible don't change.

The best poems by veterans resist facile myths about the war and keep us much more disturbed than either fiction or film—the two genres that have gained widest popular appeal. Many poems do, of course, tell war stories, but few do so without a deep sense of irony which calls attention to their distance from conventional heroic narratives. In all but the most artless, gung-ho "Boondock Bard" verses, the possibilities for heroic redemption are abrogated. For most veteran poets still drawing upon their war experiences, language is a force for struggling with the world, breaking down conventional social meanings rather than reflecting or accommodating them, as realistic fiction and film tend to do.[3] Their very effectiveness as poems, in Pinsky's terms, depends upon resisting mass cultural norms.

Many poets resist the "received cultural imagining" of the Vietnam War thematically. For instance, working free of the "old myths" (which "die hard," as he admits in the poem of that title) has been W. D. Ehrhart's main project as a poet, memoirist, editor, and advocate of other writers. Since his first involvement with Vietnam Veterans Against the War, Ehrhart has been guided by moral and political outrage and by faith in the power of writing to witness truth and resist the pernicious allure of war. At the 1985 Asia Society conference on literature and the Vietnam War, Ehrhart asserted: "I find it extremely difficult to sit here and talk about the Vietnam War as art. I don't give a goddamn about art. I'm not an artist. I'm an educator, and my writing is a tool of education. . . . if I cannot affect the course of my country as a result of my experiences, then whatever I do as a writer is an utter failure" (Lomperis 32).

Ehrhart's disclaimers belie his eloquence as a political poet, for he manages to be didactic without being preachy or propagandistic. Many poems rely on ironic understatement to make judgments. In "Time on

Target," the speaker's offhand admission that "It used to give me quite a kick / to know that I, a corporal, / could command an entire battery / to fire anywhere I said" is exposed as immoral by the war story at the poem's heart:

> One day, while on patrol,
> we passed the ruins of a house,
> beside it sat a woman
> with her left hand torn away;
> beside her lay a child, dead.

This stark imagery is immediately suppressed, however, by a return to the speaker's original tough soldier-talk, which we now read as self-derision:

> When I got back to base,
> I told the fellows in the COC;
> it gave us all a lift to know
> all those shells we fired every night
> were hitting something. (*Tired* 12–13)

Only in a compressed poem is such a complicated layering of tones possible. There is no final "truth" in this poem: soldiers *were* frustrated by not being sure of what they were firing at; they *were* just doing their jobs; dead bodies *are* a fact of life in a war zone; it *is* necessary to numb yourself to daily atrocity. The poem allows for the soldier's feelings while also rendering them specious in the face of the woman's throat-catching agony.

In poems written after his return from Vietnam, Ehrhart speaks with frank anger to break the silence that greeted the returning veteran. He rejects the cheap and sentimental consolations designed to cover up the real trauma of the war. In "The Invasion of Grenada," he refuses to glorify the war and obscure its continuing political significance: "I didn't want a monument . . . what I wanted was an end to monuments" (*Tired* 71). Above all, Ehrhart's poems warn, we are accountable to future generations; we have a choice about which values we will pass on and which stories we will tell. In "Parade Rest," a response to a ticker-tape commemoration of the ten-year anniversary of the United States' expulsion from Saigon, Ehrhart is disgusted by the sentimentality indulged in by fellow veterans:

> You'd think that any self-respecting
> vet would give the middle finger
> to the folks who thought of it
> ten years and more too late—
>
> yet there they were: the sad
> survivors, balding, overweight,
> and full of beer, weeping, grateful
> for their hour come round at last.
>
> I saw one man in camouflaged utilities;
> a boy, his son, dressed like dad;
> both proudly marching. (*Winter Bells* 3)

Many of Ehrhart's poems ask questions that preclude the possibility of putting the war to rest and enclosing it in definitive narratives. It is still part of living history, and we still have not answered questions like the one raised in "To Those Who Have Gone Home Tired": "After . . . the last loaf of bread is hammered into bullets / and the bullets / scattered among the hungry / What answers will you find / What armor will protect you / when your children ask you / Why?" (*Tired* 29). Both witness and prophet, Ehrhart provides an answer (in "Why I Don't Mind Rocking Leela to Sleep") that is not hopeful:

> What I want for my daughter
> she shall never have:
> a world without war, a life
> untouched by bigotry or hate.
> a mind free to carry a thought
> up to the light of pure
> possibility. (*Winter Bells* 13)

Other forms of resistance exploit the subversive possibilities of poetic language. Freed from the constraints of narrative structure and chronology, poetry thrives on ambiguity, puns and word play, contradiction and paradox, the sensuous qualities of words, the ritualistic motions of rhythm, and the emotional pitches of sound. In its original links to communal song, dance, and ritual, poetry cuts closer to the bone than narrative, lies deeper in the places where the body and the psyche are one (those pre- or nonrational places normally repressed in the symbolic language of the dominant culture). The nontemporal, emotional, and physical "logic" of poetry can resist and revise the cultural givens about the Vietnam War, which so often find expression in conventional war stories.

The language of John Balaban's "After Our War," for instance, challenges and overturns received perceptions of war as adventurous, purposeful, romantic, or heroic. In fact, the war only makes nightmare sense. With sinister irony, the poem shatters the comfortable order of its own seemingly logical syntax and matter-of-fact tone with a grotesque naming of parts:

> After our war, the dismembered bits
> —all those pierced eyes, ear slivers, jaw splinters,
> gouged lips, odd tibias, skin flaps, and toes—
> came squinting, wobbling, jabbering back.
> The genitals, of course, were the most bizarre,
> inching along roads like glowworms and slugs.
> The living wanted them back, but good as new.
> The dead, of course, had no use for them. (37)

More than a gratuitous litany of atrocities, this surreal horror comes alive to haunt us and taunt us. (Balaban intentionally calls this "our" war in order to implicate the reader.) The poem's dark humor gives way to anguished questions that plague a whole generation no longer able to believe the old stories or speak the old language:

> After our war, with such Cheshire cats grinning in our trees,
> will the ancient tales still tell us new truths?
> Will the myriad world surrender new metaphor?
> After our war, how will love speak? (37)

Vexing questions for writers. Many poets have confronted the dilemma of how to speak about war without reverting to the forms and language of prewar consciousness—without, that is, making it glamorous, heroic, even meaningful. For most, the answers to Balaban's questions are tentative or despairing: history and myth may not, after all, yield any truths; the world may not yield new metaphor, only compulsive repetitions; love may not speak again, certainly not in the old ways. To explore such indeterminacy and to resist easy answers, many poets have stretched toward experimental forms and structures. For critic Cary Nelson, the bankruptcy of language as moral and social currency during the Vietnam War years has forever depleted the poet's resources. History, he says, has usurped poetic language and form. Rather than acting as though language were still innocent, the successful poetry of the Vietnam War, he claims, consciously engages this problem; it will "risk more, openly contend with its coeval public history, and court its own formal dissolution" (10).

Bruce Weigl, whose war poems are collected in *Song of Napalm*, can be considered one of the consummate poets of the Vietnam War precisely because he pushes himself to take the risks Nelson describes. "Monkey" is a classic poem of dissolution. It eschews metaphor, proceeding rather through a succession of nervous, disjointed sentences—like Balaban's, syntactically correct but semantically tied to the logic of nightmare. The world "after our war" does not so much surrender "new metaphor" as yield frightening new juxtapositions. All meaningful cause and effect breaks down in the poem's disturbing associations:

> I don't remember the hard
> swallow of the lover.
> I don't remember the burial of ears.
> I don't remember
> the time of the explosion.
> This is the place curses are manufactured:
> delivered like white tablets.
> The survivor is spilling his bedpan.
> He slips a curse into your pocket,
> you're finally satisfied.
> I don't remember the heat
> in the hands,
> the heat around the neck. (22)

The reader must actively imagine the circumstances behind this very uncomfortable poem—must, in fact, feel discomfort in order to grasp it fully. Weigl talks around an experience of psychological trauma and physical injury but never narrates the events that give rise to these feelings; nor does he give us the kind of gory details that border on the voyeuristic in so much war literature. Each section begins with a semblance of meaning but quickly collapses into a jumble of memories, fears, and fantasies in which arbitrary associations of sound replace logical associations of image or syntax:

> Work eat sleep good bad work times.
> I like a certain cartoon of wounds.
> The water which refused to dry.
> I like a little unaccustomed mercy.
> Pulling the trigger is all we have.
> I hear a child. (23)

Many other poems in *Song of Napalm* reach simultaneously back toward nightmare memories and forward into fantasies of escape. Almost always, the imagined escape is finally blocked by the immutable facts of war—the endless cycle of "wounded dying" in "Monkey"; the pervasive "one smell / one word" in "Burning Shit at An Khe" (38); the horrific image of the burning girl who runs "only as far / As the napalm allows" in "Song of Napalm" (34). In such poems, the war intrudes unavoidably into present consciousness. "If there was a world more disturbing than this," Weigl writes in "Amnesia," "you don't remember it" (53). By refusing to lock the war safely in the past, Weigl's poems keep us troubled about its aftermath and ask us to share some of their dark burden of guilt and complicity.

D. F. Brown goes further than any other Vietnam veteran poet toward formal dissolution in order to deconstruct the very modes of thought and speech that permitted our involvement in Vietnam and perpetuate war's mystique. Brown's poems deny the traditional satisfactions of poetic resolution, transcendence, or reconciliation by continually deferring and undercutting final meanings. He directly engages the duplicitous nature of language, thereby holding up to the light the contradictory significations inherent in all experience and memory but especially in the Vietnam War. His strategies involve highly elliptical, anorexic lines, abrupt cuts and jumps in time, shifting perspectives and tenses, and radical dislocations of syntax. By disrupting narrative continuity and placing his poems on a horizontal plane, Brown can explore the continuing aftershocks of the war; the reader is actively involved in making meaning out of the syncopated movements of past and present.

The very title of Brown's one published volume, *Returning Fire*, is characteristically ambiguous (as a verb, shooting back; as an adjective, fire which keeps reappearing in memory). In his (unpaginated) introduction to this book, Jack Marshall points out Brown's intent to resist the artificial logic of war and the linguistic hegemony of the dominant culture:

> What follows will not be a matter of convincing through a recounting of horror stories, nor the explicit inventory of the grotesque, nor will there be encountered here any of that self-righteous comfort which comes from being involved in a disaster of such magnitude. With characteristic rigor, Brown has denied himself the tempting strategy of shock tactics since that would insidiously up the ante in an ever-accelerating repetition compulsion and instill in the reader a fascination to experience his own trial by fire and thus prove his own so-called "manhood" by perpetuating the horror. Such patent exploitation can be left to the news media.

His nonlinear techniques, Brown explains, "open the war to another reading. . . . The absence of narrative drive in the poems requires another sort of investment from my dear reader." In particular, the subversion of normal syntax serves Brown's ends: "The understanding syntax provides retards the understanding I desire. . . . Combat is something else, and to fit it to grammar is to deform it and offer it up as possibility to understand."[4] Brown's volume begins with a poem that signals these intents and prepares the reader for the war poems that follow. In "Bluto Addresses the Real," what is "real" is semiotic, eluding the fixity of symbolic language and residing in the gaps between words and actions; it can only be indicated—a condition that has long vexed poets in the romantic tradition but that here is accepted as a postmodern (and postwar) epistemological given. Establishing what will be a recurring opposition in the book—us and them—what this poem indicates is the existence of "something else," a higher order somewhere beyond what "they" say and somewhere within what "we" know. The poem's opening nonsentence immediately throws us off balance:

> This is where what then
> happens and who signifies.
> Pulling covered, over again
> and again realize. How long
> it is left in no higher order
> than grammar. Education
> works they like to say
> tell us better
> builders waiting to
> construct erect. Go on. (15)

Brown here displays his characteristic compaction and use of ambiguous syntax and line endings to suggest multiple meanings. "Tell us better," for instance, might be an imperative demand for a "higher order" of truth, or it may be modifying "builders." In either case, "they" embody the forces of convention and rigidity which obstruct truth. "Go on" might be an injunction to proceed, a taunting challenge, an expression of skepticism, or an incomplete something "to . . . go on." The poem concludes with an open-ended, unpunctuated note of possibility that "the real" might be retrieved, however fleetingly (the "real" war rescued from the reductive distortions of "grammar" and "education"):

> You have to grab before
> it gets away or how
>
> to say it, what
>
> I want. I love you. (15)

Subsequent poems play deconstructive variations on the us/them opposition, always exposing the antagonism between what "I" or "you" or "we" know (shifting pronouns also keep us off balance, sometimes including and sometimes excluding the reader) and what "they" say. Many poems struggle against and sinuously evade the fixed grammar

of war, as in "When I Am 19 I Was a Medic," whose verb tenses insist
the war is both past and present:

> I can tell true stories
> from the jungle. I never mention
> the fun, our sense of humor
> embarrasses me. Something
> warped it out of place
> and bent I drag it along—
> keeping track of time spent,
> measure what I think we have left.
> Now they tell me something else—
> I've heard it all before
> sliding through the grass
> to get here. (26)

Likewise, in "I Was Dancing Alone in Binh Dinh Province," the
speaker wearily resists the official explanations of war, which are reduced to the vague and desperate "something," which is really nothing: "There is an award for this, / a decoration, something / they want
us to believe." "This" is the actual courage and camaraderie Brown
discovers under fire. But rather than glorifying the soldiers in images
no one can "believe" anymore, Brown humanizes them and makes
them at once vulnerable infants and boys with sinister toys:

> I lose track with these guys
> how gentle they are
> rattles with machine guns
>
> Whoever holds title to this
> has a handful
> soil hearts move through. (30)

In several poems, Brown juxtaposes "their" language and images
with his own to undermine conventional war story formulas. This war
doesn't end but, as in Weigl's "Monkey," floats on the horizon of
memory and nightmare. "Still Later There Are War Stories" debunks
the myths of cowboys and "boy scout excursions" he grew up with and
permanently defers the moment when his own stories will make sense,

since there is no "now" to help us locate "later" ("still" might do double grammatical duty as an adjective and/or an adverb):

> Another buddy dead.
> There is enough dying—
> Gary Cooper will
> ride up, slow and easy
> slide off his horse
> without firing a shot
> save us all.
>
> It is a matter of waiting.
> We grow old counting the year
> in days, one by one
> each morning ritual marks
> one more, one less—
> the plane has yet to land.

When the time shifts in part 2 to "a decade / recounting days since," there are no stories, only present tense (and tense present) memories of death and psychic injury: "The jungle / loaded, nobody / comes away in one piece" (45–46).

Brown's most ambitious disruptions of conventional syntax and sense take place in several long poems in *Returning Fire*, preludes to his more radical recent work. In the title poem, Brown uses broken lines which move with the hesitant, high-strung steps of a march through a booby-trapped jungle. Many lines make plural sense as parts of preceding or succeeding lines, with no punctuation or capitalization to guide us. The reader walks point through an open linguistic field of slippery signification, abrupt drops, syntactical dislocations, and elisions—a journey that mirrors the speaker's own return, through memory, which can "take any way back / down a hot tropic / trail to good soldiers . . ." (20). There are no conventional heroic war stories in this poem, but there is a recognition shared by Larry Heinemann in *Paco's Story* and Tim O'Brien in "How to Tell a True War Story": the truest war story is both a love story and a ghost story. "Returning Fire" ends with a haunting, elegiac evocation of the ghosts who finally find the peace and renewal denied to the war's survivors. As in many of Brown's poems, the speaking "you" is both a distanced first person and an intimate address which brings living and dead (and perhaps poet and reader) together in the poem's field of vision:

> you call them
> with a motion
> a little hike
> a little while longer
> you want them
> to slip from green
> clothes wet boots
> with plenty hot water
> you would steam off mud
> get them ready for bed
> it isn't night
> empty spaces
> or the tropics
> green is nothing
> it holds the trees
> and stops sky
> it isn't guns
> or the ammo
> they sleep on knowing
> the other side
> creased
> and still white
> they never come back
> soaked off into jungle
> they rise only
> in the rough
> second growth
> that follows (22–23)

Brown goes against all the macho stereotypes and ideals of our culture by imagining himself as a nurturing figure putting his "children" to bed. This image pushes so hard against what "they" say war is that it forces a whole new way of thinking about manhood and fighting.

Most recently, Brown's poems have become more politically explicit and more radically experimental in their disruptions of conventional meaning. These are poems that deny interpretation and ask instead to be experienced as kinetic, disturbing movements of thought. They keep us off-balance and provoke our own engagement with the problems of memory and meaning. "The Other Half of Everything," which appeared in the final issue of *Ironwood*, is an intricate, eight-part poem that marches nervously across the page; the following excerpt only gives a hint of the poem's fluid richness:

> Someone in the jungle yelling in Vietnamese.
> I don't say anything about it but I can al-
> most figure what they are saying. Not what
> they are saying but what it means.
>
> Like the movie, but no music and it stink.
>
> I lost my place.
>
> You know, screw anything thirty years there's
> bound to be withdrawal.
>
> We were young and I remember.
>
> I thought I could fill enough sandbags.
>
> Leave that jungle and go straight home.
>
> 8.
> Expect to live at peace in the heart of a military
> empire. Every day martial pumped at you. White
> lines in your blue sky.
>
> Newspaper versions . . .
>
> That pile of books on Nam.
>
> One end of the wire woven to your crotch.
>
> All kinds of pain, all sorts of medicine.
>
> Remember.
>
> Ashes, ashes.

You get an E for attendance.

All of the above.

You become fucked. You are glad you made it. (179–180)

The lyrical plenitude of this poem opens it to the flux and indeterminacy of history. Poets who take this kind of risk immerse us in the full range of irreconcilable realities that was and is the Vietnam War. Admitting such a vision of reality, rather than believing what "they" tell us, might indeed be the first step toward a transformation of social and political structures. Beyond witnessing war's horror, Vietnam veteran poets call attention to how insistently our perceptions of war are determined by cultural codes, literary conventions, and received language. Actively resisting these forces, they not only keep American poetry alive and in touch with political realities, but keep us unsettled, as we still should be, about our war.

NOTES

1. For a treatment of how realistic narratives of the war are implicated in cultural and political norms, see my "Disarming the War Story" in Gilman and Smith. An excellent analysis of this issue is Thomas Prasch's "*Platoon* and the Mythology of Realism."

2. I would like to thank Dan Duffy for pointing out that American war poetry does, in fact, exist. Without tackling the complicated issue of canonicity, I would simply argue that the relative unavailability of texts makes it hard to talk about a living tradition of war poetry. As a number of people have pointed out, the British poets of World War I offer the closest affinities with the poets of the Vietnam War, but there are also important differences of idiom and sensibility. My argument rests on the idea that traditional war stories are popular because they confirm cultural norms, while many war poems disrupt those norms and therefore make us uncomfortable. It is not surprising that this tradition is submerged, given our huge emotional and political investment in perpetuating the acceptability of war.

3. Though I have quoted the poems that follow from their original volumes, most also appear in W. D. Ehrhart's excellent collection, *Carrying the Darkness: The Poetry of the Vietnam War*, recently reissued by Texas Tech University Press. The poets I discuss here—Ehrhart, John Balaban, Bruce Weigl, and D. F. Brown—are also generously represented in Ehrhart's anthology, *Unaccustomed Mercy*, also published by Texas Tech University Press in 1989.

Ehrhart deserves thanks and recognition for culling the finest poems and poets of the Vietnam War and indicating the contours of an emerging canon in this field.

4. Quoted from private correspondence with D. F. Brown.

WORKS CITED

Altieri, Charles. *Self and Sensibility in Contemporary American Poetry.* Cambridge: Cambridge University Press, 1984.

Balaban, John. *Blue Mountain.* Greensboro, N.C.: Unicorn, 1982.

Brown, D. F. *Returning Fire.* San Francisco: San Francisco State University Press, 1984.

————. "The Other Half of Everything." *Ironwood* 31/32 (1988): 171–180.

Cixous, Hélène. "The Laugh of the Medusa." *New French Feminisms.* Ed. Elaine Marks and Isabelle de Courtivron. New York: Schocken, 1981.

Ehrhart, W. D. *To Those Who Have Gone Home Tired.* New York: Thunder's Mouth, 1984.

————. *Winter Bells.* Easthampton, Mass.: Adastra, 1987.

Kowit, Steve, ed. *The Maverick Poets.* Santee, Cal.: Gorilla, 1988.

Leibowitz, Herbert. "Singing the Fin de Siècle Poetry Blues." *Parnassus: Poetry in Review* 15 (1) (1989): 5–8.

Lomperis, Timothy. *"Reading the Wind": The Literature of the Vietnam War.* Durham, N.C.: Duke University Press, 1987.

Nelson, Cary. *Our Last First Poets: Vision and History in Contemporary American Poetry.* Urbana: University of Illinois Press, 1981.

Pinsky, Robert. "Responsibilities of the Poet." *Politics and Poetic Value.* Ed. Robert von Hallberg. Chicago: University of Chicago Press, 1987.

Prasch, Thomas. *"Platoon* and the Mythology of Realism." *Search and Clear: Critical Responses to Selected Literature and Films of the Vietnam War.* Ed. William J. Searle. Bowling Green, Ohio: Popular, 1988.

Smith, Lorrie. "Disarming the War Story." *America Rediscovered: Critical Essays on Literature and Film of the Vietnam War.* Ed. Owen W. Gilman, Jr., and Lorrie Smith. New York: Garland, 1990.

Weigl, Bruce. *Song of Napalm.* New York: Atlantic, 1988.

Doing It Wrong Is

Getting It Right

America's Vietnam War Drama

O O O O O O O O O O O

Don Ringnalda

The story is told of one of Marcel Marceau's performances in which he mimed playing a cello. After the performance a somewhat bemused spectator—a real cellist—informed Marceau that his movements had been all wrong, that if anyone actually fretted and bowed a cello that way the sound produced would at best be peculiar. He then volunteered to show Marceau the correct way to mime cello playing, and Marceau taped it. After viewing the tape, both agreed that it simply did not look like someone playing a cello. Somehow, by doing things wrong Marceau had made it look right, whereas by doing things right the cellist had made it look wrong.

My contention is that even highly considered Vietnam War narrative literature and cinema get Vietnam wrong because they do the fretting and bowing right. Conversely, there is a handful of works that get Vietnam right by doing it all wrong; and one could argue, as I will, that most of them belong to war's neglected genre, namely, drama. (I might add that poetry is faring little better.) The paradoxical premise of this essay is that drama is best suited for grappling with the Vietnam War (or any war) precisely because it is the least suited. It is the best equipped for doing so because it is the least equipped. It is richly endowed with the resources needed to show the underbelly of the cliché "war is hell" precisely because it is so impoverished. It is real because it is so blatantly artificial. And because the fretting and bowing are wrong, we hear richly disturbing music which is muffled, sometimes silenced altogether, by those who do it right.

There is much confusion among Vietnam veterans and critics over how to "play" this war. More often than not, I find these veterans and critics reenacting the old story of the guy who loses his wallet but searches for it several blocks up the street because the lighting is better there. We are unseeing altogether too much of Vietnam in the clear, reassuring light of narrative artifice. The dark mythic underpinnings of the war often remain invisible in this light. We see the ominous trees in frightening technicolor, but the mythic forest of American consciousness remains invisible or at best becomes obscured. The Vietnam writer must realize that just as the mime must "do" the cello without a cello, so he or she must do the war without the war, so to speak. *Certainly* without combat. It will be difficult to convince writers of this, because there's no chance of catching the smell of napalm in the morning if you're stateside.

The well-established line of critical thought on Vietnam War literature is that the war does not fit within the tidy perimeters of the ethnocentric, traditional war narrative. Many critics have quite correctly expounded upon this, including Philip Beidler, Pearl Bell, John Hellmann, Peter Marin, Thomas Myers, Tim O'Brien, and this writer. These Chuck Norris narratives simply get Vietnam wrong by doing it wrong. That is, even though the grunt lived through a wacky postmodern experience in Vietnam, when he returns to tell his story he often tries to fit that experience within the confines of a traditional "B" narrative.

What is less well established is that critics tend to slip into a binary fallacy: writers either skew the narrative in order to make it dovetail with the reality of Vietnam or they do not. To be or not be ironic. Obviously, the skewed narrative is far more capable of expressing the disjunction between the official "reality" and what really happened to us and to Southeast Asians during the war.[1] But can any narrative ultimately connect the reader or viewer responsibly to the Vietnam War? Isn't what Irving Howe said of Holocaust writing applicable to Vietnam narratives as well? Aren't even the skewed postmodernist narratives, like Michael Herr's *Dispatches* and Stephen Wright's *Meditations in Green*, a perpetuation of a traditional aesthetic problem: "that the representation of a horrible event, especially if in drawing upon literary skills it achieves a certain graphic power, [will] serve to domesticate it, rendering it familiar and in some sense even tolerable, and thereby shearing away part of the horror. The comeliness of even the loosest literary forms is likely to soften the impact of what is being rendered" (Howe 29). As Howe would have it, therefore, aesthetic decisions have moral ramifications.

It seems to me that this aestheticizing of the war obscures a deeper, far more radical problem, like Joseph Heller's Yossarian fastidiously treating Snowden's superficial hip wound. We need to take our cue from William Broyles, Jr., from whose article "Why Men Love War" we can infer that one can properly loathe this war and be attuned to all of its monstrous atonality; one can correctly see all the stupidities, the genocides, the racisms; one can weep and rage—but still love it! Broyles says, "War is not an aberration; it is part of the family, the crazy uncle we try—in vain—to keep locked in the basement" (56).

If I may extrapolate from Simone Weil's famous essay "The *Iliad*, Poem of Might," in war narratives "the intolerable afflictions either of servitude or war endure by force of their own weight, and therefore, from the outside [the reader's point of view] they seem easy to bear; they last because they rob the resources required to throw them off" (170). Weil goes on to say that whether you win or lose a war makes no difference, for pride and humiliation are equally intoxicating (179). It makes no difference if a war story is written with patriotic zeal or disillusioned irony. Both are predicated on the assumption that the human condition is largely rational, and that at its worst, the Vietnam War was a temporary disruption of sanity. Thus, both are false expressions of the misfortunes of war. To write with patriotic zeal is to deny any wounds; to write with disillusioned irony is to treat the superficial wounds. Either way, the act of bottling war in narrative form is a tacit admission that no radical change in the writer's consciousness has taken place. Either way, as Bertolt Brecht would have it, the spectator is projected into an event rather than confronted by it (3). Either way, to use the words of Weil, it is the "subordination of the human soul to might, which is, be it finally said, to matter," the intoxicating matter of war (179–180).

The greatest example of the disillusioned ironic narrative is Michael Herr's *Dispatches*. Note that he does all the right things: he warps space and time; his structure is fragmented and jagged; he tells us the famous LURP (Long Range Reconnaisance Patrol) story; he gives us the famous deconstructive line "a lot of things had to be unlearned before you learn anything at all" (224); instead of giving the reader yet more raw material from the war's surfaces, he writes metafiction. As I've said elsewhere, Herr is a LURP writer who leaves the main trails of convention and takes us into the steamy jungles of a linguistic mine-field, in the middle of no-man's-land; his charged prose rips through pages like an M-16 on rock'n'roll. His book is so visceral, so disorienting, so frightening. And so sexy! Like "undressing a girl for the first time" (144).

Finding an aesthetic framework for the Vietnam War is indeed problematical. And it's a problem that Herr deals with ingeniously. I know of no writer who more compellingly tells me that war is hell and that hell sucks. But much more disturbingly problematical is how to stop the reader from saying, "I know it's hell, so stop it some more!" It does no good to tell alcoholics that alcohol is bad for them; they *know* it is.

The problem with the movies and novels that get war wrong by doing it right is that, to use the words of Janine Basinger, they "have it both ways with the audience" (170). They offer jeremiads and trenchant criticisms of the war but at the same time engage us by appealing to our voyeuristic appetites. In "Charlie Is a She: Kubrick's *Full Metal Jacket* and the Female Spectacle of Vietnam," Krista Walter argues that *Full Metal Jacket* (and I would suppose also Gustav Hasford's *The Short-Timers*, upon which it is based) is an exception, that it cuts the voyeuristic "orgasmicord" by eliminating most of the staples of the traditional war story: the characters are psychopaths, so we can't identify with them; they have no mission, so there's no plot to sweep us along; and the Mickey Mouse ending is anticlimactic. But no matter how skewed or starkly ironic this narrative may be, there is a much more powerful master narrative in counterpoint—a hungry narrative that will eat what is available. It does not like the taste of irony, but it will gladly eat it in order to get at the camera's seductive power to evoke the beautiful sexuality of combat, death, and massive destruction. This movie, too, has it both ways. In Howe's language, we are enthralled *because* we are appalled. Kubrick makes war deeply repulsive and deeply attractive. And for popular audiences, the latter, arguably, wins out: Army enlistments rose after this film was released.

In a fascinating article entitled "How to Tell a True War Story," Tim O'Brien seems to point the way beyond glamorizing war and having it both ways: "If at the end of a war story you feel uplifted . . . then you have been made the victim of a very old and terrible lie" (210). Indeed, we have. But what if the lie satisfies? And what do we do with O'Brien's *Going after Cacciato*, a novel so exquisitely written that I felt uplifted after reading it? O'Brien goes on to say that a true war story has an "uncompromising allegiance to the obscenity and evil of war" (210). Very good, but then so do Kubrick and Hasford in *Full Metal Jacket*. Again, O'Brien says if you believe a war story, be skeptical. This is excellent advice, but it's a bit like being told by a pathological liar that he or she is lying. Finally, O'Brien says that some war stories are "just beyond telling" (210). But aren't they all? Isn't the very act of *telling* exemplary of getting it wrong by doing it right?

Vietnam War writers and critics need to find a way beyond silently accommodating—like an alcoholic's hidden bottle—Tim Page's glamorous vision of war:

Take the glamour out of war! I mean, how the bloody hell can you do *that*? Go and take the glamour out of a Huey, go take the glamour out of a Sheridan. . . . It's like trying to take the glamour out of sex, trying to take the glamour out of the Rolling Stones. . . . I mean, you *know* that, it just *can't be done*! . . . The very *idea*! . . . Ohhh, what a laugh! Take the bloody *glamour* out of bloody war! (Herr 265–266)

The glamour of the master narrative is hard to kill. More than the family quarrel or in-house revolt of ironic narrative is required. You can't fix war narratives by tinkering with war narratives. You can no more fix the wrong tool by using that tool than you can lift your left arm with your left arm. In John Arden's brilliant antiwar play from England, *Serjeant Musgrave's Dance*, this is exactly what the title character tries to do. He wants to use the arts of violence to end violence. He tries to use what he calls his "book," (the British edition of the master narrative that encourages and dignifies the horrors of war) against itself. But as a fellow soldier says, "You can't cure the pox with further whoring" (108).

In a sense, this is the error repeated by the most gripping of the Vietnam War anti–master narrative books. What Herr calls Vietnam's "dense concentration of American energy" screaming out in "hundred-channel panic" is powerfully seductive. The urge to plug back into that energy is a powerful come-on. The writer and the reader are enticed, like Lot's wife, to give America's smoking Sodom and Gomorrah one more "eye fuck." To paraphrase the narrator of Larry Heinemann's *Paco's Story*, destruction is terrible, but it also is beautiful.

Page (in Herr's *Dispatches*) would say "Ohhh, what a laugh" to the removal of "carnalization" from carnage. But perhaps it is not such a laugh after all, for there are some seldomly heard voices out there that are taking the bloody glamour out of war. Perhaps this explains why they are so infrequently heard and critically discussed. They are the voices that do Vietnam all wrong. These error-prone "mimes" are the Vietnam War playwrights—Tom Cole, Terrence McNally, Stephen Metcalfe, John DiFusco, and of special importance Emily Mann, David Rabe, and Amlin Gray.

Each of these playwrights seems to have realized that being on location, in country, for very long is dangerous for writer and reader alike. Irving Howe comes to this same conclusion in his article about Holocaust writing. Saying that some things are too terrible to be looked at or into directly, he urges the writer to learn a lesson from Perseus, who would turn to stone if he looked directly at the serpent-headed Medusa. But he could look at her through a reflection in a mirror. This is what the Vietnam dramatists tend to do. They look at Medusa through the mirror of self-conscious artifice. For example, in John DiFusco's collaborative play *Tracers* (first performed in 1980), a pantomimed postbattlefield scene, called a "blanket party," is staged. Four grunts are assigned the task of stacking invisible dead bodies scattered all over the stage. Soon they begin locating invisible fingers, arms, and various unrecognizable body parts, which they then try to mix and match with the stacked bodies. A "food fight" ensues, and finally they place all the invisible human fragments on an invisible blanket, and with each character holding an invisible corner, they exit to the sound of "The Unknown Soldier" by the Doors. To use Jerzy Grotowski's phrase, this is "poor theatre" at its best. By not looking at the bodies directly, we actually see them more absolutely. In their palpable absence they become a sort of Platonic idea of carnage. Because the audience can't see the individual bodies, it finds itself in the overwhelming presence of the idea of death.

The actual genesis of this essay was my perplexity over why this pantomimed scene in *Tracers* had a much more unsettling effect on me than the scene of mass carnage at the end of *Platoon*. The sight of death is strangely wonderful because it is not one's own. This reaction to death is frequently documented in the novels and memoirs of the war. What makes the "blanket party" so chastening is that we can neither stare at death voyeuristically nor close a second, protective eyelid to shield us. Instead we stare at the ultimate incarnation of death: emptiness filled with itself. The indirect look at death becomes painfully direct through the ritual of flaunted make-believe: theater.

One of the most important differences between Vietnam narratives and plays is that none of the latter looks at Vietnam directly. Very few even take place in country. (By contrast, almost all Vietnam fiction and cinema do.) Only *Tracers*, Terrence McNally's *Botticelli*, and Amlin Gray's *How I Got That Story* are set in Vietnam. And of David Rabe's four Vietnam plays, only *The Basic Training of Pavlo Hummel* is set in Vietnam, and then only briefly. Furthermore, even those that are "on location" are, like *Tracers*, so blatantly artificial and stylized that there is no possibility of seduction. There is no rerunning of the war. This frees the playwright to reflect the subtexts of the war, to raise what James Reston, Jr., calls "generational questions" about the master narrative, to confront Americans with their own duplicity and complicity. As Emily Mann says in a note to her play *Still Life*, Vietnam War plays are pleas for examination and self-examination of our own violence. The battles that these playwrights fight are not the ones in Khe Sanh, Pleiku, or An Loc. Their battlefield is one located between the war and the home-front epistemology that started, maintained, and lost it. Their battlefield reflects the conflicting realities of the master narrative, now out in a new edition, and the antinovel that was Vietnam. Using a metaphor from Rabe's *Sticks and Bones*, the Vietnam playwright traces either the fallout or the roots of the war back to the myth of innocence enshrined in Harriet Nelson's kitchen of immaculate deception. The Vietnam plays bring the war back home where it started and is still being waged. We could give these plays the composite title of Paul Hoover's recent novel, *Saigon, Illinois*, or Bobbie Ann Mason's *In Country*, where "in country" means America. To emphasize this connection between home and Vietnam, Rabe in two of his plays (*The Basic Training of Pavlo Hummel* and *Streamers*) calls for a stage that slants downward, rather threateningly, toward the audience.

And what a different "movie" we get when the "cello" is removed from the stage; when the screaming Phantoms just above tree level, the thudding rotors of the Huey, the vision of multicolored flares and tracers are all edited out. Most important, what a different "movie" we get when combat is edited out. Theater simply cannot do combat without being plain silly. (Neither can cinema, but it has the technology to create the illusion that it can.) But this limitation is one of theater's strengths, because trying to get Vietnam right by spending millions of technological dollars on the latest special effects is tantamount to fighting the wrong war, wrongly again. What is needed is a guerrilla genre, as it were. Unlike the military planners and Hollywood producers, who have so many toys that they try to play with all of them at once, this genre is quite satisfied with a rice ball, a little nuoc mam, and a carbine. Unlike the narratives of cinema and fiction, theater, as Grotowski says in *Towards a Poor Theatre*, is like sculpture (39). The playwright and the director reveal essence by taking away not adding on. They remove what is concealing the essence instead of building it up. They reveal by removing Snowden's flak jacket. What is left after their sculpting is the elemental stage. What Peter Brook says about Elizabethan theater could be said about Vietnam theater: "Absence of scenery in the Elizabethan theater was one of its greatest freedoms" (86).

The paucity of scenery on the Vietnam stage creates a new relationship between author and audience, a new contract with new responsibilities for both parties. Once we no longer have a cello decorating the stage, we have a whole new agenda that differs radically from any on-location war narrative. Without the dead bodies, the jobs of the playwright and spectator become quite different from those of the narrator and reader or the moviemaker and spectator. The narrator enables the reader to see the seen, whereas the playwright enables the spectator to see the unseen mythic tracks that led to Vietnam and back to Harriet's split-level. Whereas the rich narrative is very user friendly in that it does a great deal of the work for the passive reader as it fills in the Medusan Vietnam canvas, the poor theater is user disturbing; eliminating the wealth, it requires a great deal from the necessarily active spectator.

There is a sense in which both actors and spectators are vulnerable in the absence of scenery. That absence signifies that what happens in this theater is active presentation and investigation, not passive representation; enactment, not reenactment. It is live, disturbingly so because everyone involved (including the audience) knows that in production theatre can easily go wrong if either party fails to embrace the special contract demanded by the genre. Distinguishing between the artifice of cinema and theater, Brook says:

> The cinema flashes on to a screen images from the past. As this is what the mind does to itself all through life, the cinema seems intimately real. Of course, it is nothing of the sort—it is a satisfying and enjoyable extension of the unreality of everyday perception. The theatre, on the other hand, always asserts itself in the present. This is what can make it more real [getting it right by doing it wrong] than the normal stream of consciousness. This also is what can make it so disturbing. (99)

Brook argues that theater is disquieting because the spectator cannot get beyond the medium itself. The medium *is* the message. The authentic Vietnam theater is *about* theater, about making the unseen seen, about how we see. It is artifice that flaunts its artificiality. Compare this to what Northrup Frye says about the artifice of narrative.

He likens it to a plate-glass window between shoppers and a department store display. The glass is so clean and polished that the shoppers are unaware of it. Unconsciously they pass right through its invisibility to the content on the other side (265). This is what happens to the readers of Vietnam War narratives. Enticed and distracted by the content, they are unaware of how the intervening form is processing and translating that content. Polished and repolished by long use, narrative—and language itself—seems completely natural and neutral. Seeing only the seen, readers are unaware of the intervening filtering lens. In a word, Vietnam narratives can very easily become what Roland Barthes and Neil Postman mean by myth, "a way of thinking so deeply embedded in our consciousness that it is invisible"(Postman 79).

At the 1984 Vietnam Writers Conference in New York City, John Clark Pratt, author of *The Laotian Fragments*, voiced his concern that Vietnam was actually being understood the way traditional novels are written. In other words, events seem real only to the extent that they are organized into a plot. Meanwhile, the processing medium goes about its window washing—unseen; the interpretive tool becomes the mythic reality, and the unseen artifice of realism actually is identified as "authenticity," the buzzword of critics and veterans.

In these post-Vietnam years, we can ill afford to ignore how dangerously easy it is to remythologize the war, which I think Michael Herr has done, quite unintentionally, with his magnificent book. The Vietnam playwrights seem to have recognized this, for they are demythologizers of war's glamour, of militarism, of violence, of machismo, of the whole apparatus of *Bildungsroman*, of the media that process us and tell us who Americans are. On their relatively bare, detechnologized stages they never let us forget the artifice and the illusion of transparency. We never get around or through the opaque medium; it takes up all of our time. To translate another Brechtian term, these playwrights "alienate" us at every turn, breaking all the rules of verisimilitude. Blatantly tossing away any pretense of being real, they insist on the being of real pretense—the imaginary cello.[2]

Emily Mann's *Still Life* (first performed in 1980) is one of the most effective examples of a play as the being of real pretense. It consists of three characters: Mark, a guilt-ridden marine combat veteran, now a struggling, tormented artist; Cheryl, his willfully politically naive, passive-aggressive wife; and Nadine, Mark's somewhat cynical older friend, artist, and social activist. Soon after the play begins, Mark says, "I don't want this to come off as a combat story" (222). One can infer that he has done very little *but* rerun combat stories since his discharge, and he knows that these stories simply plug him back into something he can't process: nostalgia, and therefore guilt, for the seductive power of having been able to do horrible things—legally— while in Vietnam. The point is, Mann doesn't allow her play to turn into a combat story. She cuts the orgasmicord by staging a Brechtian play loaded with alienation effects. Somewhat reminiscent of Beckett's play simply called *Play*, *Still Life*'s characters speak—much to our discomfort—directly to the audience, and rather than speak *to* each other, they speak *about* each other in the third person. Rarely do they even seem aware of each other's presence. Their voices collide with each other and overlap, undermine, and deflect each other ironically. Occasionally they even drown each other out. And because the audience is repeatedly and directly told we all are implicated in the Vietnam War, we have a fourth "voice" added to this polyphonic collage of colliding traumatic memories of the sixties and seventies and explorations of an untenable present.

What Mann achieves with the contrapuntal voicings is that no single voice can ever build up narrative momentum and stake out a claim for the spectator's sympathy. The content of this play is not any or all of the voices; instead it is the charged, silent spaces between the voices. Almost like a musical score, this play is an investigation of consonant and dissonant relationships. Thus, Mark can share fragments from his Vietnam experiences without the play becoming his univocal "melody." Many of these fragments are slides of war photographs that Mark projects on a screen throughout the play. As such, they are offered up as *still* lifes, operating on the spectator's mind in conjunction with the "still lifes" of Nadine and Cheryl. I emphasize "still" to distinguish Mark's Vietnam slides from the movement and life of narrative art. Whereas narrative art presupposes either linear or nonlinear continuity, the still lifes underscore rupture.

Mann's point is that the tangled, ruptured voices allow (and force) the audience to see the real theater of Vietnam where we all were "it." The real Vietnam is not other, not an isolated, sickly surreal aberration of the American identity. Instead, as Mann presents the war, it is a logical continuation, a mere symptom of violence masked by seemingly respectable values, marriages, fatherhood, motherhood, even the church. Dysfunctional families and social institutions are seen here virtually as basic training for Vietnam. For Mann and for the Vietnam playwright in general, the Vietnam War was not a short circuit. Rather it was all systems on go. Everything went according to plan. The crazy uncle simply had to walk up the stairs. He did.

Mann's collage of domestic voices *is* Vietnam. It *is* its formula. Of course, this collage once again does Vietnam all wrong: it muffles the universal siren call; it pulls it off location; it devotes two-thirds of the play to women; it is written by a woman who hasn't even set foot in Vietnam; finally, it is an internal affairs investigation, not an adventure. Mann's stage directions call for a "poor theatre" set that looks like a conference room or a trial room.

She concludes her play with a microcosmic slide projected on a screen. It is Mark's still-life collage, and it reveals the Vietnam that can exist only when the one done right is replaced by the one done wrong. At first it looks like a classic Zurbarán still life: wholesome grapefruit, an orange, delicious fresh bread. But with her melody-destroying improper "fretting and bowing," Mann also includes a grenade, a broken egg, and a fly on the fruit. That fly, broken egg, and grenade are not meant simply to represent the ticking trip-wire marine veteran suffering from posttraumatic stress disorder, they are a commentary on the American mythic jungle as well. If anything, Mann would have us see the fruit and bread as Mark's, the rest of the collage as Nadine's, Cheryl's, and the audience's. "We've all done it." Mark's final line—"I didn't know what I was doing"—reminds one of Friedrich Dürrenmatt, who upon surveying the first fifty-four years of the twentieth century, declared, "In the Punch-and-Judy show of our century . . . everything is dragged along and everyone gets caught somewhere in the sweep of events. We are all collectively guilty, collectively bogged down in the sins of our fathers and of our forefathers . . . " (31).

All of David Rabe's Vietnam-related plays (*The Basic Training of Pavlo Hummel*, 1971; *Sticks and Bones*, 1972; *Streamers*, 1976; and *Hurlyburly*, 1984) are seemingly incongruous collages of the voices that led us to Vietnam. Once again, it is juxtaposition, not continuity, that forms the structure of *Pavlo Hummel*. Rabe refuses even to write an anti-*Bildungsroman*, for that would still give us the seductive continuity of so many Vietnam War narratives: naive young man's initiation leads not to new wisdom but to cynicism. Rabe will have none of that in his plays. In effect, he announces this to his audience one minute into *Pavlo Hummel* by having his "hero" die the first of several deaths. The beginning is the end. The title character is Rabe's new American mythic Everyman: a creature who dies over and over, pointlessly and absurdly. As Ardell, his stud alter-ego, says, we're "thin as paper. We melt; we tear and rip apart. Membrane, baby. Cellophane. Ain't that some shit" (96).

It is as if Pavlo is caught in the middle of the very chaotic game of hurlyburly, and Rabe's collagelike structure reinforces this. If Mann gives us a Dali still life, Rabe gives us one of Jean Tinguely's motorized, self-destructing sculptures, coughing, hissing, belching, lurching, and smoking, with the grinding of unaligned gears. *Pavlo Hummel* is frantic and frenetic. I know of no play that makes such a shambles of Aristotle's three unities. Action, place, and time are so scrambled that sometimes we are in Vietnam in the jungle, in a whorehouse, in a hospital; we are at Fort Gordon, in a day room, in the physical training area, in a barracks, at the rifle range; we are in New York, in Pavlo's brother's apartment, in Pavlo's mother's apartment—all virtually simultaneously, without any significant set changes. At one point Pavlo undresses, dresses, has a prostitute undress him in his brother's room, which is his mother's place, which is a Vietnamese whorehouse, where a wounded GI calls to Pavlo from his hospital bed while Pavlo's drill instructor yells training instructions, and so on.

Of course cinema can do these same cuts. In fact it can do them much better, but this wealth often is its poverty. Whereas in cinema the cuts are demarcated from one discrete space to another, in *Pavlo Hummel* the dirt is dragged from space to space, until they merge, messily, in a mise-en-scène collage of fractured space and time.

Whereas the voicings are a tenuously controlled polyphony in *Still Life*, in *Pavlo Hummel* they are strident, raucous, and cacophonous. The volume is set at fortissimo, the tempo at prestissimo. Para-

doxically, however, all these quick movements and sharp juxtapositions bring the play to a silent halt. They destroy any possibility of
momentum. Appropriately, following eight staccatoed, crescendoing
repetitions of the word "shit," Rabe's composition climaxes with a
very long, sustained note, a note that sums up the lessons learned
from Pavlo's basic training. Dying for the fourth time, Pavlo howls
"SHHHHHHHHIIIIIIIIIITTTTTTTTTTTttttttt!—certainly the most
protracted use of the word in the history of the theater.[3]

How do we interpret this moment of epiphany? We can infer from
Rabe's note to the play that Pavlo, one of many thousands of middle-
class kids who went to Vietnam, finally comes to the realization that
he is lost and always has been lost. However, he does not learn "how,
why, or even where" (110).

Like most of Rabe's characters (David Nelson is somewhat of an
exception in *Sticks and Bones*), Pavlo finds himself in a world where
linguistic certainties no longer obtain. His line "I DON'T KNOW WHAT
YOU'RE TALKING ABOUT!" (97) expresses the extremely limited point
of view of these characters. Similarly, what Rabe says in his afterword
to *Hurlyburly* reminds one of *Still Life*, and it applies to all of his
plays: "It has no 'mouthpiece' character. [What play responsible to its
genre does?] No one in it knows what it is about. It has no character
who is its spokesman. The main character [Eddie] does not understand
it" (169). Rabe's characters search for an author, for anything that will
locate them in a world where language meaningfully connects them to
a seemingly accidental sequence of events, for which Vietnam was the
"ON" button. In fact, one could say that Rabe's plays are Tinguely
accidents, not constructed plots. They are the antithesis of narrative.
Trapped within that antithesis we find characters on an elemental
stage, who like stroke victims need to start from scratch, without sus-
taining props, to rediscover language, voice, and movement. To draw
attention to this loss of language, in *Hurlyburly* Rabe has his characters fill silence by being repeatedly reduced to uttering such phrases
as "whatchamacallit," "thingamajig," and "blahblahblah." As Rabe
says in his stage directions, "These are phrases used by the characters
to keep themselves talking and should be said unhesitatingly with authority and conviction . . ." (13), as in A squared plus B squared
equals whatchamacallit.

But if Rabe does not allow his characters to pilot their way through a linguistic wasteland, he does allow his spectators to come to some understanding of how, why, and where America got lost. The answer in all three cases is the same: Hollywood. Not for nothing does the refrain "I don't think I'm going to like this movie" echo throughout Vietnam War literature. Hollywood is in the background (the foreground in *Hurlyburly*) of all Rabe's plays. Talking about Hollywood, a character in *Hurlyburly* says:

> "They take an interesting story, right? They distort it, right? Cut whatever little truth there might be in it out on the basis of it's unappealing, but leave the surface so it looks familiar—cars, hats, trucks, trees. So, they got their scam, but to push it they have to flesh it out, so this is where you come in, because then they need a lot of authentic sounding and looking people—high-quality people such as yourself, who need a buck. So like every other whore in this town, myself included, you have to learn to lend your little dab of whatever truth you can scrounge up in yourself to this total, this systematic sham—so that the fucking viewer will be exonerated from ever having to confront directly the fact that he is spending his life face to face with total shit." (29)

Later he adds, "Phil, you're background, don't you know that? They just take you on for background. . . . Don't you know that? You're a prop" (114). A prop in a mythic landscape immaculately conceived by Hollywood.

In *Pavlo Hummel*, Rabe would have us see that Hollywood infiltrates and poisons the family, where mothers and fathers pass on a schizophrenic legacy to their children. In fact, in this play Hollywood becomes a father substitute. After Pavlo asks his mother who his father is, she answers, "You had many fathers, many men, movie men, filmdom's great—all of them, those grand old men of yesteryear, they were your fathers" (75).

Rabe's plays are explorations into the mythic landscapes where he searches for connections between the network of trails and voices that led to Vietnam. In *Sticks and Bones* he pinpoints one very important source: the TV, spic-and-spanned, tidy-bowled, endusted, perfectly middle-classed home of Ozzie and Harriet Nelson. David Nelson, a combat veteran blinded in the war, says, "I am—a young . . . blind man in a room . . . in a house in the dark, raising nothing in a gesture of no meaning toward two voices who are not speaking of a certain . . . incredible . . . *connection!*" (162). Not so paradoxically, like Tiresias, David does come to see the connection, precisely because he is blind. Being blind, he gets Vietnam right. He is no longer distracted by the seductive, "systematic sham." Because he is blind, only he can see the tortured images of his Vietnam War home movie. Because he is blind, only he can see the specter of a dispossessed Vietnamese girl floating through the walls of Ozzie and Harriet's home. Because he is blind, only he can see that the walls of his parents' home are constructed from coffins filled with the war-dead. He sees the total complicity of his Hollywoodized family. And now he understands the hows, whys, and wheres. Now he sees the collage of voices that led to Vietnam. He says, "There were old voices inside me I had trusted all my life as if they were my own. I didn't know I shouldn't hear them. So reasonable and calm they seemed a source of wisdom" (177). We hear all these voices within the Nelson home. They are the voices of racism, xenophobia, ethnocentrism, technology, consumerism, sexism, patriarchal theism, and narrative revisionism.

Rabe may grant David a bit of understanding that he denies Pavlo in *Pavlo Hummel*, Billy in *Streamers*, and Eddie in *Hurlyburly*, but he is no sentimentalist. The myth of the master narrative is indestructible in *Sticks and Bones*. It contains its own antibodies which destroy any bacteria that threaten its healthy sickness. Finally, even Ozzie has to admit the presence of Vietnam in his house of coffins. When he does finally see Zung, the Vietnamese girl, he strangles her to death and drags her out of sight and mind. Even Harriet comes to see that David's presence will undo her fudge and cookie bulimic regimen. So she fetches the silver pans and the kitsch towels with roosters on them and watches, with growing contentment and calm, as David slits his wrists. As David's blood flows, the voices of Ozzie, Harriet, and Ricky almost literally begin to purr.

Amlin Gray's *How I Got That Story* (first performed in 1979) is ultimate "poor theatre," and this very poverty enables Gray to expose the artifice behind the Hollywoodization of the Vietnam War. Although the play shows us an entire war-torn society in Vietnam (called Am-bo

Land here), it uses only two actors. One plays a naive Iowa reporter whose previous journalistic feat was to cover the western part of East Dubuque. The other plays the entire Historical Event, which involves twenty-one different roles, including soldiers, both American and Vietnamese, peasants, a crazed Tim Page-like photographer, a nun, prostitutes, and the Am-bo Land Empress, Madame Ing—all without makeup. Furthermore, this actor does all the sound effects: rock music, gunfire, a self-immolating monk, an airplane dive-bombing. As one can easily imagine, this is all done quite wrong!

But as Jack Kroll said in his review of the play, Gray's "impulse is not so much to see as it is to see through—everything and everybody" (68). What Gray sees through is the myth that war can be truthfully rendered into war stories. The irony of *How I Got That Story* is that there is no story.[4] As the reporter puts it, "All I found out as a reporter was I'd never find out anything" (107). How can you write a story about something that dissolves even as you begin to write about it? How can you write about a labyrinth where the walls change position with each step you take? Gray's reporter thinks he will get his story. He arrives in country with the traditional bag filled with linguistic agent orange. He thinks he has all the necessary weapons. He has names for them: truth, reality, document, fact, objectivity, news, answers. But as he desperately searches for a hook, an angle, a way to render the war in narrative form, he is totally done in by the protean Historical Event. There simply are too many masks and dissembling voices between the reporter and reality, too many layers of artifice between him and the edifice. To call attention to this, Gray puts Vietnam's backstage upstage, in Brechtian fashion. The opaque, artificially contrived medium becomes the message of the play, just as it was the unacknowledged, subtextual message of the war itself. Thus, Gray implodes rather than explodes the falseness of the whole Vietnam endeavor, the duplicity, and the overlapping entangled contingencies. Gray's message is that Vietnam was a farce, not a tragedy, and certainly not a narrative. The story that Americans did get back home was therefore less real than the Historical Event crumpling paper to imitate the sound of a monk on fire. So by seemingly doing everything wrong, Gray gets the war right, as perhaps only the playwright can.

Reporter Michael Herr and Amlin Gray's Am-bo Land reporter both come to the conclusion that they went to cover the war but the war ended up covering them instead. But the difference is that Herr eventually did get a story, Gray's reporter did not. As the play comes to an end, we see the photographer, now legless and one-armed because of his insane efforts to do Vietnam right, pulling himself forward on a dolly. He sees the reporter dressed in peasant pajamas, crumpled on the floor in "a position that suggests a drunken stupor or a state of shock" (117). Delighted by the presence of this former reporter in search of a narrative, he takes a flash photo. At the same instant, a picture of the reporter appears on a screen. "It is the head and shoulders of a body in the same position of the reporter's, dressed identically. The face is that of the Event" (117). The coverage now complete, Gray pushes his irony one final step: a new slide appears on the screen, bearing the words "HOW I GOT THAT STORY." And then, blackout. Narrative is expunged.

One of the implicit lessons of this and many other Vietnam War plays is that when a nation's mythic hunger twists a farce into narrative real people start dying from real bullets and bombs. The real war would never even have started were it not for the fact that Americans saw themselves as the protagonists in that most linear of narratives: the domino theory. Long before the war started, we were a people pretending to be characters in a false, superimposed genre. And when this paper genre disintegrated, we left hundreds of thousands of Vietnam veterans without a book and without an author. Not for nothing does a character in *Tracers* say that he feels like a character out of Pirandello. To his credit, he at least gets the genre right.

Earlier I alluded to Thomas Myers's book, *Walking Point*, an excellent critical study of Vietnam War narratives. As a critic, Myers himself does a pretty good job of walking point. The metaphor itself certainly is apt. Like most of the point-walking novelists he discusses, Myers has a keen awareness that "the point man seldom knows the strength or the location of his adversaries. In the thick undergrowth of mythic space, however, the enemy is clearly positioned and well equipped, a foe of prodigious power with a familiar face" (8). Myers has a pretty good nose for this mythic undergrowth. And he is about as wary of what is on his flanks as one can be: the myths of popular culture to one side, official airbrushings and reifications on the other.

But let him and us keep our eyes on the rear. Let all of us be on the alert for friendly fire, fraggings, and the long-term effects of agent orange—in short, our own mythical ordnance. Let all of us not overestimate the firepower and effectiveness of the predominate Vietnam War "field weapon"—narrative. Let all of us realize that the "foe of prodigious power with a familiar face" has a more familiar face than we may have first thought. And especially, let all of us realize that the point man, as watchful and responsible for others as he was, sometimes was allowed to pass in order to trap the entire patrol within the enemy's field of fire.

Predictably, none of those who gets things right by doing them wrong is among Myers's pantheon of point walkers. This is saddening. It is the point walkers turned civilian dramatists who most need to be watched and listened to. Watch and listen as they do the cello without a cello, so wrong and so right as they strive to understand their confusion.

NOTES

1. In his book *Walking Point*, Thomas Myers argues that this official reality flourished in order to force the war to dovetail with America's mythic identity. Myers calls this deluded identity America's "master narrative." Elsewhere ("Unlearning to Remember Vietnam") I have referred to it as "the American book."

2. Even the seemingly conventional *Streamers* is Brechtian. As I have said, the stage threatens to spill into an implicated audience. Beyond that, although the play might seem at first simply to be a study of characters nervously awaiting reassignment to Vietnam, it is actually something quite different. The main character is not Richie, Carlyle, Billy, Roger, Cokes, or Rooney. Instead it is the claustrophobic physical space of the theater that Rabe confines them and us in. Rabe denies the master narrative the open space it needs to thrive. For audience and actors the play thus becomes a no-exit confrontation without, as it were, the mitigating backgrounding of Barber's *Adagio*. Without giving anyone any cover, Rabe thrusts the myths of male initiation and barracks camaraderie into the foreground where they self-destruct.

3. Interestingly, this is also the dying word of Nick DelCorso, Philip Caputo's photojournalist in *DelCorso's Gallery* (New York: Holt, 1983). Like Pavlo, Nick ends his quest for a sense of purpose with an inarticulate obscenity.

4. The very title of Gray's play is an ironic inside joke, for it is identical to

that of a 1967 self-congratulatory book edited by David Brown and W. Richard Bruner in which thirty-six foreign correspondents tell of the intrepid cunning they practiced in order to get their exclusive stories. Compare the disillusionment of Gray's reporter with the dauntless confidence with which many of these correspondents conclude their stories about their stories: "We sat down on two boxes, used a trunk for a desk, and wrote the story." "And once more Mac had proved that the word 'impossible' is nonsense." "I had taken 'the bull by the horns'—and a big one at that—and won." "I had the satisfaction associated with getting out a story nobody else had. Every newsman and woman knows the feeling!" "I had realized the newspaperman's dream of a lifetime—a world scoop."

WORKS CITED

Arden, John. *Serjeant Musgrave's Dance. Plays: One*. John Arden. New York: Grove, 1977.

Basinger, Janine. *The World War II Combat Film: Anatomy of a Genre*. New York: Columbia University Press, 1986.

Beidler, Philip. *American Literature and the Experience of Vietnam*. Athens: University of Georgia Press, 1982.

Bell, Pearl K. "Writing about Vietnam." *Commentary*, Oct. 1978, 74–77.

Brecht, Bertolt. "Theatre for Pleasure or Theatre for Learning?" Trans. Edith Anderson. *Mainstream* 12(2) (1958): 3.

Brook, Peter. *The Empty Space*. New York: Atheneum, 1969.

Brown, David, and W. Richard Bruner, eds. *How I Got That Story*. New York: Dutton, 1967.

Broyles, William, Jr. "Why Men Love War." *Esquire*, Nov. 1984, 55–65.

DiFusco, John, et al. *Tracers*. New York: Hill and Wang, 1986.

Dürrenmatt, Friedrich. *Problems of the Theatre*. Trans. Gerhard Nellhaus. New York: Grove, 1964.

Frye, Northrup. *Anatomy of Criticism*. New York: Atheneum, 1969.

Gray, Amlin. *How I Got That Story. Coming to Terms: American Plays and the Vietnam War*. New York: Theatre Communications Group, 1985.

Grotowski, Jerzy. *Towards a Poor Theatre*. Trans. T. K. Wiewiorowski. New York: Simon, 1968.

Hellmann, John. "The New Journalism and Vietnam: Memory as Structure in Michael Herr's *Dispatches*." *South Atlantic Quarterly* 79 (1980): 141–151.

Herr, Michael. *Dispatches*. 1977. New York: Avon, 1978.

Howe, Irving. "Writing and the Holocaust." *The New Republic*, Oct. 1986, 27–39.

Kroll, Jack. Review of *How I Got That Story*, by Amlin Gray. *Newsweek*, March 1, 1982, 68.

Mann, Emily. *Still Life.* In *Coming to Terms.*

Marin, Peter. "Coming to Terms with Vietnam." *Harpers,* Dec. 1980, 41–56.

Myers, Thomas. *Walking Point: American Narratives of Vietnam.* New York: Oxford University Press, 1988.

O'Brien, Tim. "How to Tell a True War Story." *Esquire,* Oct. 1987, 208–212.

Postman, Neil. *Amusing Ourselves to Death.* New York: Penguin, 1985.

Pratt, John Clark. Panelist. *Back in the World: Writing after Vietnam.* Audiotape. New York: American Arts Project, 1984.

Rabe, David. *The Basic Training of Pavlo Hummel* and *Sticks and Bones.* 1973. New York: Penguin, 1978.

———. *Hurlyburly.* New York: Grove, 1985.

Reston, James. Introduction. In *Coming to Terms.*

Ringnalda, Don. "Fighting and Writing: America's Vietnam War Literature." *Journal of American Studies* 22(1) (1988): 25–42.

———. "Unlearning to Remember Vietnam." *America Rediscovered: Critical Essays on Literature and Film of the Vietnam War.* Ed. Owen W. Gilman, Jr., and Lorrie Smith. New York: Garland, 1990.

Walter, Krista. "Charlie Is a She: Kubrick's *Full Metal Jacket* and the Female Spectacle of Vietnam." *CineAction!* (Spring 1988): 19–22.

Weil, Simone. *The Simone Weil Reader.* New York: McKay, 1977.

Yossarian's Legacy

Catch-22 and the Vietnam War

○ ○ ○ ○ ○ ○ ○ ○ ○ ○ ○ ○ ○ ○

John Clark Pratt

At the outset, I must confess to some unintentional skullduggery. When going to Vietnam in the summer of 1969, I took with me a copy of *Catch-22*. From what I knew then about the war, I suspected that reviewing the plight of Yossarian from time to time might provide some continued reassurance that my world at war would not really be any more insane than Joseph Heller's.

I could not know, of course, that the colonel seated next to me throughout that long, ominous flight would comment on my choice of fiction and provide me with some early material for my novel, *The Laotian Fragments*. In *Fragments*, Major Bill Blake also reads *Catch-22* on the flight over, and when the colonel asks about the book (obviously not having heard of it), Blake tells him only that it is "a novel about World War II." Returning for his second tour, the colonel observes, "That was a real war . . . not like this one" (9). Later, Blake signs many of his official memos "Love, Yossarian."

Naturally, those of us who knew *Catch-22* could not help but see some obvious parallels to Vietnam, and almost all of them involved the fact of conflicting realities that lie at the core of Heller's vision of the modern world. Vietnam was a "conflict" that was neither a war nor a Korean "police action." In Vietnam, many of us became involved in operations that we could not talk about, even to people who were also involved in often contiguous operations that they couldn't talk about either. We discovered that the war had been going on longer than even many of the senior commanders knew and that it was being fought in and by countries that professed neutrality and noninvolvement. What FNG (Fucking New Guy) who knew *Catch-22* could help but wonder, when visiting either the Saigon exchanges or the stalls in Cholon, where Milo Minderbinder might be? And who of us can ever forget the sense of incredible irony when we exited the aircraft that had brought us to Vietnam and heard the phrase that only Heller could have written, spoken perfunctorily by an obviously veteran stewardess: "Hope you enjoyed your flight. See you in a year."

General comparisons are one thing, but the unreal reality, the actuality of *Catch-22* provided specifics as well to all of us who knew the novel—so many, so often, and so incredibly true that the book should properly be seen as a paradigm for the Vietnam War itself. When looking at the "facts" as well as at the fiction written about the war, to ignore what Heller has written is to obfuscate, misunderstand, and more dangerously, I think, distort what the Vietnam experience really was.

Let us look first at the "fact," then at the fiction. In *Dispatches*, Michael Herr said it best: "You couldn't avoid the way in which things got mixed, the war itself with those parts of the war that were just like the movies, just like *The Quiet American* or *Catch-22* (a Nam standard because it said that in a war everybody thinks that everybody else is crazy) . . ." (210). It's Yossarian, of course, who tells the chaplain, "Everybody is crazy but us" (14), a feeling that I know was held by many of the pilots who flew north from Thailand (a country *not* at war) into the Red River Valley or against the Thanh Hoa bridge, taking the same routes at the same times day after day, experiencing ever-increasing flak from antiaircraft artillery and surface-to-air missile sites that had been off-limits for enough time to allow the North Vietnamese to make them operational. Still classified, for instance, are the details about a senior officer's being relieved of command because he authorized and planned an attack against SAM sites under construction, but just as the armed aircraft were readying for takeoff, the mission was canceled from Washington. In all this, one recalls Milo's having alerted the German antiaircraft artillery in order to "be fair to both sides" during the attack on the highway bridge at Orvieto (261).

There were the medals, too. In *Catch-22*, "men went mad and were rewarded with medals" (16), often for deeds they never did. So too in Vietnam, where a Bronze Star was practically assured, especially to Saigon desk soldiers who had typewriters, and many of the medals, even though deserved, were awarded for fictional heroics because the actual sites of the events were not officially admitted to be in the war zone. Even today, many heroes cannot reveal that the citations on their truly deserved awards are invented. Similarly, and more paradoxical, is the fact of the missing names from the Vietnam War Memorial, names of those Americans killed in action while in combat against the VC, North Vietnamese, or Pathet Lao before the "official" date of U.S. involvement in Vietnam. Any one of these men would have made a fitting tentmate for Yossarian, like "Mudd the unknown soldier who had never had a chance." As was Mudd, these men are "really unknown" (112) and should be recognized.

The parallels continue. Although few pilots were privy to the facts of the regular "Tuesday lunch" in Washington where all missions into North Vietnam were approved personally by the president, some of the fighter pilots' songs such as "Mañana" showed that someone, at least, understood:

> Before we fly a mission
> And everything's o.k.
> Mac[namara] has to get permission from
> Flight Leader LBJ. (Pratt, *Voices* 248)

One is reminded of Clevinger's quivering rationalization, "But it's not for us to determine what targets must be destroyed or who's to destroy them. . . . There are men entrusted with winning the war who are in a much better position than we are to decide what targets have to be bombed" (127). A major target in North Vietnam was, of course, the Thanh Hoa bridge, which was not destroyed until the last days of the war despite ingenious attempts such as Project "Carolina Moon" on May 30, 1966. A specially modified C-130 was to drop 5,000-pound "pancake" bombs about 8 feet in diameter. At night, at 400 feet and 150 knots, the C-130 delivered five bombs near the bridge, then returned to base despite heavy groundfire. The next day's reconnaissance revealed no sign of damage or exploded bombs. One wonders if Yossarian would have returned to the target that night, as another C-130 did "with only slight modification in its route of flight." This aircraft disappeared and was never heard from again (LaValle 52–55). Yossarian made his second bombing run over the bridge on the river Po, and when asked why, he replies, "We'd have had to go back there again. . . . And maybe there would have been more losses, with the bridge still left standing" (142).

Not only bridges but mountain passes too provide irony for both *Catch-22* and the Vietnam War. In *Catch-22*, an attempt is made to interdict a road in order to block two armored divisions coming down from Austria. The plan is to destroy a small mountain village that "will certainly tumble right down and pile up on the road." Dunbar objects: "What the hell difference will it make? . . . It will only take them a couple of days to clear it" (335). Colonel Korn refuses to listen. "We don't care about the roadblock," he says. "Colonel Cathcart wants to come out of this mission with a good, clean aerial photograph he won't be ashamed to send through channels" (337). The hundreds of air force and navy pilots who flew missions against Vietnam's Mu Gia or Ban Karai passes may see some real truth here.

There are many more episodes in *Catch-22* that seemed to prefigure the facts of aerial combat in Vietnam, not the least of which is the question of the number of missions, the basis of the concept of the phrase "Catch-22" itself. To document the various Vietnam War mission requirements for awards and decorations and for rotation home would require a book-length computer printout; it is enough to say that some missions counted, others did not, depending upon the dates they were flown, the country to which they were directed, and the Rules of

Engagement at the time. I often heard pilots say "Catch-22" when these rules were changed, but thanks to their understanding of Heller's concept, most of them accepted with grace what they knew was craziness. As one F-4 pilot put it:

> Flew on Dave Connett's wing on his final mission. It was a spectacular display for his finale. The night was moonless and we were using napalm and CBU's on a storage area. The above mission turned out to be my final one also. I completed 102 in all but, because of a ruling halfway through the tour, some of the missions into Laos didn't count after 1 February 1966. (Pratt, *Voices* 239)

Other events of note are the sad prefiguring of fragging in the plot to kill Colonel Cathcart, and the unpublicized, but severe infighting among and within the Central Intelligence Agency, State Department, and Department of Defense as well as among the services, as can be seen in General Peckem's plan to grab control of all commands. There is also the frightening rationality of Ex-PFC Wintergreen when we first meet him in the novel. He has no objection to digging holes at Lowry field "as long as there was a war going on." His reason: "It's a matter of duty, . . . and we each have our own to perform. My duty is to keep digging these holes, and I've been doing such a good job of it that I've just been recommended for the Good Conduct Medal. Your duty is to screw around in cadet school and hope the war ends before you get out" (108–109). It is a recorded fact that candidates for admission to the service academies presented higher and higher test scores as the Vietnam War progressed, and that when the draft was rescinded in 1972, resignations of cadets suddenly increased. While teaching *Catch-22* during this period at the United States Air Force Academy, I heard many slightly embarrassed laughs from my draft-exempt students when I highlighted Wintergreen's credo. One cannot argue with reason—or with Ex-PFC Wintergreen, wherever he may be today.

It's quite apparent, then, that in both general and specific areas, *Catch-22* did indeed provide a paradigm for many aspects of the Vietnam War. And as those just starting in the military during the mid-1950s snidely called some commanders Captain Queeg, so did the names Colonel Cathcart and Major Major pass often from the lips of the Vietnam-era military men. *Catch-22* as novel had influenced our thinking, but Vietnam as Catch-22 itself affected our immediate existence.

I believe, too, that knowing Heller's work, seeing such irony and paradox come alive, made many of us more able to cope with the unreal reality of Vietnam. Nothing but *Catch-22* could have prepared us, for instance, for the initially unreported firing of General John D. LaVelle, Commander of Seventh Air Force, Saigon. His testimony before Congress in June 1972 has dialogue that could have been written by Heller himself. Having authorized "protective reaction" (a Helleresque term) air strikes against a buildup of North Vietnamese missiles and equipment in an area near the Laos–North Vietnam border, LaVelle explained his actions. A questioner (Mr. Pike) asked:

> Were you concerned that the bomb damage report showed damage to trucks or a SAM transporter or to POL, rather than to something [the missiles themselves] that you were allowed to hit?
>
> GENERAL LAVELLE: No, sir.
>
> MR. PIKE: Tell us why. You said they were missile-related equipment. Is that it?
>
> GENERAL LAVELLE: Yes, sir.
>
> MR. PIKE: Did you feel that under the rules of engagement, as you interpreted them, your right to attack missiles would include a missile on a transporter?
>
> GENERAL LAVELLE: Yes, sir.
>
> MR. PIKE: When you say these trucks were missile-related equipment, how were they missile-related equipment?
>
> GENERAL LAVELLE: We had picked up, or identified by reconnaissance, missiles on transporters parked along-side the road, waiting for the bad weather, to come through the pass, to come into Laos. They were never alone. The missiles had associated equipment, generator, vans, fuel, or just equipment for the personnel. But we never found a missile on a transporter by itself. We found missiles and trucks with them. . . .
>
> MR. PIKE: Would it have been permissible for you to have hit those targets between the 26th and the 31st of December?
>
> GENERAL LAVELLE: 26th and 31st; yes, sir.

MR. PIKE: Would it have been permissible for you to have hit those targets on the 17th and 18th of February?

GENERAL LAVELLE: No, sir, because of their location. (Pratt, *Voices* 521–522)

These incidents, taken primarily from air force experiences, show the pervasive quality of Catch-22ness in Vietnam, but there are so many more examples. Perhaps some future article will portray the colonel, in charge of a classified research project in Saigon, who would stride like Cathcart up and down the aisle between two rows of diligent writers, screaming, "Do not say that an F-4 cannot hit a truck. Do not say . . ." I hope, too, that someone, sometime will find, declassify, and write the story about the discovery during the height of the bombing of a yacht being transported down the Ho Chi Minh trail as a gift from the Chinese government to the leader of Cambodia, Prince Sihanouk, or about the episode of the seeding of a wetting agent on the same trail complex to create continuous mud, leading one high official to comment that it was "better to make mud, not war." Unfortunately, the rains washed out the experiment. Or the time a pilot who was not supposed to be stationed in Vientiane, Laos, had an affair with the daughter of the North Vietnamese ambassador. There are so many of these stories, and they are all sadly and wonderfully ironic. So Catch-22.

Many fiction writers have, however, attempted to apply *Catch-22* to the Vietnam War by direct reference, analogy, echo, and in a few instances parody. In the vast literature of the war (more than four hundred novels, hundreds of poems, short stories, and plays), the existence of *Catch-22* appears to be a given, but some writers believe that Heller did not go far enough. In Charles Durden's *No Bugles, No Drums*, for example, PFC Jamie Hawkins begins to feel "like I was ODing on absurdity. . . . Things get so outa hand that nothin' makes sense. . . . Alice in Wonderland was gettin' to be timid shit next to this." He remembers "readin' a book called *Catch-22*" and believing that "this dude's gotta be crazy. He was. But he wasn't crazy enough" (207). Similarly, Ward Just, in *To What End*, reflects on "the similarity of the soldier and the war correspondent, the basic text for which comes from Joseph Heller's novel, *Catch-22*. On the one hand, no one wants to get ambushed or to be where bullets are fired in anger. On the other, if nothing happens there is no story. If the patrol does meet the enemy you are likely to be killed or wounded, or at the very least scared to death. Catch-23" (181).

Critic and veteran Philip Beidler (who first identified the above *Catch-22* references) believes that writers had difficulty portraying post-*Catch-22* Vietnam because they could not write "a *Catch-22* about Catch-22." "At best," Beidler says, "*Catch-22*, with its almost sublime spirit of absurd apocalypse, seemed to bear on the attempt to make literary sense of Vietnam only insofar as it suggested something like a set of mathematical upper limits" (11). Because Vietnam became "*Catch-22* come giddily real" (145), Beidler feels that those who wrote about the war as Heller had done for World War II produced works that were only "Catch-21 1/2 or 3/4 or 7/8" (63).

It is certainly true that Heller's chaplain had already seemed to set the Vietnam experience in concrete: "So many monstrous events were occurring that he was no longer positive which events *were* monstrous and which *were* really taking place" (287). But I think that Beidler's assessment needs emending. Many writers did try to equal Heller, and some, I think, succeeded, simply by writing about the war as they saw it. Of the nine major novels that would probably not have been written without *Catch-22* as a model, five are essentially realistic (with *Catch-22* situations, characters, and overtones), while only four use Pianosa-like settings and characters that, in Heller's words, "could obviously not accommodate all of the actions described" (5). These four are the fanciful *Ears of the Jungle*, 1972, by Pierre Boule; *Gangland*, 1982, by David Winn; *Brandywine's War*, 1971, by Robert Vaughn and Monroe Lynch; and the remarkable novel *Bridge Fall Down*, 1985, by Nicholas Rinaldi. The other novels, listed in order of their internally dateable realism, are *The Land of a Million Elephants*, 1970, by Asa Baber (1960–1961); *Parthian Shot*, 1975, by Lloyd Little (1964); *Incident at Muc Wa*, 1967, by Daniel Ford (1964), *The Only War We've Got*, 1970, by Derek Maitland (1967); and *The Bamboo Bed*, 1969, by William Eastlake (1967–1968). Each of these novels moves so deftly from the real to the surreal and back again that a reader not versed in many of the facts of the Vietnam War does not know when he or she is reading fiction or when the events are real—an effect the writers intended. As a result, these books succeed differently than does *Catch-22* and become particularly representative of the real unreality of the Vietnam War.

In any of these nine novels, however, one needs only to meet the characters to recognize whose world—Joseph Heller's—they are entering. In Baber's *The Land of a Million Elephants*, for instance, a U.S. colonel spends most of his time in Chanda (Laos) on a roof watching the beautiful Wampoon, mistress to the king; Nadolsky, the Russian agent, gets excited by listening on his electronic device to his CIA counterpart make love; M/Sgt Campo keeps looking for the nonexistent PX; and Coakley, the effeminate State Department clerk, prances throughout the novel. There are also Indian, North Vietnamese, American, and Laotian characters who constantly protest each other's truce violations. Many of these characters, however, are thinly veiled satires of actual participants in the unbelievable events of 1960–1961 Laos, and if one knows the history, one will recognize the little Captain Kong Le playing himself.

Parthian Shot begins with Special Forces Team A-376 being notified that it has been shipped home two weeks earlier; thus it is no longer in Vietnam. The team contains a second lieutenant who can't be promoted, he suspects, because his voice is too high and a sergeant who starts Hoa Hoa Unlimited, Ltd., first to make VC flags, then to manufacture fake AK-47s. Hoa Hoa Unlimited, Ltd., later branches out into brassieres and blouses, sells stock, receives a Small Business Administration loan, and finally commissions a RAND Corporation study that advises them to cooperate with both the VC and the U.S. commands. Eventually, their enterprise becomes international in scope.

Similarly, *Incident at Muc Wa*, a novel that was billed as "The *Catch-22* of the War in Southeast Asia," introduces a general who has no unit patch on his shoulder but who chews everyone out for not wearing one, a Christian Scientist medic who juices vegetables and even field grass for his health, and a captain who will do anything to get a combat infantryman's badge. In this novel, the Americans shoot most of the Vietnamese they encounter, in part because the major has ordered them to report two enemy casualties for every one of their own, while in sector headquarters everyone keeps watching the "master mosquito-control chart."

Although called by the *Times Literary Supplement* "The *Catch-22* of the 1970's," Maitland's *The Only War We've Got* becomes Heller-esque more from its selection of fact-based targets of satire than from the inventiveness of its author. Commanding General Windy asks his secretary to spy on his second-in-command, General Cretan, "to find out what he's plot . . . I mean thinking" (34), while General Cretan's secretary is doing the same thing to him. There are two U.S. ambassadors to Saigon, each of whom thinks he is in charge. One of them devises a plan to dress everyone in VC pajamas for security reasons and trumpets his intention to defoliate the entire country. Also appearing are an NVA unit that loves the Hershey bars left behind by Americans; a soldier named Leaping Prick Smith who, because of his few drops of Sioux blood, keeps cheering the outcome of Custer movie reruns; and the great "Happy Hour Shutdown" when no American aircraft are available for combat.

Of these realistically centered novels, Eastlake's *The Bamboo Bed* is probably the most like *Catch-22*. The title refers both to the underground love nest of the mysterious and beautiful Madame Dieudonné and to the helicopter in which Captain Knightbridge and the nurse keep setting altitude records for having sex. Captain Clancy goes into battle wearing a plumed helmet and sword, marching to the beat of his drummerboy. B-52 crews drink martinis on their way to a mission, while below, the hippies Bethany and Pike are on their "way to the front to give flowers to the troops" (73–74). There is also a black sergeant who wants to surrender all the white men in his company to the VC; and Captain Knightbridge's crew consists of men named Disraeli Pong, Lavender the Purple Negro, and Ozz, his copilot, who like his *Catch-22* namesake Orr, has a "secret dream." Only the location is different. Ozz wants "to fly to Katmandu and declare himself neutral" (132).

Although the fanciful *Catch-22* follow-on novels are patently unrealistic in setting as well as character, each shares a common subject: the use and impact of U.S. technology not only in the war but also (often by not too subtle association) on the future of the world as well. These novels are all darkly prophetic, and each is really a warning more about the future (as is *Catch-22* itself) than it is about the war in which it is supposedly set.

Pierre Boule's *Ears of the Jungle*, for instance, while probably the most simplistic, inaccurate, and juvenile of any of the novels, does offer an apocalyptic vision of technology defeating itself. Based loosely on Task Force Alpha, the electronic nerve center of the Air Force's Laotian bombing efforts, Boule's novel shows what can happen when a beautiful NVA spy manages to compromise the electronic targeting system by placing audiotapes beside truck-spotting sensors. Madame Ngha also manages to reprogram the center's computer to call in airstrikes on itself, but she manages to get herself blown up as well. In this novel, U.S. air raids kill enough water buffalo to feed the North Vietnamese, an American officer waits to destroy a hamlet until his tanks can have their carburetors adjusted to reduce air pollution, and Air Force pilots read detective stories while flying missions.

Much more incisive (although patently derivative) is Vaughn and Lynch's *Brandywine's War*, which is really *Catch-22* set in Vietnam and which perfectly exemplifies what Beidler has cited as the difficulty of writing *Catch-22* about Catch-22. CWO Brandywine, a helicopter pilot, generates insane memos and telephone calls that everyone believes. Characters include Sgt. Percival, NCOIC of Defecation Elimination, and the hippie "unsoldier" who is in Vietnam by mistake and has an "unfile" that he can't inspect. The "unsoldier" eventually expands his marijuana business into an international cartel, but can never be sent home because he's not officially assigned to Vietnam. There are also General Deegle, who is obsessed with his rashes and keeps sprinkling baby powder in his crotch, and Lt. Soverign, the chaplain misassigned as a helicopter pilot who, like Yossarian, runs away in the end. An indictment of practically everything about the Vietnam War, this novel lacks *Catch-22*'s overwhelming sense of humanity and merely stops, implying the endlessness of the war and the authors' conviction that nothing will change.

The last two novels to be noted here go far beyond the Vietnam War. They are to the war what the war was to *Catch-22*; in other words, they show that the absurdity and craziness seen in Vietnam have become a part of the present and, alarmingly, the future as well. Most of Winn's *Gangland* takes place in post–Vietnam War California, where the Women's Defense League patrols the streets with M-16s, the Fastfood Marxists are everywhere, and the lotzl's (young female medical students) give the men backrubs and, flaunting their sexuality, live chaste lives while eating only health food. As it conducted (rather imperfectly) the Vietnam War, so does the master computer ANIMA still control the present as it sends personal LED messages to Dunkle, the protagonist, on any available video screen. No one except Dunkle appreciates what the Vietnam experience, referred to again and again as "the greatest adventure of our generation," really means. In the Vietnam scenes, ANIMA is linked with the Weary Weasel box in the company compound, and because of this black box, the men are able to take pictures and "interpret" the meaning of the war's development. Unfortunately, power outages and faulty data predominate, so no one really knows anything, not even how Dunkle's friend has died. Two of the significant characters are Madame Verrukteswerke, who is in Vietnam writing a "series on the children of the Americans left in the military" (104), and the Green Man, "who looks like a disease-wasted gas station mechanic." Everyone knows, however, that he is really a colonel (99). By the end of the novel, Dunkle has admitted that "things are hopeless" and that any change will "probably be for the worse, so the best thing to do is mind your own business as best you can" (221).

Finally, it seems entirely appropriate that the ultimate *Catch-22* novel about the Vietnam War is actually, despite many reviewers' attributions, not about the Vietnam War at all—but it has to be, even if it isn't. *Bridge Fall Down*, author Rinaldi tells us carefully in phrases scattered throughout the novel, is *not* set in Africa, but it does take place somewhere near the equator in a tropical, Asiatic country where the "monkeys from the North" are trying, with the help of all Communist countries, to conquer the "monkeys from the South," assisted by the Americans. One character mentions that some time ago, "the French were here" (92), and the mad general who leads the patrol is about fifty and had served during the Korean War when he was twenty-seven years old. Nowhere is Vietnam ever mentioned—but the subject is really the Vietnam War made timeless, much like Joe Haldeman's use of Vietnam as paradigm in his futuristic novel *The Forever War*, published in 1974.

In *Bridge Fall Down*, a patrol that includes two women, one of whom is the group's sharpshooter, is on a mission to blow up a vital enemy bridge (one immediately thinks of Thanh Hoa). Their meals are delivered by air, cooked by the pilot-chef Sugarman who apologizes for not bringing caviar to supplement his gourmet offerings of steak, swordfish, or scallopini. Under continual but sporadic attack from friend and foe, the patrol is being constantly filmed by Meyerbeer, who many suspect is actually running the war from his rainbow-painted helicopter. More randomly than in *Incident at Muc Wa*, these American soldiers kill even the friendly "monkeys" indiscriminately, and every time they pass a village, the brutal Sugg rapes someone. Central to their mission is the "black box," a small computer carried by a man known only as Merlin, who uses it to communicate with headquarters, to navigate, to forecast the weather, to spot the enemy (but like the Weary Weasel box of *Gangland* this one doesn't always work), and to carry on a running chess game with a Russian master. When Merlin is killed, no one else knows how to use the box—so the patrol is forced to complete its mission on its own. During a journey that often resembles a mad *Odyssey* set in Wonderland, the patrol passes a symbolic tree covered with hanging skeletons, meets the Queen of Skulls, escapes from the Falling Down disease, is tracked by a UFO, and has a battle at the Resort on the Lake, where vacationers from all parts of the world have come to swim, sunbathe, water ski, and relax. One might say that *Bridge Fall Down*, like *The Forever War*, concerns what might have happened if the U.S. had remained in Vietnam—but unlike Haldeman's book, Rinaldi's novel contains all the ingredients of both *Catch-22* and the Vietnam War and also presents characters (like Heller's) who really matter.

Other Vietnam novels also contain references to and echoes of *Catch-22*, but these nine seem to me to be the most obvious in their derivation. The first five differ most, though, in their realistic bases. Often, such as in Baber's *The Land of a Million Elephants* or in Maitland's *The Only War We've Got*, one can recognize the real people being satirized. In *Elephants*, for instance, Colonel Kelly is based on Colonel "Bull" Simons who commanded the clandestine "White Star" teams in Laos, whose mission was to train the Lao against the North Vietnamese and Pathet Lao. Also, much of the apparent madness such as Russians and Americans both training the same people or Kong Le's vacillating politics and actions actually did happen. Maitland's General Windy is based on General "Westy" Westmoreland, and Windy's deputy and successor, General Cretan, is a parody of General Creighton Abrams, who succeeded Westmoreland as commander of U.S.

forces in Vietnam. Also, there actually were two U.S. ambassadors in Saigon, and Maitland's portrait of Ambassador Risher satirizes Special Ambassador Komer who initiated and directed the controversial CORDS project for revolutionary development. Likewise in *Parthian Shot*, the base camp in the delta is entirely realistic, and many of the unit's activities ring true. The camp at Muc Wa, too, derives from actual plans for such outposts, and the relationships between the American advisers and their Montagnard raiders are poignantly accurate. Even in *The Bamboo Bed*, as many Vietnam veterans will attest, much of the apparent madness is real, especially the ground combat scenes.

What one sees, I think, in the best Vietnam novels is precisely what Beidler identifies as "*Catch-22* come giddily real." Consider this interchange in *Incident at Muc Wa*. Two officers are discussing the impending attack against the recently built outpost. Says Major Barber, "Charlie's thrown a whole battalion against Muc Wa—would he be doing that if it wasn't important to him?" Captain Olivetti replies, "Well, sir, maybe he's thinking the same thing. Maybe he's throwing men in there because he thinks it's important to us" (146). As in an earlier novel, Jonathan Rubin's *The Barking Deer* (1974), one side is reacting to what it sees the other side doing—the effect becomes the cause—and the real reason for the action does not exist. Catch-22, verily.

There are many other examples of *Catch-22* dilemmas in the fiction, usually expressed in equally authentic *Catch-22* dialogue. In *The Land of a Million Elephants*, as they watch the entire population of the capital of Chanda (Laos) flee to the countryside, the king, U.S. Colonel Kelly, and the Russian Nadolsky reflect on their respective predicaments. Says the king, "How can I be king without my people?" Complains Colonel Kelly, "How can we advise an army we haven't got?" Reflects Nadolsky, "How can the confrontation of the Twentieth Century be brought to conclusion in dialectical terms, if we have no people to sway?" (208). The answers are identical, of course, but each will continue trying to succeed, even if he knows he can't.

Beidler notes one of the most obvious examples of *Catch-22* dialogue in *The Bamboo Bed*. Two characters talk:

"Why are you shooting at them?"
"Because they are shooting at us."

"Who is shooting at whom?"

"Everyone is shooting at each other."

"Why?"

"War." (Beidler 54)

My favorite passage in the same novel is this interchange which, like so many of Heller's, sets up a comic perspective, develops it, and then abruptly presents a horrible resolution. Two soldiers discuss the news:

"I heard on the radio transmitter this morning that Clancy's outfit got wiped out," Oliver said.

"You mean all killed? Not Clancy too?"

"We reckon."

"Did you report this to Captain Knightbridge?"

"No."

"That's supposed to be our job."

"I didn't want him to feel bad," Oliver said.

"Our job is to report what we hear on the transmitter."

"I didn't want to make the captain feel bad," Oliver said.

"How is Search and Rescue going to rescue people if you don't report who needs to be rescued?"

"They don't need to be rescued."

"Explain. Explain."

"They're all dead," Oliver said. (Eastlake 41)

Likewise in *Brandywine's War*, the following discussion involves Lt. Soverign, the chaplain who has been mistakenly sent to Vietnam as a pilot:

"I'm not a pilot," Soverign told the check-out pilot that afternoon as they started their ascent.

"He's not a pilot," the check-out pilot told Major Casey after he had barely managed to recover the aircraft from a near-crash landing.

"He's not a pilot," Major Casey told General Deegle after he had talked to the check-out pilot.

General Deegle had the Department of the Army TWX'd. They pulled Soverign's data card . . . and inserted it into their UNIVAC.

"He's a pilot," DA told General Deegle.

"You will fly," Major Casey told Lieutenant Soverign.

"*I'll get killed!*" Soverign protested.

"A lot of pilots are getting killed," Major Casey said. . . .

"I'm afraid to fly."

"A lot of pilots are afraid to fly." (22–23)

Hardly afraid, but just as derivative, is North Vietnamese Colonel Khanh in Maitland's *The Only War We've Got*. Having been smuggled into Saigon in a coffin, Khanh is told by his local cadre commander, "We read in the newspaper that your regiment had been wiped out in the Central Highlands." Khanh replies:

> "My dear sir . . . If we took the time to add up all the Communists the Americans claimed to have killed so far in this war, South Vietnam would be a nation of ghosts."
>
> "Colonel," said Tran, "I would like to introduce you to Nguyen Hue, who is directing the funerals. Nguyen Hue's various, er enterprises in Saigon have served us well." Nguyen Hue stepped forward and bowed low.
>
> "It is an honor to . . ."
>
> "Shoot him," Colonel Khanh snapped.
>
> "What?"
>
> "Shoot him. He knows too much. We cannot risk jeopardizing our mission."
>
> "But we cannot shoot him," Tran protested. "Not yet. . . ."
>
> "Hmmmmmmmmmmmmm," Khanh breathed. "O.K. We'll shoot him in the morning." (233)

In the same novel, General Windy is upset when two American platoons are wiped out by the enemy while only four NVA are reported killed. He is relieved, however, when he is told:

> "It's like this, sir. The official body count was only four, the intelligence officer said that unofficially it could be as high as four hundred and seventy-five—you know, blood trails, fire ratio, allowances for wounded and all that."
>
> The General's color rushed back into his cheeks, and he sighed with relief. "Phew. That's better. Then it's not really a defeat, is it?"
>
> "I guess not, sir."

"And if it's not really a defeat, it must be victory."

"I guess you're right, sir." (79)

Such conflicting realities are seen often in the *Catch-22*-influenced fiction. Perhaps the most ironic occurs in *Parthian Shot*, where an American general meets a North Vietnamese general at the invitation of Hoa Hoa Unlimited, Ltd. Both generals are interested in investing in the enterprise, and both have been told that the other is a defector to his cause. They talk about the "enemy," and NVA General Phat asks, "Between us, Arlington [a rather funereal name], how soon do you think we can defeat them?" The American replies, "To be honest, Phat, I don't know. We can win, but the enemy is tough. And persistent. They're a lot tougher than we figured." Thinking that Arlington the "defector" is on his side, General Phat replies, "You're right there. Our original timetable to win this war was five years. We never thought they would commit as many men and supplies as they have" (270). The bottom line, however, turns out to be profit when the Communist and capitalist generals both buy stock in Hoa Hoa Unlimited, Ltd., because of the same, convincingly apolitical sales pitch: "All of this . . . was built and paid for by the people themselves. And the people get the profits" (268). Everybody, as Milo Minderbinder would say, gets a share.

Similarly, in *Bridge Fall Down*, Meyerbeer is officially filming the attempt to blow up the bridge for the Corps and has established interlocking corporations in Hollywood, West Berlin, and Tokyo to produce and distribute his movie. He sells stock to everyone but plans to liquidate the companies at the war's end and force his stockholders into bankruptcy. His sales pitch: "When you get back to the states, you can retire and live off the dividends" (45).

Likewise in *Brandywine's War*, Sergeant Coty, who has requisitioned thousands of yards of Astroturf for one of his ventures, trades his Vietnamese real-estate holdings for a half share of the "unsoldier's" marijuana business, and together they form the Greater East Asian Company Prosperity Sphere conglomerate, which rents a Saigon villa to the local VC commander. And like the business ventures of *Parthian Shot*, one unit in this novel also makes VC flags for extra money.

At least one outfit has problems that even Milo Minderbinder might not be able to solve. In *The Bamboo Bed*, the SAR unit has been issued two bridges for one river, so it sells one to the VC, who have none. Because of political considerations, the VC want to sell their bridge back to the Americans so that they can have a bridge to blow up, because they've blown up all the other ones around.

As did the real war, the fiction of the U.S. involvement in Vietnam presents startling individual echoes of *Catch-22*. In addition to the dialogue, the emphasis on "business," and the obvious character echoes, one should consider the following parallels. On the war in general: "The problem with this war is that it is out of human control" (Eastlake 251). On the bombing of one's own troops, like Milo's attack on his own base: in *Incident at Muc Wa*, Corporal Conney leads his Montagnard raiders on a fake attack against Muc Wa in order to impress the visiting U.S. General Hardnetz, but they find themselves a part of a real NVA attack on the base, thus disrupting the statistics of the Saigon-based "Incident-Flow-Priority-Indicator." In *Bridge Fall Down*, even General Trask cannot call off a programmed B-52 strike (which Meyerbeer films) against his own troops. The only casualty—reminding one of Elpenor, the lost sailor in the *Odyssey*—is a man named Polymer, from Plastic, Idaho.

As for promotion problems similar to those of Major Major, that of the tenor lieutenant in *Parthian Shot* has already been noted. In addition, Captain Carmondy in *Brandywine's War* will never make major because General Deegle likes "the alliteration of the phrase. . . . Captain Carmondy was doomed to remain a captain forever, trapped by the poetry of his name" (49).

Echoing the old Italian's view in *Catch-22* of eventual victory by losing is the village chief in *Bridge Fall Down*, who claims that his people are "friendly with anybody who's willing to be friends. They're even friendly with their enemies [the northern 'monkeys']. They have no guns and know they'd lose any war they got involved in, so for them . . . war is a bad idea" (93).

Even the inquisition of *Catch-22*'s chaplain is echoed in the trial of *Brandywine's War*'s B. Dowling Mudd (one suspects dual derivation here), and what Heller presents as one naked man at war becomes a full-scale battle in *Parthian Shot* when a VC unit strips in order better to be able to identify its enemy, but then the South Vietnamese unit does likewise. *Brandywine's War*, too, has an important PFC, but unlike Ex-PFC Wintergreen, PFC Hill operates in the foreground and, claiming to be the son of the secretary of defense, controls General Deegle and as result the whole Vietnam War.

What permeates all of these Vietnam novels is the *Catch-22* concept of craziness, mentioned earlier as Yossarian's belief that "everyone is crazy but us." To Simon in *Bridge Fall Down*, the war becomes a "madness, a wild, blistering insanity that he didn't understand, and wanted desperately to get away from" (104). In *The Bamboo Bed*, Captain Knightbridge thinks "he must be going crazy." Except for the Asians in his helicopter unit (all of whom are actually VC agents), he believes that "all the rest are after me. Picture a naked man being chased by seventy-eight million Asians" (147). Yossarian, at least, could take refuge in a tree. Most derivative, however, is the craziness of Weintraub, the former war protester in the same novel, who says that he feels "fine" after dropping napalm:

> "That is why I want to check and see if I'm going crazy," Weintraub said.
>
> "You're not going crazy, Weintraub," Appelfinger said.
>
> "Sure?"
>
> "Yes. I know enough about evolution to know that man adapts."
>
> "You mean that if he adapts to insanity he's not going crazy?"
>
> "Yes," Appelfinger said.
>
> "But he's crazy if he doesn't become crazy? If everyone else is crazy?"
>
> "Yes."
>
> "Why is that?"
>
> "Because we have to set a norm," Appelfinger said.
>
> "Even if that norm is crazy, it's called a mean. . . ."
>
> "It's an interesting theory. That I am not crazy."
>
> "It's not a theory, it's a fact. . . . I promise you it's a fact."
>
> "Why did everybody laugh when I said the Bamboo Bed was our conscience?"
>
> "Because," Appelfinger said, "those guys in the Bamboo Bed are crazy. They are against both sides and they are for both sides. In any book, that's crazy."
>
> "Yes, I guess it is," Weintraub said. (296)

Says Philip Beidler, writing about Ward Just's "real" vision of the Vietnam War as expressed in *To What End*, "Joseph Heller could have written it, but he could not have written it better, because it was already true" (62). Well, Heller did foresee the major contradictions of the Vietnam War, but he built better than perhaps he knew, and he also presented a protagonist, Yossarian, with a final choice that is denied his fictional legatees. In the majority of the novels not mentioned in this essay, many of the characters do embark on a quest similar to Yossarian's—and for much the same reason—"to survive" (Heller 30). In Tim O'Brien's *Going after Cacciato*, for instance, Private Paul Berlin has but one goal: "to live long enough to establish goals worth living still longer for" (27); and in many of the Vietnam War novels that do *not* use *Catch-22* as a point of departure, the major characters engage in the same quest for survival as does Yossarian.

Not so in the novels discussed above. If any of the characters survive, they do so by chance, and their main objectives are to exist *within* the madness, not escape it. Even if they do survive the war, they will encounter a similar environment at home. For them, no Swedish sanctuary exists. Although Yossarian's initial goal is only to get to Rome, he like his alter ego Chief Bromden in Ken Kesey's *One Flew over the Cuckoo's Nest*, still is able to get *out*. Not so fortunate are their fictional heirs.

One need only to compare the endings of the novels discussed in this essay to see how different their authors' visions are from Heller's vision. In *The Bamboo Bed*, for instance, everyone dies in a surrealistic assimilation of the helicopter with nature: "When the Bamboo Bed came out on the other side there was nothing left . . . forever lost, disappeared, eaten by tigers, enveloped in the gentle, tomblike Asian night" (350). In *Parthian Shot*, the entire village, including the Americans who have stayed to run Hoa Hoa Unlimited, Ltd., which has so improved the local conditions, is obliterated by a misdirected American bombing strike. *Brandywine's War*, as noted earlier, merely stops, its truncated ending showing that nothing will change. In the final scene of *Incident at Muc Wa*, all die, including the American adviser who might have escaped but chooses to return to see if any of his indigenous friends are still alive. In *The Land of a Million Elephants*, the American solution, a nuclear airstrike, is thwarted only by the local "phi," the spirits of the land and the country, and instead of destruction, the bombs create only flowers and little mushrooms. The people of *Ears of the Jungle* destroy themselves, and the protagonist of *Gangland*, one of the few survivors in these apocalyptic novels, wants only to be let alone in a crazy world that is bound to get even worse.

Another main character survives, too, but at tremendous cost. Jonathan Wilkinson of *The Only War We've Got* leaves Vietnam for his native England (note that he is not an American), but the horror of the war has come home:

> Where was the rabid Socialist who'd stomped up and down the country, wild-eyed and frothing forth dissent, disgust, revulsion at what the Americans were doing? Where was the brave soul who'd stood by the strength of his own convictions at the point of Capt. Beau Hinkle's pistol? Wilkinson could summon up many reasons for leaving—disgust, revulsion, extreme cynicism, escapism, were some of them. But his real nemesis was fear, Wilkinson was scared; and he was scared because on the night of Chua Ben, war had suddenly become real—as real as the crimson tracers that poured into the rice paddy; as real as the horrible death dance of the trapped Viet Cong; the artillery blasts and boiling napalm that all but leveled the little hamlet of Chua Ben. All that had gone before now meant nothing. War meant death and destruction, and no amount of brave moral argument could change that. Words went in one ear and out the other, but bullets killed and shrapnel maimed and napalm left hideous burns. And there was no room for talk. (261)

The two "lovers," Tess and Simon, of *Bridge Fall Down* also survive the massacre of their patrol after first blowing up the bridge, then discovering that their entire mission has been a diversionary action for another attack on a munitions factory. It is Meyerbeer the filmmaker who rescues them, and in an ending similar to but more hopeless than that of *Gangland*, Simon realizes that the madness will continue: he understands at last that Meyerbeer "wasn't just filming the war, recording it, but inventing it, creating it, or at least co-creating it with the ones who had the detonators and knew how to blow things up" (275). A few moments later, Meyerbeer speaks:

I'll give it to you straight. It's film, folks. Film and videotape are remaking the world. Haven't you simpletons noticed? Image. Appearance. What you see. It's here to stay, so you might as well get used to it. . . . It makes and remakes, twists and turns, shapes and reshapes. It's the divine energy—pulse and power. It gives life and takes it away. Film is God. (277)

Ex-PFC Wintergreen has indeed left a legacy to Meyerbeer, but the latter's control is much more inclusive. Accordingly, close inspection of the Vietnam War fiction that evolved from *Catch-22* does indeed show a darkening vision and growing despair over the progress of the modern world. Primarily, I think, the authors despair in our ability to perceive what we are doing to ourselves, especially with our dependence upon technology and media. Like Heller, these novelists point toward a future that is indeed *Catch-22* come real. In almost everything that has happened in the past twenty-five years, Heller was really quite prophetic, even to his remarkable insight (developed in greater depth by Rinaldi) into why Americans in particular elevate people to higher office. One has only to look at 1980s' politics from Carmel, California, to the highest office in Washington, D.C., and remember that Major Major is promoted in *Catch-22* only because he either looks like or actually is—movie star Henry Fonda. Nurtured by, derived from, and dependent upon the greatness of *Catch-22*, the subsequent fiction about the Vietnam War shows that there is no longer an equivalent to Yossarian and Orr's World War II Sweden, no place left for Americans to escape even from themselves.

WORKS CITED

Baber, Asa. *The Land of a Million Elephants*. New York: Morrow, 1970.
Beidler, Philip. *American Literature and the Experience of Vietnam*.
   Athens: University of Georgia Press, 1982.
Boule, Pierre. *Ears of the Jungle*. New York: Vanguard, 1972.
Durden, Charles. *No Bugles, No Drums*. New York: Viking, 1976.
Eastlake, William. *The Bamboo Bed*. New York: Simon, 1969.
Ford, Daniel. *Incident at Muc Wa*. 1967. New York: Pyramid, 1968.
Haldeman, Joe. *The Forever War*. New York: Ballantine, 1974.
Heller, Joseph. *Catch-22*. 1961. New York: Dell, 1974.

Herr, Michael. *Dispatches*. New York: Knopf, 1977.

Just, Ward. *To What End*. Boston: Houghton, 1968.

LaValle, Major A. J. C., ed. *The Tale of Two Bridges*. Vol. 1, USAF Southeast Asia Monograph Series. Washington, D.C.: U.S. Government Printing Office, 1976.

Little, Lloyd. *Parthian Shot*. New York: Viking, 1975.

Maitland, Derek. *The Only War We've Got*. New York: Morrow, 1970.

O'Brien, Tim. *Going after Cacciato*. New York: Delacorte, 1978.

Pratt, John Clark. *The Laotian Fragments*. 1974. New York: Avon, 1985.

——. *Vietnam Voices*. New York: Viking, 1984.

Rinaldi, Nicholas. *Bridge Fall Down*. New York: Marek–St. Martins, 1985.

Rubin, Jonathan. *The Barking Deer*. New York: Braziller, 1974.

Vaughn, Robert, and Monroe Lynch. *Brandywine's War*. New York: Bartholomew House, 1971.

Winn, David. *Gangland*. New York: Knopf, 1982.

Conradian Darkness in
John Clark Pratt's
The Laotian Fragments

O   O   O   O   O   O   O   O   O   O

James R. Aubrey

Even though Joseph Conrad did not receive any screen credit, film reviewers in 1979 were well aware that *Heart of Darkness* had helped to shape the production of Francis Ford Coppola's film *Apocalypse Now*.[1] There was certainly no attempt by Coppola to hide the parallels with Conrad, or he would have renamed Colonel Kurtz who, like Conrad's "Mistah" Kurtz, exceeds his authority in waging a private, jungle war. And if Coppola intended his film to be a judgment against the war in Southeast Asia, whose futility had become clear with the U.S. withdrawal in 1975, the film's transfer of Conrad's location from the Congo to the Mekong River inside Cambodia was a rhetorical masterstroke. For film-watchers aware of the Conrad parallels, Coppola was implying a critique of the war because, as one critic has wryly observed, "it is a truth universally acknowledged" that *Heart of Darkness* is an indictment of colonialism (Singh 41). Coppola's equivalent of colonial "darkness" in *Apocalypse Now* would be, of course, the geopolitical system that provides similarly noble-sounding motives for an ignoble war in his own time.

What critics have not noticed is that John Clark Pratt's 1974 war novel, *The Laotian Fragments*, employs the same rhetorical strategy as the film: Pratt uses Conrad's *Heart of Darkness* as a pattern for his narrative about the war in Southeast Asia.[2] It is possible that Pratt had heard about John Milius's script for *Apocalypse Now*, written in 1969 (Hagen 295), but it is equally possible that Pratt, an English professor and air force officer at the time he wrote the book, independently noticed the rich analogies between Marlow's experiences and his own experiences in Vietnam and Laos from 1969 to 1970, when he had been assigned there.[3] For example, Pratt updates Conrad's image of military ineffectuality rendered as a French man-of-war off the coast of Africa, "shelling the bush" with its cannons, "firing into a continent" (17). Pratt borrows this image to describe a campaign "where we'd been bombing for weeks without visible results. The bombs would disappear under the jungle canopy, sucked in it seemed, like the shells from a lone patrol boat firing into a jungle shoreline" (208).[4] Further evidence indicates that Pratt used Conrad's book as more than a source of images and ideas, however. *Heart of Darkness* is an extended parallel text to *The Laotian Fragments*, and for a reader aware of Conrad's presence behind the immediate scene, Pratt's novel can evoke a response similar to what one feels watching *Apocalypse Now* with Conrad in mind: a sense that something mysteriously wrong is going on in Southeast Asia. As with Coppola's film, Pratt's book does not acknowledge the debt to Conrad; indeed, for reasons I will go into, Pratt may have deliberately obscured the connection.[5]

Like *Heart of Darkness*, *The Laotian Fragments* begins with a narrative frame, supposedly written by a political science professor named York Harding, who has acquired the personal papers of former student William Blake after he disappears on a flying mission over Laos. The papers include some tape recordings but are mostly documentary. There are a few real articles quoted with permission from 1970 issues of *Time* magazine and the *Washington Post*, as well as various pseudodocuments made up by Pratt to sound like cables, memos, letters, and intelligence messages found in the belongings of his Blake character. These documents constitute the "fragments" of a mysterious whole picture of clandestine activity—in all, a book that reads less like a war novel and more like *The Pentagon Papers*.[6] As editor of these materials, Professor Harding resembles the anonymous narrator of *Heart of Darkness*, sitting on a boat anchored on the Thames, who says he feels "fated, before the ebb began to run, to hear about one of Marlow's inconclusive experiences" (11). One reason Marlow's story seems inconclusive, like Harding's (or like *The Pentagon Papers*, for that matter), is that it represents the narrator's impressions of Kurtz as he listened to Marlow's tale, based on puzzling bits of evidence mentioned by Marlow but never made completely clear by him to the narrator.

Pratt's novel is equally impressionistic and inconclusive, providing only fragments of information which we try to integrate and understand. For example, the first chapter describes how Major Blake's journal records his firsthand impressions of Southeast Asia. Professor Harding observes that earlier pages of the journal contain notes from an undergraduate philosophy course called "Asian Thought," which end "with an entry in heavy pencil, underlined and apparently retraced many times. . . . Approximately two inches in height, spanning five or six lines, and followed by eleven exclamation points, this two-word entry reads, 'FUCK IT!!!!!!!!!!!' " (7). Although a first-time reader might never guess, this is the Laotian "fragment" equivalent in *Heart of Darkness* to the pamphlet by Kurtz that contains seventeen pages of high-minded rhetoric on the suppression of local customs, annotated later with the scrawled expression of disillusion: "Exterminate all the brutes" (51).

Like Conrad's novel, Pratt's novel has little conventional plot, although there is a psychological progression similar to Marlow's by William Blake, the central character, from innocence to experience. The literariness of the name may affect some readers who are unable to avoid thinking of the English poet (just as some moviegoers are unable to forget that Colonel Kurtz is being played by Marlon Brando). Blake is by no means the only character in *The Laotian Fragments* with a literary name; York Harding's name is evidently an homage to Graham Greene, who mentions the writings of a fictional York Harding in *The Quiet American*.[7] Less literary names might have promoted the illusion that Pratt's "fragments" are genuine documents instead of fictions. Pratt chose to undercut this kind of realism by playing literary games—perhaps in the spirit of postmodernism, which views traditional realism as a trifle naive. Surely having a character named William Blake read *Catch-22* on his flight from the U.S. to Vietnam is a cue for readers that this novel is to be read as a self-consciously literary journey, full of allusions and literary names, whose meanings are intertextual.

A more important literary aspect of *The Laotian Fragments* than that constituted by the names, however, is the book's relation to *Heart of Darkness*. When, for example, Blake arrives at Tan Son Nhut Airport, Vietnam, he compares the reception room to "a Toonerville railroad station" (9). The word "station" is an echo from Conrad, and Saigon is Pratt's equivalent of Conrad's "outer station" in *Heart of Darkness*, with "Vietnamese clustered quietly" much like the black slaves at the coastal station in the Congo (20–21). Blake proceeds six months later to Vientiane, Laos, the counterpart of Conrad's "central station." In an homage to Conradian details such as grass growing through the ribs of Fresleven or "a boiler wallowing in the grass" along with other "pieces of decaying machinery" (19), Pratt describes the Vientiane airport with "grass growing through cracks in the concrete and what looked like old hulks of airplanes sagging off to the sides—C-46s and C-45s, some without wings—in the weeds" (28). In a military crisis several months later, Blake assumes duties at the "inner station" of Long Tieng, near the Plain of Jars in north-central Laos, from where Major General Vang Pao and his army of Meo tribesmen are resisting an offensive by the Pathet Lao and North Vietnamese forces in fighting that threatens to go beyond the traditional seasonal exchange of territory.

This struggle is the one that became known in the news media as the CIA's "secret war" in Laos. *The Laotian Fragments* never mentions the CIA directly, but it does contain several references to "the Company," a phrase which is the traditional euphemistic nickname for the CIA.[8] Serendipitously for Pratt's purposes, the phrase is also used by Belgian traders in *Heart of Darkness* to refer to their colonial headquarters in Brussels (61). Pratt may signal his awareness of this ironic coincidence when, in a discussion of how CIA employees behave differently from military personnel, Blake mentions the rumor that the Laotian ambassador had once been "a Company man in the Congo" (69). As an honorary Raven FAC, or Forward Air Controller, who had flown on missions directing strikes in support of CIA operations in Laos, Pratt could hardly have failed to note this irony when he reread *Heart of Darkness* with his Air Force Academy students in the early 1970s; perhaps Conrad's use of the term "company" gave Pratt the original idea of translating the heart of darkness from Africa to Southeast Asia.

Unlike most war novels, *The Laotian Fragments* is deliberately anticlimactic. Pratt tells about how the Communist forces moved further than ever before into territory traditionally held by General Vang Pao and his troops, only to withdraw mysteriously when they have an opportunity to overrun his headquarters and deal a significant defeat to the American war effort in Laos. In a supposed draft of a summary for the Defense Intelligence Agency, the U.S. air attaché writes, "There is an air of deepening mystery infusing the entire operation" (223). Blake has earlier noted, with reference to books about Laos, that "no one really has access to all the facts, anyway" (137). The idea that truth is inaccessible, if it even exists, is an important theme in Pratt's book, as it is in Conrad's. Marlow interrupts his narrative to express similar concern that the fragmentary impressions he is providing do not mean anything, as he asks his listeners, "Do you see him? Do you see the story? Do you see anything?" (27). Pratt acknowledges the inadequacy of language in other ways. He includes as one of the "fragments" an excerpt from *Time* magazine called "The Tiger in the Pagoda," which Blake deconstructs line by line, revealing hidden or invalid assumptions as well as inaccuracies, concluding that "no matter who's telling the story, you've got to read between the lines" (88). Other "facts" seem deliberately distorted, as when the targets first described as six trucks and a tank become in the bomb damage report "14 trucks and 3 tanks destroyed" (93). And one of Blake's last statements in the novel is a rambling speech into a tape recorder, where he comments on his own commentary: "What could I really say? The truth? The facts, ma'am? The way it really was? Or is my goddamn drunk and heat-oppressed brain conjuring up another fucking fiction on this tape?" (214). The literal last word of Pratt's book is "truth," which has been conspicuous by its elusiveness in the novel—in spite of the novel's claim to a certain nonfictional status for much of what it reports. It seems that for Blake, the more he learns about the war, the less he feels he knows. Like Marlow, as Blake moves psychologically to an increasing awareness of how noble-sounding policies are being carried out, he feels a decreasing confidence that any meaning underlies the discussions, military activities, and policy disputes—in short, the fragments. The absence of cosmic purpose which Marlow glimpses in the colonial scheme of *Heart of Darkness* parallels the absence sensed by Blake of a geopolitical vision informing the inconclusive military activity in *The Laotian Fragments*.

Pratt does not follow Conrad's model systematically, however. It is not even clear who the Kurtz figure is in *The Laotian Fragments*. In one of the most obvious departures from Conrad's script, Pratt gives attributes of Kurtz to several of his characters. A reader conscious of the presence of Conrad in Pratt's novel might expect to find the Kurtz figure at Long Tieng, the Laotian "inner station." In *Heart of Darkness*, Kurtz is instigating tribal wars or, less charitably, raids on other villages in an effort to acquire a mass of ivory. In Pratt's novel, even if General Vang Pao is involved in the smuggling of opium, as the air attaché's daughter tells Blake "everybody knows" he is doing (57), Vang Pao's status as one of the local chieftains prevents him from carrying the kind of moral weight an American would have as the equivalent of Kurtz, the European running amok at the heart of the Belgian colonial empire. Abraham Horowitz, evidently the CIA station chief, is "directing the scenario" (131) and has a name that echoes the word "horror," associated with Kurtz. However, Horowitz is normally back at the central station of Vientiane.

On the other hand, Pratt's American base commander at the inner station of Long Tieng, Major Dante Hamilton, is a strong candidate. Besides being found at the center of the war effort, Hamilton's "unorthodox manner" (42) suggests Kurtz's use of "unsound method" (63). Hamilton is to be replaced by Blake, as other traders assume that Kurtz is to be replaced by Marlow. Also like Kurtz, Hamilton has "gone native" to the extent that he "can eat Lao food regularly, and he even has a 'wife' who has been given him by Vang Pao" (42). Hamilton is not a clear parallel to Conrad's Kurtz either, however, because Pratt has assigned other attributes of Kurtz clearly to Blake himself, including the relationship with a distant, white female. Kurtz has his Intended in Europe and a concubine in Africa; Hamilton may have a Laotian concubine, as Kurtz does, but the female we hear about back in America is not Hamilton's but Blake's wife. In a letter Blake doesn't mail, he refers to her as a "princess" and as a woman who can't understand what he's doing—not unlike Kurtz's fiancée, who must be protected from the truth. In sum, Pratt seems to have given characteristics of Kurtz to Horowitz, Hamilton, and Blake—a move which requires Blake, in turn, to be a composite figure, part Kurtz as well as part Marlow.

When Blake apparently dies, as Kurtz certainly does in *Heart of Darkness*, the narrator must take the news back to Blake's wife at the end of the novel. Indeed, the last few pages of *The Laotian Fragments* contain the most obvious parallels to Conrad's *Heart of Darkness*. Blake has sent Harding a letter asking him to give his wife a call and to "let her know that I'm still alive and well in Indochina" (240). Of course, by the time Harding pays this visit Blake has been declared missing in action. Even Harding's thoughts as he decides to make the visit are word-for-word the same as Marlow's (except for the first "that"):

> I had no clear perception of what it was that I really wanted. Perhaps it was an impulse of unconscious loyalty, or the fulfillment of one of those ironic necessities that lurk in the facts of human existence. I don't know. I can't tell. But I went. (241; cf. Conrad 71–72)

As the episode develops, Pratt continues to borrow from Conrad for the setting and dialogue. In *Heart of Darkness*, as Marlow arrives at the house of Kurtz's Intended, "dusk [is] falling." Marlow observes "the tall marble fireplace." He places a package Kurtz has asked him to give her on a table. She comments, "'It was impossible to know him and not to admire him.'" When asked what Kurtz's last words were, Marlow can hear them: "The horror! The horror!" but he lies and tells her, "'The last word he pronounced was—your name'" (72–75). In *The Laotian Fragments*, as Harding arrives at Mrs. Blake's house, it is "growing dark." He observes "the red brick hearth." He thinks about how Blake's "voice had spoken to me after a silence of many years, but nowhere had he given me the slightest hint of the dangers he had experienced or the horrors he would only too shortly undergo." Mrs. Blake begins the conversation with Harding by remarking, "I admired him so." When Harding places Blake's letter on the table, she asks,

> "Did he say anything about me?"
> "No," I lied. "I'm sorry." I replaced the letter in my inside jacket pocket.
> "Ironic," she said. "The last thing he wrote was your name on the envelope."

Pratt has his own sense of irony, for the lie does not protect "frail womanhood," as Marlow's does; indeed, in a reversal of Conrad, Mrs. Blake has initiated divorce proceedings, is a fiancée in reverse, an "intended" nonwife (241–243).

These parallel passages indicate that Pratt's writing of *The Laotian Fragments* was deeply involved in his reading of Conrad's *Heart of Darkness*. And if we read *The Laotian Fragments* with Conrad's text in mind, our interpretation is inevitably affected. Read without awareness of this intertextuality, Pratt's novel might seem to be an elegy for some mute, inglorious pilot lost over Laos rather than a critique of the war. After all, Pratt dedicates his novel to the Raven FACs with whom he flew. And the book's dust jacket shows a rugged-looking Pratt in the cockpit of an OV-10 and identifies him as a subsequently promoted lieutenant colonel as well as "a former pilot in the clandestine war over Laos." I infer that he feels proud of his flying career and feels comradeship with the Ravens. I further imagine that some of Pratt's own attitudes emerge through the voice of Blake, who writes to his wife, "Regardless of *why* we're here, I am a military officer and I'm doing my job" (37).

Individual Ravens must have felt genuine concern for the Meo tribesmen, who depended on the Ravens to direct U.S. aircraft against their enemies—the same aircraft which the increasing American emphasis on interdiction would inevitably divert away from Meo battlegrounds in northern Laos to the Ho Chi Minh trail in the south, bombing trucks en route from North to South Vietnam. A reader can sense a tendency for Pratt to see policy through Western eyes when Blake refers to the Meo tribesmen as "the little guys" and the NVA as "the bad guys" (208), or when Blake delights in telling the legendary story about the North Vietnamese soldier overheard on acoustic sensors making love to a nurse, or the one about a soldier who tries to recover a sensor hanging in a tree and is monitored cutting off the limb he's sitting on. Pratt's sympathies seem unlikely to extend so far as those of his character Colonel Lunderberg, however, who wants to "nuke" Hanoi until it is a deep-water port. Pratt's views probably align themselves fairly closely with the dutiful skepticism of Blake, who notes, "I see no overall sense of purpose reflected in the daily actions of the men, yet they do their jobs—and some die doing them—it's only when a lack of purpose from above starts shining through that the guys start fidgeting" (209).

As an English professor at the time he wrote the book, Pratt might be expected—as an academic and author—to have played literary games with a canonized text like *Heart of Darkness*. One outcome of this approach needs to be contemplated, however: by constructing Blake as a composite of both Marlow and Kurtz, he implicates Blake in "darkness" more fully than Conrad does Marlow. In *Heart of Darkness*, Marlow says that he was able to pull back from the void and cling to his saving illusions. When Pratt's Blake disappears, he becomes literally lost in the heart of Laotian darkness, as Kurtz loses his moral bearings in the Congo. It is possible, then, to see the death of Blake either as a parallel event to the death of Kurtz or as a submission of the Marlow character to the powers of darkness, as if Conrad's Marlow had gone ashore for a howl and a dance and never returned. By situating Blake as he does, Pratt invites any reader aware of the Conrad parallels to see the whole Southeast Asian war effort as the moral equivalent of colonialism.

This equivalence is close to the classic Marxist critique of the U.S. war effort as capitalist imperialism, and I find it difficult to imagine that Major John Pratt thought of himself as a writer on the antiwar left. On the other hand, Professor John Pratt must have recognized the implications of what he was doing. I consider his book to be a working out of his own ambivalent feelings about the war in Southeast Asia, an ambivalence perhaps related to a view he once expressed that to be an air force officer and an English professor at the same time requires a kind of "creative schizophrenia." Pratt was something of a conundrum when he taught at the Air Force Academy, an officer with a keen sense of military professionalism and an equally keen sense of intellectual cynicism, a maverick who relished administrative subversions such as refusing to stop wearing his coat and tie to class after the dean prescribed a less-formal dress code.[9] Pratt's attitude toward duty and the mission was not so different from the attitude expressed above by his character Blake, which might be paraphrased, "Do your duty well, even if the system is screwed up." I can see Pratt's "schizophrenic" ambivalence in his combining of Marlow and Kurtz into the dual personality of Blake, who expressed Professor John Pratt and Major John Pratt, humanist and warrior. Part of Pratt's attraction to *Heart of Darkness* may have been Conrad's recognition that Kurtz is a psychological double of Marlow, a subversive aspect of his personality or, to use phrases important to Conrad, a secret sharer or a secret agent. This last phrase is particularly appropriate, of course, in that Pratt's association with the CIA makes him a literal secret agent.

It is tempting to imagine that Pratt saw himself as a secret agent literarily as well as literally, for *The Laotian Fragments* may have constituted a sort of publishing conspiracy. On the surface, it is a story about a dutiful military officer and a skeptical civilian professor—both of whom are "cover" identities, personae which mask the true identity of the author, whose negative assessment of the war is further disguised by embedding his critique in an intertextual relation with a literary classic. Discerning the "real" John Pratt behind the masks and the "cover story" is as difficult as trying to figure out who is working for which side in a spy novel. If Pratt had not been subtle with his critique of the war, his book might have been suppressed or his air force career jeopardized. As it turns out, no one penetrated the publishing conspiracy.

According to Malcolm Cowley's endorsement on the dust jacket, Pratt's novel was "invented with such knowledge of the facts as to convince the Pentagon, for a time, that the documents had been taken from its files." On the inside of the dust jacket, a "high-ranking source" reports that Pratt's manuscript was considered "so classified in Washington that the author was not allowed to see his own manuscript."

Perhaps government reviewers were so concerned over the possibility that Pratt had used classified sources (less than three years after the "conspiracy" to publish *The Pentagon Papers*) that they overlooked Pratt's key, unclassified source: *Heart of Darkness*. I doubt that the official reviewers would finally have released the manuscript for publication if they had realized that it contained an antiwar subtext, the Conradian intertext, for the novel's connection with Conrad makes *The Laotian Fragments* into as much a critique of American government policy as Conrad's novel is a critique of colonialism. Since the U.S. government's own reviewers and security monitors failed to recognize and break this political code, thus uncovering Pratt's "double agency," it is time for textual critics to do so.

NOTES

1. William M. Hagen explains how the film came to omit any reference to Conrad in his article, "*Heart of Darkness* and the Process of *Apocalypse Now*," reprinted in the 1988 Norton critical edition of *Heart of Darkness*. Noting the film's connection with Conrad was standard in reviews of the film.

2. The only critical essay treating Pratt's novel is Kathleen M. Puhr's "Four Fictional Faces of the Vietnam War." Puhr calls *The Laotian Fragments* "perhaps the most stylistically unusual of the Vietnam War novels" (115). She has nothing to say about Conrad.

3. Jack M. Shuttleworth, one of Pratt's colleagues at the Air Force Academy in the late sixties and early seventies, recalls that Pratt was assigned to Project CHECO (Contemporary Historical Examination of Current Operations) in Vietnam. Pratt evidently obtained some material for *The Laotian Fragments* when he flew several missions over Laos with the Raven FACs (Forward Air Controllers), ostensibly civilian pilots in light planes who marked targets in northern Laos for other aircraft carrying bombs. Named an "Honorary Raven," Pratt must have been liked by the members of this secretive and somewhat eccentric unit.

4. Besides this seeming echo of Conrad, there are other references to ineffectual bombing as "blowing up all those trees" (79), "blowing up trees" (139), and "pounding every tree in sight" (161). Conrad elsewhere refers to the pilgrims' response to the attack on Marlow's steamer as "simply squirting lead into that bush" (46). Skeptical references to U.S. bombing as destruction of trees and monkeys were commonplace during the air war in Southeast Asia (in which I served as an intelligence officer), but Pratt's other references to Conrad will make clear that such similarities are more than coincidental.

5. In his bibliographic commentary to *"Reading the Wind": The Literature of the Vietnam War*, Pratt comments on his own novel without mentioning Conrad (146).

6. Pratt may have been inspired by *The Pentagon Papers* to present his story as a collection of documents. Neil Sheehan, coauthor of *The Pentagon Papers*, similarly chose not to shape official materials into a conventional, historical narrative but instead let them speak for themselves, even though, as he explains in his introduction, "the very selection and arrangement of facts, whether in a history or in a newspaper article, inevitably mirrors a point of view or state of mind" (xvii). Pratt's editor-character York Harding concludes the novel's epilogue with a similar justification for presenting the "fragments" as he found them: "This method is, after all, the only objective way, even though any selection and arrangement of facts, whether in a newspaper article, a tape recording, or a private document, inevitably mirrors someone's point of view or state of mind" (245). The identical phrasing would seem to constitute a discreet homage to Neil Sheehan, today best-known for *A Bright Shining Lie: John Paul Vann and America in Vietnam* (New York: Random, 1988).

7. Although both York Hardings are political scientists, Pratt's character is struggling to understand what Greene's character is an expert on: Southeast Asia. Greene's "quiet American" admires Harding and owns all of his books: *The Advance of Red China, The Challenge to Democracy*, and *The Role of the West* (21, 28). Kathleen Puhr has noted Pratt's "respect for literary figures" and points out the origin of the name York Harding. She also notes that Air Attaché Jake Barnes "hasn't got any balls" and that Captain Robert Browning is killed early in his career. Other literary names include Major Dante Hamilton who, like the Italian poet, reaches the center of the war in Laos (and "war is hell," as everyone knows). Like the author of *Slaughterhouse-Five*, Pratt's Lieutenant Colonel Vonnegut has previous experience in strategic bombing (151). Some names are selected for their religious implications: Blake's wife, Mary Joseph, is Catholic; Colonel Gabriel gives intelligence briefings; Lieutenant Colonel Raphael is "an Army man". One name seems historical rather than literary: like William Jennings Bryan, advocate of the gold standard, Pratt's W. J. Bryan requests that the Laos attaché get him a four seasons bracelet, an item of black-market Laotian gold jewelry. Pratt is also fond of allusions to literary works: *Slaughterhouse-Five* (185), "Dover Beach" (180), "Ozymandias" (234), *All Quiet on the Western Front* (126), *Dombey and Son* (51), *Hamlet* (38), *Catch-22* (9, 20, 37), and a double allusion to "The Rime of the Ancient Mariner" and "La Belle Dame sans Merci" (213). The walk in the rain at the end recalls *A Farewell to Arms*, and the "fragments" of Pratt's title recall the end of *The Waste Land*.

8. Kathleen Puhr assumes that these references to "the Company" are in-

deed references to the CIA (116), and the same connection is made by David P. Calleo in "The Company We Keep," his review of a book about the CIA. Indeed, this meaning of "the Company" is part of American mass consciousness.

9. Pratt was my colleague during his last two years in the air force and my first two years at the Air Force Academy Department of English, 1973 to 1975.

WORKS CITED

Calleo, David P. "The Company We Keep." Review of *The CIA and American Democracy*, by Rhodri Jeffreys-Jones. *New York Times Book Review*, March 5, 1989, 14–15.

Conrad, Joseph. *Heart of Darkness: An Authoritative Text, Backgrounds and Sources, Criticism*. Ed. Robert Kimbrough. 3d ed. New York: Norton, 1988.

Greene, Graham. *The Quiet American*. 1955. New York: Viking, 1956.

Hagen, William M. "*Heart of Darkness* and the Process of *Apocalypse Now*." *Conradiana* 13 (1981): 45–54.

Pratt, John Clark. "Bibliographic Commentary: From the Fiction, Some Truths." *"Reading the Wind": The Literature of the Vietnam War*. Timothy J. Lomperis. Durham, N.C.: Duke University Press, 1987.

———. *The Laotian Fragments*. New York: Viking, 1974.

Puhr, Kathleen M. "Four Fictional Faces of the Vietnam War." *Modern Fiction Studies* 30(1) (1984): 99–117.

Sheehan, Neil, Hedrick Smith, E. N. Kenworthy, and Fox Butterfield. *The Pentagon Papers*. New York: Quadrangle, 1971.

Singh, Frances B. "The Colonialistic Bias of *Heart of Darkness*." *Conradiana* 10 (1978): 41–54.

Vietnam and John Winthrop's

Vision of Community

Owen W. Gilman, Jr.

When the Vietnam conundrum went up (or down) in the loss column, American culture reached an important turning point. The profusion of texts, literary and cinematic, that have revivified Vietnam in the last decade suggests that we are not destined soon to dispatch this part of our past out of mind. All-out forward progress now seems to circle backward, a pattern of turning movement quite alien to the Emersonian side of our character that places the present state of the individual above all else. As we swoop backward again and again, each going alone but all potentially arriving at some common ground akin to the mystical center point of the Vietnam Veterans Memorial in Washington, we are invited to see specters of earlier pasts, moments of significance long before Vietnam.

When we venture backward in this way, the fictive record of Vietnam may loom before us as a typological experience, one with roots in a frame of mind evident early in our history. To weigh this possibility, it will be necessary to consider a set of ideas about how a community must function in times of trouble, a legacy of notions planted in the New World by the Puritans. Certain Puritan views generated as the land was first subsumed in a cosmic pattern seem almost to have been devised for the experience of Vietnam.

In a study illustrating how Southerners distinctively focus upon history in the exercise of imagination, C. Hugh Holman notes the contrary tendency evident in the Puritan scheme of things: "The imagination of the Puritans was essentially typological, catching fire as it saw men and events as types of Christian principles" (1). The Bible served to provide the Puritan settlers of the early seventeenth century with all the types (or models) necessary to decode their engagement with the world—and simultaneously to encode their disengagement from the world. They practiced a kind of exegesis by living, caught up as they were with fulfilling their inscribed destiny.

Because the Puritans were excruciatingly rational and rigorous in their attempts to establish a God-centered society, one aligned in every detail with original types of visible saints, they left a powerful trail of documents, the residual power of which may still influence judgment of our affairs more than three centuries after they broached the wilderness. The Puritan histories embedded the present into types of the past, and their sermons translated the types of the past into the living experience of a new world.

Of all the surviving documents from the early Puritans, perhaps John Winthrop's "A Modell of Christian Charity," in all likelihood delivered to his congregation on the *Arbella* during sea passage to the new land, stands as the most ferociously haunting. In fact, many of our Vietnam novels have a starting point in Winthrop's text. The key issue as framed by Winthrop, one which transcends time in the American record, involves the fundamental primacy of community.

Winthrop began by acknowledging the wide variability of God's people; they naturally diverged in rank and character—a divergence that has been compounded many times over in the years between his time and our own. Winthrop did not quibble with this design. He accepted it as God's wisdom. But he intuitively knew that all this diversity might well make for hard days and harder nights whenever a group of people assembled to make a community of common purpose, even a people who shared one God. The only hope, Winthrop reasoned, would rest in placing responsibility to others above the inherently divisive responsibility to self. As a solution, Winthrop offered a vision of a "Modell" community, the very community he hoped to see established when the *Arbella* discharged its passengers onto the land.

In the process of his reasoning, several phrases stand out, all reflecting in some way the guiding principles of Christian charity. He noted, for example, "that every man might haue need of other, and from hence they might be all knitt more nearly together in the Bond of brotherly affeccion" (28). He recalled the commandment for each person to "love his neighbor himself vpon this ground stands all the precepts of the morrall lawe, which concernes our dealings with men" (28). And from this condition, he quickly drew an application: "This lawe requires two things first that every man afford his help to another in every want or distresse. Secondly, That hee performe this out of the same affeccion, which makes him carefull of his owne good according to that of our Saviour Math [7.12]: Whatsoever ye would that men should doe to you . . ." (28–29). At every turn, Winthrop extracted the notion that full and generous accountability to (and for) others was the finest standard that could be set for the function of a people together.

Midway in the argument, Winthrop began to feature the attractiveness inherent in this orientation to others: "There is noe body but consistes of partes and that which knitts these partes together giues the body its perfeccion, because it makes eache parte soe contiguous to other as thereby they doe mutually participate with eache other, both in strengthe and infirmity in pleasure and paine . . ." (29). Perfection, which was an objective for the Puritans and which still lurks as a distant goal somewhere in the American psyche, could be realized in only one way: cohesive togetherness.

The theme of togetherness, of community, was sounded again and again as Winthrop worked to establish a lasting standard for the enterprise being undertaken by the Puritans. The theory had to be discernible in practice, the practice had to be regular, and it could not be conditional. A new standard of community accountability was asserted, and failure would be perilous, for "neither must wee think that the lord will beare with such faileings at our hands as hee dothe from those among whome wee haue lived . . ." (31).

In that last clause, Winthrop added the sense of moral imperative that has had us looking anxiously over our shoulders at our record of experience for a long time, and now, in the aftermath of Vietnam, we look back compulsively. Winthrop's conclusion was written in such a way as to make crystal clear the absolute litmus test for success in the Puritan settlement endeavor. The Puritans had "entered into Covenant with him [God] for this worke," had "taken out a Commission," and everything, including most particularly any final judgment, would hang in the balance. Winthrop availed himself of the most natural metaphor (shipwreck) readily at hand in order to accentuate the either/or condition that attended his flock's obligation to make a community, and in his conclusion, with its well-known "Citty vpon a Hill" phrase, he asserted that "the eies of all people are vppon vs; soe that if wee shall deale falsely with our god in this worke wee have vndertaken and soe cause him to withdraw his present help from us, wee shall be made a story and a by-word through the world . . ." (32).

Would that Winthrop had equivocated in lining up the test for the future record of his people. Or if only he had somehow found a way to put the burden of responsibility on each individual, alone and apart from others. The ensuing record would then have been far more consistent—and far less full of anxiety about failure. But, as we have seen, Winthrop put the value of community at the center of it all, and from that position have ensued ten thousand tons of brooding anxiety, to say nothing of stories full of indictment about failure to reach the standard articulated in the originating vision of New World settlement.

The record shows that, even from the beginning, Winthrop's "Modell" was a hard sell. By the close of his years as governor for the Massachusetts Bay Colony, the jeremiad had emerged as a predominant form of discourse—a ritualistic but ever-evolving system of fault-finding—necessitated always by abundant evidence that God's people were not measuring up adequately to the standard of perfection voiced by Winthrop. Over time and space (the space enlarged steadily as the idea of community yielded to another mission, the "errand into the wilderness," an idea much more self-serving if one looks behind the surface to discern hidden agendas) of the first hundred years, Winthrop's hope for a people bonded with a charitable spirit of togetherness remained just that: a hope. Somehow the community of Winthrop's sermon proved elusive, always just out of reach, and yet the standard remained, a haunting presence that questioned—sometimes even mocked—the reality of a competitive, factious, highly individualistic people.

Thus it happened that a pure community in the new land came into existence as an idea—a typological "Modell"—early in the seventeenth century but passed into the failure column almost immediately. For this challenging vision, the "in" door was hard by the "out" door. Community in Winthrop's terms proved balefully ephemeral.

By the time Alexis de Tocqueville studied American life in the nineteenth century and wrote *Democracy in America*, individualism had been embraced as a governing alternative to community. Tocqueville's definition of individualism makes this shift clear: "Individualism is a mature and calm feeling, which disposes each member of the community to sever himself from the mass of his fellows, and to draw apart with his family and his friends; so that, after he has thus formed a little circle of his own, he willingly leaves society at large to itself" (193).

How small the "circle" might be, of course, varies. In *The American Jeremiad*, a provocative study of New-World–style fault-finding, Sacvan Bercovitch allowed a place for even Henry David Thoreau with his *Walden*. Thoreau stood the original community vision on end: society was now the villain, natural enemy of the pure individual. Hence Thoreau composed a vision of the smallest complete circle imaginable, with himself as both center and circumference. Ralph Waldo Emerson argued along similar lines in his essay on "Self-Reliance," although Emerson documented his case less specifically than Thoreau. More recently, in *Habits of the Heart*, Robert Bellah and his coauthors have sketched out the long slide away from community in a scope that includes many American voices from the last decade; in many forms, Bellah found evidence of "life style enclaves," most of which entail self-centeredness to one degree or another.

And yet, never has the fleeting, tantalizing ideal of community disappeared from American culture. Sporadic efforts have been made to revivify the spirit of togetherness, and periodically there have been historical moments when Americans set aside their self-centeredness in favor of commitment to the community as a whole. The commonest circumstance for this occasional brush with the community idea is war. A totally cynical view might even allow that Americans have gone to war regularly because only engagement with an external adversary creates the conditions necessary for the sensation of community in American life. Despite the cynicism involved, such a conclusion perhaps deserves serious scrutiny.

At this point, however, it is time to consider communities as they were constituted during the Vietnam War years. More specifically, against the typological background of Puritan ideas about community, we might examine the small "unit" communities of U.S. soldiers in combat in Vietnam. But first, to allay obvious misgivings anyone might have about comparing military combat units in Vietnam with what Winthrop had in mind as he and the Puritans readied themselves to establish a viable enterprise in a new land, the following points must be noted: first, while the original Puritans were volunteers all, the Vietnam forces were composed of a mix of volunteers and soldiers who were drafted (only marine units would typically be made up of soldiers who had explicitly chosen to be marines); and second, many Vietnam combat units were continuously subject to planned recomposition. That is, through a command-initiated practice of periodic rotation—generally involving a year's tour of duty—individual soldiers moved into and out of units on a regular basis, a policy which had the effect of diminishing the sense of solidarity that had been part of combat units in earlier wars.

Moreover, the extent to which Vietnam combat units were micro-scale versions of a larger idea of national community changed considerably over the course of the war. In the early years (perhaps nearly up to the 1968 Tet offensive), combat units in Vietnam seemed to be part of a comprehensive structure of values and institutions that constituted the American community at large, but as the war evolved, the home front community broke up into warring subcommunities. At this point, the combat units were, in essence, on their own—a world apart. And on their own, they faced the obligation to try to sustain some spirit of togetherness, all on a scale not unlike the one known to Winthrop and his companions.

Despite these reservations, we might well look at Vietnam as a grotesque laboratory where Winthrop's ideas about a true community
were subjected to the most severe testing conceivable. I would argue
that a community test pattern serves to make a good number of imaginative texts on the war lastingly meaningful; among them is Gustav
Hasford's *The Short-Timers*, which vividly opens up the typological
dimension of Vietnam fiction.

The title of Hasford's novel is an obvious clue to the whole text, for
it highlights the consequences of a fixed tour of duty. In the nightmarish uncertainty of combat, any clear rules that can be discerned
are potent. Much about the Vietnam War was rule-less, and the absence of reassuring kinds of certainty created grounds for rampant
anxiety. As an antidote to this flux, there was a rotation date, the
DEROS (date of expected rotation from overseas), with each soldier
having just one year to survive in Vietnam. The rotation date was a
matter of individual concern and record; each soldier counted his own
days as they passed, each one bringing him twenty-four hours closer
to safe exit from Vietnam. As the time to remain in country dimin-
ished—ever so slowly—the impulse for individual survival increased
proportionately. Sooner or later, the short-timer's countdown put the
individual at odds with all others in time, and self-preservation became
all-consuming. This pressure placed any sense of community (unit) obligation at extreme risk.

As the opening section of Hasford's novel shows, this preoccupation
with self was not, on the surface at least, in accord with a vision of
togetherness proffered to recruits during marine basic training. Indeed, everything that Gunnery Sergeant Gerheim says and does is
meant to eradicate the self and replace it with zealous devotion to community, to the Corps. Gerheim puts the message in plain talk: "My
orders are to weed out all nonhackers who do not pack the gear to
serve in my beloved Corps" (5). Through an oppressive system of psychological and physical abuse, Gerheim plans to eliminate anyone who
does not fit the marines. He wants a pure community, and as an en-
ticement, he offers his trainees the classic benefits of community: "I
will **give** you motivation. You have no *esprit de corps*. I will **give** you
esprit de corps. You have no traditions. I will **give** you traditions. And
I will show you how to live up to them" (5). In short, those who pass

muster will truly belong to something infinitely larger than the individual self, something more glorious, something of transcendent virtue—something that will justify any possible consequence of action done for the community. You want to be part of a true community? Gerheim will teach you.

But the basic-training section of *The Short-Timers* also reveals the guiding commandments of this particular community. The first section's heading, "The Spirit of the Bayonet," lets us know that the marines are grouped with a purpose contrary to the one imaged for the community in Winthrop's "Modell of Christian Charity." In fact, as voiced by Gerheim, who strikes the reader as being authoritative (quite comparable to Winthrop in function), the Corps in its work is consistently in opposition to all Christian principles. Gerheim wants hate, not love, for "the more you hate me, the more you will learn" (5). Gerheim works diligently to create hard hearts, for "it is the hard heart that kills" (13). Any weakness is scorned. Gerheim makes an imaginative case for programmed atavism. Meekness, a Christian virtue, is anathema to him: "If the meek ever inherit the earth the strong will take it away from them. The meek exist to be devoured by the strong" (14–15). Any bow in the direction of more traditional religious attitudes is superficial: "Sergeant Gerheim assures us that the Marine Corps was here before God. . . . 'You can give your heart to Jesus but your ass belongs to the Corps'" (19). Throughout "The Spirit of the Bayonet," Hasford emphasizes the gulf between the ethos of the Marine Corps and the ethos of Christianity.

Nevertheless, all communities need leaders. Someone must provide the visions and values that will become the bonding agents for those who join together to make a group. The Massachusetts Bay Colony had John Winthrop; the marine basic trainees in *The Short-Timers* have Sergeant Gerheim. He articulates the gospel of marine behavior, and he wins converts to his gospel, though his victory is costly. The chief virtue of the marines is a hard heart, and in Gerheim's developing community, many hearts harden. There is resistance, though, to the systematic eradication of individuality and any human softness. The character Joker is an allegorical type, and his individual defensive mechanism is humor. The Joker's irreverence keeps him at some distance from doing his marine devotions with the fervent belief of the prophet Gerheim, and yet Joker eventually succumbs to the "hard heart" patterning preached in basic training. Joker's last act in the narrative epitomizes the effect of Gerheim's instruction, even as it reveals the fatal flaw of the marine system of community in Vietnam.

Long before that act, however, the system's problematic side has become evident. In the "success" of Sergeant Gerheim's efforts to mold Leonard Pratt, sarcastically dubbed Gomer Pyle (a prefiguring of the new-name syndrome in Vietnam), into a true marine, the failure of the marine (American community) episode in Vietnam is paradoxically foreshadowed. Leonard is not good basic material for Gerheim's vision. He is soft in too many ways. But eventually, by turning the nascent community hard, hard, hard upon Leonard in his ineptitude, Gerheim sees Leonard's conversion realized. After brutalization by his fellow trainees, Leonard becomes a model soldier or, as Gerheim declares, the "most motivated prive in my herd" (23). Leonard becomes a zealous fanatic, and in true fanatic form, his last act of hard heartedness is one of self-extinction, following by moments his assassination of the prophet Gerheim. All of this comes just a few hours after the highly ritualized celebration of the recruits' passage into the world of the marines, a graduation ceremony capped by the following words from the commanding general of Parris Island: "Have you seen the light? The white light? The great light? The guiding light? Do you have the vision?" (25). In short order, Gerheim sees the white-light muzzle fire from Leonard's darling Charlene and joins marine heaven. Leonard puts on "the final grin that is on the face of death" (31). And the rest of the community heads off on the trail to Vietnam.

Joker goes to Vietnam as a writer. In the modern world, jokers are writers and writers are jokers. Either way, the result is someone who is typically at some distance from the community of a given moment. Thus it is for Joker. His work as a "combat correspondent assigned to the First Marine Division" (37) reflects much more detachment than attachment. The war is a sick joke, ready material for his joker's stance. While in this alienated mode—an individual at odds with the hard heart marine spirit—he is able to act according to principles slightly more in line with those advocated by Winthrop. During the battle for Hue, Joker is reunited with Cowboy, one of his chums from basic. Cowboy is fully part of a marine community, the Lusthog squad, which is endangered during the city-scene combat by a sniper with deadly aim.

Eventually, Joker, Rafter Man (Joker's buddy-killing pal), Cowboy, and the other surviving members of the Lusthog squad locate the sniper, a young girl. She has been mortally wounded in the battle, but her death will come slowly as the blood drains from her body. She pleads, in a foreign tongue but in an international human language, for the mercy of a quick death. A hard heart would have none of this, but Joker's lingering individualism gives him the courage to act mercifully. Though the others see the action as being "hard," readers know differently, and Hasford offers a signal that remnants of a softer vision of community were sometimes part of the Vietnam War.

Nevertheless, Hue—at least with its American presence—is no "Citty vpon a Hill" (or beside still waters, for that matter). With language meant to reverberate within the context of antecedent Christian typological works, Hasford points to the woeful irony embedded in the liberation of this once-glorious city: "The sun that rises in Hue on the morning of February 25, 1968, illuminates a dead city. . . . Wise, like Solomon, we have converted Hue into rubble in order to save it" (122). Although America composed a community to sustain its vision in Vietnam, the underlying principles therein were antithetical to those advocated by Winthrop for the first American community. The results were a travesty, not a glory.

Full Metal Jacket, Stanley Kubrick's film adaptation of *The Short-Timers*, comes to a close immediately after Joker's mercy-killing of the sniper. As the soldiers move in a mass through smoldering ruins, a community is spontaneously formed. They join in a club song, one which some few years earlier had united the youths of America through television, marvel of electronic connectedness that it is. The "Mickey Mouse Club" theme song, in this surreal context, has bitterly ironic overtones, but a community is constituted nevertheless, just as the singing of "God Bless America" by Mike and the other survivors in Michael Cimino's *The Deer Hunter* emphasized the deep-seated need that people have for community.

However, Hasford's own ending is not so comforting about the presence of community in the aftermath of action in Vietnam. In *The Short-Timers*, Joker has one more mission. His joking irreverence for the *semper fi* marine ethos eventually results in punishment; he is sent to a grunt unit for the final countdown to his DEROS. He joins the Lusthog squad, now under the leadership of Cowboy. The Lusthogs are a community bonded by desperation, and their motto, inscribed on a shopping bag carried by Alice, their premier point man, shows again how far afield this community is from the one conceived by Winthrop: "Lusthogs Delta 1/5 We Deal in Death and Yea, though I walk through the valley of death, I shall fear no evil, for I am the evil" (154).

Joker is short—"twenty-two days and a wake-up left in country" (147)—when the Lusthogs march off "into God's green furnace" (150), a phrase by which Hasford's text admits the presence of an authoritative, even judgmental God, not so different from the figure who managed the wilderness broached by the Puritan community in Winthrop's time, although Hasford's style is relentlessly sardonic, not reverential. Thus the Lusthogs enter a tradition, albeit from a radically different perspective than the one that governed the Puritans. There must be standards, and survivors like Joker will be judged accordingly. They will know failure, guilt, and lasting pain by their falling short of binding standards. The chief standard is community—commitment to others. About this standard, the marines allow no ambiguity.

In the novel's concluding action, another sniper has the Lusthog squad in his power. Once the point man Alice is cut down, wounded but not dead, the others must act to reclaim him, to bring him back to the community of the unit. As Animal Mother asserts dogmatically, "Marines *never* abandon their dead or wounded, Mr. Squad Leader, *sir!*" (173). One after another—Doc Jay, New Guy, Cowboy—members of the squad venture forth into the open where the sniper can shoot them. The sniper knows the power of community for marines. He only needs to have one wounded man alive to draw out the rest, and at times the jungle is filled with hysterical laughter about the consequences of community morality. But individualism and the force of self-preservation are present too, mainly in the joker short-timer. Joker finally breaks the chain of togetherness that would doom them all, one at a time.

As Cowboy lies wounded in the clearing, Joker assumes the leadership role he has so long avoided with his comedic posturing. He does what Kubrick could not put on the large screen for Americans to confront: Joker kills Cowboy in cold blood to save himself. No matter how this action is softened, and Cowboy does his best by giving Joker one last taunt ("I NEVER LIKED YOU, JOKER. I NEVER THOUGHT YOU WERE FUNNY—" [178]), the act epitomizes the triumph of self over community. Yes, others will live as a result of his action, but his motivation is intensely and logically personal. The survival of others is incidental to his own preservation. At this point we can clearly see the consequences of survival under conditions that Vietnam placed before groups of men who had horrifically competing impulses—on the one hand, a natural need for community; on the other, a natural need for self-preservation. The short-timer syndrome often enough tipped the balance toward the self. Memories of that tilt might be repressed, and maybe, sometime, there might be some sort of cathartic escape from guilt spawned by the self-preservation impulse, but in the meantime (probably a long time), the war's effects would surely linger, a point that Joker himself has already grasped: "Those of us who survive to be short-timers will fly the Freedom Bird back to hometown America. But home won't be there anymore and we won't be there either. Upon each of our brains the war has lodged itself, a black crab feeding" (176).

The image of the black crab feeding is bleak, and anyone suffering from such horrors embedded within the reaches of memory will have a hard time joining other communities. Hence the central test for the people of the New World, a community of real togetherness, is carried forward by Gustav Hasford from John Winthrop's "Modell" to a modern setting involving Vietnam and its aftermath. Any failure in this test, regardless of what variations it might take, leads to being "made a story and a by-word through the world." I would add, a lot of stories—hundreds of them now having tumbled out of the Vietnam repository.

Not all of the stories, of course, are as bleak as *The Short-Timers*. A different tone is struck, for example, by Tim O'Brien's *Going after Cacciato*, which may become the classic text of the Vietnam War. O'Brien takes up the community issue as seriously as Hasford, but the results are different. Ultimately, his vision is hopeful. Imagination serves as the key for O'Brien, for the best community in his novel exists in the mind of his protagonist, Paul Berlin, whose character and circumstances rather closely parallel O'Brien's own as recorded in *If I*

Die in a Combat Zone, the memoir that preceded *Going after Cacciato*. Such was the case, it is worth remembering, with Winthrop, too. Winthrop's "Citty vpon a Hill" did not exist in reality, but its power was inspiring nonetheless. Much the same is true of Paul Berlin's Third Squad as it treks "eight thousand six hundred statute miles" (18) in order to reach its full complement by bringing the elusive Cacciato again into the fold in a celebrated city of lights, Paris.

Throughout the novel Paris symbolizes a community at peace— Paris, capital of the French, who had once been caught in an Asian war and had removed themselves; Paris, site of the American/North Vietnamese peace talks that eventually led to the removal of American soldiers from Vietnam. Paris—an ideal place that anyone who had experienced Vietnam would desire. Paris—a place to serve as the focal point for the idea of coming together to make a harmonious whole.

But as O'Brien makes clear at the outset of *Going after Cacciato*, Vietnam was a place so dominated by fragmentation (including the Third Squad's fragging of their inept lieutenant) that any idea of wholeness could only be entertained in a dream. Death was one of the facts of Vietnam that obstructed community togetherness, a fact that gives the narrative its point of departure:

> It was a bad time. Billy Boy Watkins was dead, and so was Frenchie Tucker. Billy Boy had died of fright, scared to death on the field of battle, and Frenchie Tucker had been shot through the nose. Bernie Lynn and Lieutenant Sidney Martin had died in tunnels. Pederson was dead and Rudy Chassler was dead. Buff was dead. Ready Mix was dead. They were all among the dead. (13)

O'Brien's opening is a calculated variation on a well-known beginning from another writer in another country of another century: "It was the best of times, it was the worst of times." However, the balance allowed by Dickens is not allowed by O'Brien; only the worst is acknowledged. Death.

To cope with death and its attendant anxiety, the soldiers of Vietnam had only the defensive mechanism of jokes (a motif already noted in Hasford's novel). Jokes provided a life-support system in the war, and sharing jokes forged a kind of desperate community, but the jokes made dark laughter, uncertain laughter—laughter meant to keep the spectre of death at bay:

> There was a joke about Oscar. There were many jokes about Billy Boy Watkins, the way he'd collapsed of fright on the field of battle. Another joke was about the lieutenant's dysentery, and another about Paul Berlin's purple biles. There were jokes about the postcard pictures of Christ that Jim Pederson used to carry, and Stick's ringworm, and the way Buff's helmet filled with life after death. Some of the jokes were about Cacciato. Dumb as a bullet, Stink said. Dumb as a month-old oyster fart, said Harold Murphy. (14)

No one should ever underestimate the bonding capacity of humor. It might have been a good thing if Winthrop and the Puritans had allowed themselves the public indulgence of jokes (surely they did joke in private . . . once in a while). Yet *Going after Cacciato* shows that more, much more, than humor is needed to keep a community alive and well in the face of life's (and death's) challenges.

The "more" that is needed comes in Paul Berlin's imagination, an imagination derived from that of Tim O'Brien, Vietnam veteran extraordinaire. Even as the form of *Going after Cacciato* represents the essential fragmentation of Vietnam (part visionary dreaming about the pursuit of goodness, part remembrance of torturous past happenings, part anxious watchfulness over the present darkness), the visionary dream predominates. O'Brien's enthusiasm for the imagined journey to Paris is palpable in the serendipity of details provided to flesh out his picaresque tale. Wholeness is to be gained by incremental additions as one treks along.

In the "eight thousand six hundred" miles between Vietnam and Paris, there are many additions. With an Alice-in-Wonderland fall into the Mother Earth, the Third Squad gains an illuminating perspective (that of the enemy) on the war above/below. With the added presence of Sarkin Aung Wan, Paul Berlin gains a sense of the feminine perspective on life. And with subsequent stops in New Delhi and Tehran, exposure to other cultures—ancient and antecedent to western civilization—is gained. It is as if the Third Squad replicates the evolution-ary history of humankind, and through this imagined journey, O'Brien makes a subtle case for world togetherness, a community of the whole earth. Not a bad visionary idea given the grotesque ignorance about Southeast Asia with which America ventured forth into combat in the 1960s.

Nevertheless, when the Third Squad arrives at the symbolic center of enlightened wholeness, a final stumbling block is discovered. Ironically, the blockage involves community—the heartland American community of Paul Berlin's past. In Paris, at the very point of reclaiming Cacciato for the squad and with Sarkin Aung Wan offering strong arguments to forgo the conclusive action that would involve a return to Vietnam, Berlin confronts the reason that placed him in Vietnam in the first place:

> More than any positive sense of obligation, I confess that what dominates is the dread of abandoning all that I hold dear. I am afraid of exile. I fear what might be thought of me by those I love. I fear the loss of their respect. I fear the loss of my own reputation. Reputation, as read in the eyes of my father and mother, the people in my hometown, my friends. I fear being an outcast. I fear being thought of as a coward. I fear that even more than cowardice itself. (377)

Albeit in a passive or fearful mode, Berlin recognizes that he is a creature of community. He does not want to go it alone, to indulge himself and his views by declaring independence from the community of his origin. He fears alienation, and he accepts his need to be accepted by those near and dear to him. Such a condition is where most of us meet the idea of community, and no exercise of the imagination—no matter how powerful—can displace the natural need for the approval of others. As Berlin notes, "Even in imagination we must obey the logic of what we started. Even in imagination we must be true to our obligations, for, even in imagination, obligation cannot be outrun. Imagination, like reality, has its limits" (378).

This declaration brings Paul Berlin and Sarkin Aung Wan to an impasse. In a dramatic fashion, O'Brien spotlights the individual departures of Paul and this woman of enchanting possibilities, one from the

other. She leaves. He leaves by a separate exit. A wonderfully innocent and special community is no more.

> Spotlight dims: An electric hum fills the Salle des Fetes. The
> amplification system buzzes indifferently.
> Spotlight off.
> Imagine it. (378)

There is no celebrating in this hall of festivals. Lights out in the city
of lights. We are given something to imagine here distinctly unlike the
vision meant to be summoned by another work of the same era that is
cued on the same word, John Lennon's "Imagine." Lennon would have
us imagine a better world, a world of greater goodness.

But, ultimately, so would Tim O'Brien. With the imperative "Imagine it," O'Brien throws the responsibility for dreaming to his readers.
We naturally do not want to imagine that cold, dark room with its
buzzing indifference. We want something better than that. O'Brien
sets us up perfectly; he gives us a point of departure, right where Paul
Berlin falls back into a community project that led him and others to
the miseries and moral complexities of Vietnam.

We are invited to imagine, and the only thing we can imagine is a
better community, one larger in spirit, one less likely to plunge into
catastrophe. The community of homeland America placed Paul Berlin
in Vietnam. That action was a misstep, but the idea of community is
still worth pursuing. Going after it is the key. The first step is a vision,
work of the imagination.

John Winthrop's "Modell of Christian Charity" outlined a type of
ideal community. The imaginative texts of Vietnam show us something
close to the reverse. While Hasford's *The Short-Timers* reveals un-
equivocally the despair that prevails when the community disintegrates into a nihilism of selves in isolation, O'Brien's *Going after Cacciato* reaffirms the spirit that vitalized Winthrop's text: the good
begins in dreams. The good is first projected imaginatively. Now, in
our time—no less than in the time of the Puritan settlers—there must
be dreams. Our best dreams must join us with others. The scope of
our vision must be as large as we can make it. It will never be easy.
But it must be. Imagine it.

Thus O'Brien's challenge is pointedly clear, especially so when his text is measured within the context of the typological imagination, a dimension of reality extant in America for a long time and one likely to postpone almost indefinitely the loss of Vietnam from our sense of moral purpose.

WORKS CITED

Bellah, Robert N., Richard Madsen, William M. Sullivan, Ann Swidler, and Steven M. Tipton. *Habits of the Heart: Individualism and Commitment in American Life*. 1985. New York: Perennial, 1986.

Bercovitch, Sacvan. *The American Jeremiad*. Madison: University of Wisconsin Press, 1978.

Hasford, Gustav. *The Short-Timers*. 1979. New York: Bantam, 1980.

Holman, C. Hugh. *The Immoderate Past: The Southern Writer and History*. Athens: University of Georgia Press, 1977.

O'Brien, Tim. *Going after Cacciato*. 1978. New York: Dell, 1979.

Tocqueville, Alexis de. *Democracy in America*. Ed. Richard D. Heffner. New York: Mentor-NAL, 1956.

Winthrop, John. "A Modell of Christian Charity." In *Puritanism and the American Experience*. Ed. Michael McGiffert. Reading, Mass.: Addison-Wesley, 1969.

The (Hidden) Antiwar Activist

in Vietnam War Fiction

O O O O O O O O O O O O

Jacqueline R. Smetak

The Vietnam War is receiving much, perhaps too much, coverage these days. We have monuments and television shows, feature films, documentaries, histories, novels, scholarly journals, and course packets all designed to walk us through a public trauma so intense that for many years it couldn't be talked about at all. There is something morbid in this obsessiveness, something as morbid as the vision reflected in the titles chosen for books about the war: *The Wounded Generation, The Haunted Generation, The Long Dark Night of the Soul, A Contagion of War*. This recurrent metaphor of disease echoes an old political cartoon in which Lyndon Johnson pulls up his shirt to expose the mark of his gall bladder operation only to show us a scar in the shape of Vietnam. But in the midst of all this scrutiny, something is missing. Almost all of the material is about the war over there. Very little focuses attention on the war that was right here.

This relative silence is odd because more people were involved in the war-against-the-war at home than were sent to Vietnam. The 1969 moratorium, in fact, attracted more people than were actually stationed in Indochina at the time. Why is it that the wartime experience of all these people has found hardly any voice at all?

An easy answer would have to do with genre. The war story, as such, is a very old form, highly conventionalized and relatively easy to tell. The story of political opposition is more difficult because it has no convenient a priori structure to appropriate. But this is only a partial answer. Any story can be told if people want badly enough to tell it. The rest of the answer most likely has to do with the peculiarities of the antiwar movement itself and what happened to it.[1]

The movement was in many ways a mirror image of the war itself, dependent on the war for its very being. This relationship was acknowledged at the time in the bits and pieces of military clothing many protesters chose to wear and in such books as Norman Mailer's *Armies of the Night*. These people, as Mailer points out, went forth "to wage a war on corporation-land" (110). That war should have made for an interesting story, but the story rarely got told except in terms of failure. Perhaps the difficulty of confronting the experience of resistance resides in the traumatic realization that one's own country was using guns and bayonets to protect itself from its own, largely unarmed, people. The close identification with the Vietnamese as victim and of America as perpetrator of monstrosities beyond imagination left many of those who had resisted in a terrifying nightmare equally compounded of fear and guilt.

"Bring the War Home," said the leaflets, but the war didn't need to be brought home. It was already here. Nevertheless, attempts to tell its story from the vantage point of "here" were problematic. The war at home was not a war as such, merely war's image—a play war with few people killed or even badly injured. With few exceptions, the story of the war here had to be told from over there.

The closest we come is Robert Stone's *Dog Soldiers*, a novel about American civilians first in Vietnam and later back in the States, but the civilians in question are heavily involved in the drug trade not the peace movement. Although the protagonist's wife is a red-diaper baby and her father a "veteran of *New Masses* and the Abraham Lincoln

Brigade," their political behavior has degenerated into a jaded fascination with perversity. The old man now publishes "A Weekly Tabloid
with a Heavy Emphasis on Sex," his daughter works in a triple-X
movie house, and his son-in-law (Converse) is a failed playwright with
a bogus press pass that gets him access to heroin rather than the news.
Perhaps the story is intended as a warning about what happens when
a political movement gets sidetracked.

Granted, something of the sort did happen to the antiwar movement
as thousands of kids flooded into Students for a Democratic Society
under the mistaken impression that *Time* and *Newsweek* were correct
in saying that antiwar activists and hippies were somehow the same
and that, therefore, drug use and opposition to the war were also
somehow the same. However, that was not quite what the movement
was—only what it was thought to be by people who didn't understand
it. Thus Stone's novel, though it has much that is eerily familiar, contains nothing to justify or make sense of the experience of political
opposition.

On the other hand, the book gives us a place to start because Converse is built out of a specific construct. Antiwar activists were
thought to be somehow defective. This stereotyping was a maneuver
on the part of those in power to discredit those who disagreed with
them. As noted by Michael Parenti in *Inventing Reality: The Politics
of the Mass Media*:

> After initially downplaying the war and the protests, the media
> began giving serious attention to both [after 1966]. Unable either
> to prevent or to ignore mass protests, the opinion manufacturers
> set about to misrepresent, discredit, and contain a political move-
> ment that was raising serious questions about "democratic capi-
> talism." . . . [Although there were] moments of coverage . . .
> when protesters were occasionally treated with some sympathy
> and insight . . . the *cumulative impact* of press coverage was to
> create the impression that these "kids" were crazy, violent, ex-
> tremist, and dangerous to society. Thus the protesters were made
> the issue rather than the things they were protesting. (90)

In brief, the activists were marginalized, portrayed as a tiny mi-
nority—violent, irrational, drug-addicted communists, or even worse,

mere students, even though the majority of activists were nothing of the sort. In fact, according to polling information analyzed by Milton Rosenberg et al. in *Vietnam and the Silent Majority*, the most hawkish demographic group at the time was white male college students. But the original constructed version of the activist stuck, so that by the 1980s Stanley Rothman and S. Robert Lichter could, in *Roots of Radicalism*, characterize the New Left as a "seething cauldron of narcissism, self-hatred, sexual inadequacy, declining ego strength, irrational power drives, and other unpleasant characteristics" without much rebuttal.[2] However, studies of activists done at the time, such as Kenneth Keniston's *Young Radicals: Notes on Committed Youth*, found that most activists were quite well adjusted. Keniston also found that there was no such thing as the "generation gap," that the vast majority of student activists held views similar to those of their parents and, indeed, seemed to be "living out expressed but unimplemented parental values" (309).

While this sort of information is very interesting, it creates a problem for the storyteller who must deal in the plausible, not necessarily the real. So ingrained is the vision of the activist as a mass of crippling neuroses that a story about activists as they really were might be as impossible to accept as a story about a Vietnam veteran *not* suffering from severe posttraumatic stress disorder. John Wheeler, in *Touched with Fire*, argues that the tendency to depict Vietnam veterans as "cripples" is symptomatic of fear: "It is fear of the health in Vietnam veterans. . . . It is fear of potency and authority evidenced and earned in a hard way by Vietnam veterans. . . . The more afraid one is, the more fearsome others become. The more hurt, angry, and worthy of punishment one feels, the more natural it is to replace oneself as the hurt, angry, and guilty one" (166). Though Wheeler limits his remarks to the public perception and construction of the veteran, by extension the same thing could be said of the activist since, as Philip Caputo acknowledges, "We—all of us—went through something together" (Wheeler 117). The assumption here is that those who were not involved in the war or who did not oppose it are projecting their own quagmire of emotions in the form of a "crippled vet" or a neurotic activist.

Ironically, most Vietnam War fiction, much of it written by veterans, follows this same pattern. In these works, the writers' attempt is not to justify common misperceptions but to use them to defend veterans against the accusation that they are defective, to undermine what can be called "the ideology of individualism," the notion that the individual, not the system or the circumstances, is responsible for whatever happens. Much of this fiction also makes use of characters who are either antiwar activists or are constructed as activists. In this regard, the four novels I have chosen to examine are fairly typical. Two of them, James Webb's *Fields of Fire* and Philip Caputo's *Indian Country*, have protagonists who are torn by conflicting loyalties. Each has, to an extent, internalized another character who is overtly an activist. Tim O'Brien's *Going after Cacciato* and Jack Fuller's *Fragments* have characters who, though they are soldiers, seem more like those who opposed the war than those who fought in it.

In *Fields of Fire*, James Webb blends these traits in the character of Goodrich, a marine who has never fully left his civilian sensibilities behind and thus has internalized two mutually exclusive value systems. Goodrich is unusual. He is a Harvard man in a war that people from places like Harvard just did not fight in.[3] Not only that, but Harvard at the time was a hotbed of antiwar activity.[4] In keeping with this, most of Goodrich's Harvard friends are antiwar. His best friend, Mark Solomon, had gone to Canada. The rest "went to grad school." But Webb takes none of these young men seriously, and he is determined that we should not either. One of them, Tim Forbes, who will someday "confess his boondoggle" and be admired for "his honesty," is a swipe at former Harvard student and antiwar activist James Fallows, whose "What Did You Do in the Class War, Daddy?" appeared in the October 1975 issue of *Washington Monthly*.

How seriously the real war resisters should be taken is open to question. Myra MacPherson, in *Long Time Passing: Vietnam and the Haunted Generation*, reports 172,000 were granted conscientious objector status and some 250,000 challenged draft laws head-on, but her tone, though less hostile, indicates that she agrees with Webb. These were nineteen- and twenty-year-old kids, she seems to be saying, how much selfless commitment can one reasonably expect? Indeed, Goodrich is one of them. He "did not care about anything. . . . Leaving school was the first decision he had ever made" (90). He joins the marines not to fight for his country but because the Peace Corps had rejected him as "too militant." Joining the marines was a good way to mend fences with his father, a World War II navy veteran, and avoid combat. He assumes, when he signs the papers, that he will play in the Marine Corps band.

He ends up, however, in a combat zone with a lot of working-class kids he has difficulty understanding. Besides that, he's soft. He explains his last name by comparing himself to the Goodyear blimp. "You *look* like a goddamn blimp," the soldier he's talking to exclaims. "How much you weigh, man?" (66). Goodrich has problems handling combat. He loses control of his bowels. He throws up. His fellow soldiers, on the other hand, are neither fat nor weak in the gut. And they have reasons for joining the marines. Snake joins because he likes to fight, Hodges because he is descended from a long line of warriors, Bagger because he does it for "the team," and Cat Man because he was "meant to do these things."

There is a heady neoromanticism about this, a conviction that there is something more important than the individual, discrete and isolated, living in a civilian world where people are neither alive nor with honor: "You do not sue a man who insults you. How much is honor worth? You destroy him" (Webb 210). It's a simple code with no room for a person who agonizes or questions. Even Ogre's handmade peace symbol becomes an ironic comment on the questions Ogre had apparently never asked when the VC shot out his eyes.

It is not country these men fight for. It is something more elemental because their country betrays and abandons them. It is a people they fight for, a people composed of themselves. Garry Wills, in *Nixon Agonistes*, discusses this identification in terms of Robert E. Lee's decision to join his home state of Virginia and lead the Confederate Army:

> Lee did not think of the nation as a legal unit indivisible, a judicial entity with one National Will. . . . Nor did he justify his choice on the grounds that he had a new country, the Confederacy, established by right of self-determination. This whole cast of thought was foreign to him. . . . He was not fighting for any Cause, for slavery or the Confederacy. For him, country *meant* one's

friends—the bond of affection that exists among countrymen; and when a rift opened in this union of persons, he had to choose those to whom he was bound by primary rather than secondary ties. (441)

These men understand this, but Goodrich, contaminated by the alien values of a corrupt civilian world, never quite learns.

Part of Goodrich's problem is that he has primary ties to two diametrically opposed groups. Mark Solomon keeps sending him letters: "I see pictures of the patrols burning down homes . . . and I just can't picture you there. . . . I sure can't see *you* burning people, or standing by while someone else does" (88). Eventually Mark's letters will force Goodrich to choose. When Baby Cakes and Ogre are executed by two VC disguised as villagers, the other marines force the two Vietnamese to stand beside the graves they had dug before shooting them. Goodrich objects but is told to keep his mouth shut. This war crime is justified by Webb in terms closer to the values of ancient Greece than modern America—"a gut-wrenched funeral procession that had avenged the murders of its kin" (244). Goodrich goes into a funk, alternating between being sullen and being obnoxious, and accuses Hodges, who had been wounded but voluntarily returns to the Combat Zone, of coming back because "there ain't any . . . kills on Okinawa" (262, ellipses Webb's), thus misunderstanding entirely why Hodges had come back—"his men were on patrol, or digging new perimeters, or dying, and he was nothing if he did not share that misery" (258).

But for Goodrich, none of that matters. These people are not his people, and the simulacrum of loyalty he achieves—he does keep his mouth shut—stems more from a lack of courage than anything else. Finally, a letter from Mark containing a clipping from the *New York Times* about a massacre of civilians, a reference to My Lai,[5] puts Goodrich in an untenable position: "We can't administer street justice—what the hell: bush justice—to every Vietnamese who pisses us off" (277). So he goes to the legal officer, files a report which in turn is itself filed. Nothing happens.

At this point the story could take any one of several turns depending on the value system Webb is trying to express. The story could hinge on a classically tragic conflict involving the necessity of choice, in this case the choice between loyalty to one's friends or to a minimum level of human decency. Instead, Webb chooses to justify what most people would call murder. Nothing happens with Goodrich's report for a while, but eventually it does surface after a firefight in which most of the men who participated in the executions are either killed or wounded. The legal officer in charge is most concerned, because the general is most concerned, about "political difficulties." The company commander is worried about his career. Snake, who had initiated the executions and had died in the firefight, would be denied the recommended posthumous Medal of Honor, his grieving mother denied the only thing that would comfort her.

Clearly, Goodrich had blundered. Snake had saved his life, and his own injuries, the loss of a leg and partial paralysis of one arm, are a penance and a mark of Cain, permanently excluding him from both the military and the civilian world. His problem, then, becomes one of reintegration.

The first step is taken not by Goodrich but by his father. When Mark comes to visit, Goodrich notes an ironic similarity in the attitude of his draft-dodging friend and that of his former marine comrades: "You might not believe this, Mark, but you sound a lot like some of the Marines I served with. . . . They used to ask, what kind of law is it that allows a person who doesn't understand your motivations to say you're right or wrong? They never said it that way, but it was the same" (328). For a brief moment, the activist and the soldier merge, but that merging is Goodrich's misinterpretation. Mark, as Goodrich's father points out, isn't "a fighter anyway. He's a runner" (330). The old man turns Mark over to the police and justifies this betrayal by saying, "We've lost a sense of responsibility. . . . People seem to have forgotten that a part of our strength comes from each person surrendering a portion of his individual urges to the common good. And the common good is defined by who wins at the polls, and the policies they make. Like it or lump it" (332). In a nutshell, good marines are those who put the unit above themselves and do what they are told. Mark is no marine, and neither is Goodrich because he ratted on his fellows.

At the end of the novel, Goodrich participates in an antiwar demonstration on the Harvard campus, manipulated into it by people who, contemptuous of the values for which Goodrich had fought and his friends had died, are eager to use him as a stage prop for their anti-American show. But this will be the turning point away from people like Mark and toward people like Snake and Bagger and Hodges, the people he had betrayed by going to the legal officer. In the middle of his speech, he stops, accuses the protesters of playing "THESE GOD-DAMN GAMES," and leaves. "Hey, Braverman," he says to one of the organizers, pointing his crutch, "Pow" (338–339).

While it is easy to criticize Webb's description of the demonstration—his focus makes it seem more like a clip out of the film *Woodstock* than anything authentic—it is not easy to answer his accusations. In general, Harvard kids who opposed the war did not go. Working-class kids did, and though in this book the activist and soldier merge in the divided self of Goodrich, they coexist there in an uneasy nonalliance that literally makes Goodrich sick. The implication is that he will never be well until he kills the one to become the other. So he points his crutch and "Pow."

Is Webb successful in defending those he served with, who fought a war for "some goddamned amorphous reason" that could not be articulated? It depends. The anger is palpable, but Goodrich's desire at the end of the novel to hunt down the seven-year-old child who had led him and the others into that final ambush and "blow her away" is a bit much. It is as if for Webb the mere fact of war justified all actions because the war itself had simply stopped making sense except on the most basic level where anyone and everyone who was not part of the primary group was ipso facto the enemy. Thus, for a certain type of reader, identification with the soldiers and their plight, while not impossible, is difficult.

Tim O'Brien's autobiography, *If I Die in a Combat Zone*, is more successful in establishing identification primarily because he sidesteps the issues of placing blame or defending either the war or anyone who participated in it. The war simply was and, for him, the issue is not the war but courage. For Socrates, courage is wise endurance, but O'Brien concludes that his has been foolish. Foolish endurance seems to have been the primary factor in the My Lai massacre of March 16, 1968: ". . . if a man can squirm in a meadow, he can shoot children. Neither are examples of courage" (136). When O'Brien lucks-out after six months in the field, he is shipped to the rear to shuffle papers under the command of a Major Callicles who is convinced the war is going badly because of "mustaches, prostitution, pot, and sideburns" in that order. My Lai hit the major hard, and his attempts to justify the massacre make him sound at times like a deranged parody of the narrative voice in *Fields of Fire*, becoming more and more strange in his rage and personal hurt until finally he burns down the local whorehouse and is given two hours to get out of the area: "It hurt him, leaving" (201). O'Brien, on the other hand, is not at all sorry to leave when his tour of duty is up. On the plane home he puts on civilian clothes and stuffs his uniform into his suitcase. The problem, though, is that he has only one pair of shoes: "Much as you hate it, you don't have civilian shoes, but no one will notice. It's impossible to go home barefoot" (205).

Ostensibly, the shoes refer to the truism that O'Brien can't stuff his experiences as easily as he can stuff his clothes, but the emphasis on feet is significant. Unlike the fictive Goodrich, O'Brien goes home with both legs still attached, a major stroke of luck considering that he was stationed in an area where each day two or three of his mates had their legs taken off by mines. But his unscarred feet become stigmata, marking him as different in much the same way Goodrich is marked as different—through the feet or legs.

There is something oddly appropriate about this kind of wound, whether literal or symbolic. It contains echoes of Odysseus's scar, high enough up on the inside of his thigh to give one pause, or of Achilles, his vulnerable heel coupled with his refusal to fight. Indeed, an injury to the legs or feet has both literal and symbolic (displaced castration) significance. Thus Webb's description is meant to suggest that Goodrich is sexually dysfunctional: "He stood uneasily on the platform, agonizingly self-conscious of his legless state. Just below him a girl in cut-off jeans sat comfortably on someone's shoulders. . . . Goodrich watched the breasts bounce merrily and tried to remember if he had ever experienced such lovelies. He hadn't" (337).

Goodrich's wound is in part the result of his conflicted status as both marine and activist—a surrogate Mark Solomon—in that it is the result of "months of frustration, of fighting with himself" (299). In that last firefight, he had thrown himself between one of his comrades and a Vietnamese child he had wrongly presumed to be a civilian, thus exposing the entire unit to attack, a pacifist's gesture that gets half of them killed. If the marines make men, then a man who won't fight is a man who can't fuck and a man who can't fuck is a woman. Achilles was kept out of the Trojan War, at least for a time, by the fact that his mother disguised him as a girl.

That male antiwar activists were constructed as sexually dysfunctional and womanish men should be obvious even without reference to Rothman and Lichter's analysis in *Roots of Radicalism*. The army, on some level making the connection between men who wouldn't fight and women, seemed to have been obsessive in its efforts to separate the men from the "girls." O'Brien tells of his drill sergeant in basic training discovering that he had not one but two college graduates in his unit and exploding: "You're a pussy, huh? You afraid to be in the war, a goddamn pussy, a goddamn lezzie? You know what we do with pussies, huh? We fuck 'em. In the army we just fuck 'em and straighten 'em out" (*If I Die* 54). The sergeant in his homophobic, woman-phobic mania is only making the obvious connections. But it goes beyond that. A womanish man who will not fight is bad enough, but women are even worse: "There is no such thing named love in the world. Women are dinks. Women are villains. They are creatures akin to Communists and yellow-skinned people and hippies" (52).

There is room to speculate as to the role of the vagina dentata in all of this, and the Bouncing Betty land mine which, when stepped on, leaps high enough in the air to take off a man's balls (disintegrating his legs in the process) certainly fits that role. But it is more than that because women, after the manner of Circe, can lure a man away from the fields of fire. O'Brien speaks of a dream in which he escapes from prison and encounters a beautiful woman:

I looked into the valley below me, and a carnival was there. A beautiful woman . . . was charming snakes. With her stick she prodded the creatures, making them dance and writhe and perform. I hollered down to her, 'Which way to freedom? Which way home?' . . . She lifted the stick and pointed the way down a road. I loved the woman, snakes and stick and tanned skin. I followed the road, the rain became heavier, I whistled and felt happy and in love. (92)

Clearly, sex and women, carnival and battle are mutually exclusive because giving in to that kind of pleasure entails a transfer of the phallus—the stick and snakes—from the man to the woman. A male warrior holds his stick in his own hand.

But O'Brien is not interested in maintaining that kind of exclusionary control. When he expanded the dream into a novel, *Going after Cacciato*, he reversed the signifiers. The ultimate act of courage is not to stay and fight, as it is in Webb's novel, but to run away. O'Brien's story is of Cacciato, the deserter, who heads out of the war zone to be trailed by the Third Squad all the way to Paris. Cacciato is depicted as being as soft as Webb's Goodrich: "Open-faced and naive and plump, Cacciato lacked the fine detail that maturity ordinarily marks on a boy of seventeen years. The result was blurred and uncolored and bland" (21). In Webb's story, Goodrich's softness, a certain effeminacy, signals Goodrich's essential gutlessness. But Cacciato's doesn't: "You can't say he ran away because he was scared. . . . You can't say he wasn't brave" (29). Indeed, *not* following him is a mark of cowardice.

One of the men, Murphy, refuses to cross into Laos after Cacciato because such an act would be desertion: "I say we get our butts back to the war before things get worse" (54). Obviously, Murphy is afraid. Soldiers don't stay in a war because they are brave or have a purpose. As Doc puts it, "We stick it out because we're afraid of what'll happen to our reputations. Our own egos" (240). Soldiers also stay because of the trouble they would face if they ran. And they stay because they are incapable of freely choosing to do otherwise. Lt. Sidney Martin might view his troops' climb up a mountain as an example of "fortitude, discipline, loyalty, self-control, courage, toughness. The greatest gift of God . . . freedom of will" (203), but PFC Paul Berlin, who is doing the climbing, has a different reaction: "He was dull of mind, blunt of spirit, numb of history, and struck with wonder that he could not stop climbing the red road toward the mountains" (204).

Berlin, however, will find a way out by taking the hand of a Vietnamese woman, Sarkin Aung Wan, and falling down the rabbit hole. In order "to go home," he becomes, like her, a refugee (75). Here we enter the realm of myth where women are emblematic of the primal feminine containing within themselves aspects of the other, the earth, the source of life and healing, the mother, and the home. They are also that which is courage. And courage, as it was in *If I Die in a Combat Zone*, is the issue, not fearlessness but "how to act wisely in spite of fear" (101). In Webb's novel women divide roughly into two groups: those who castrate the male warrior and those—Hodges's grandmother, mother, and wife—who breed more warriors to die in battle before their own children are born. In O'Brien's novel it is not women who do the castrating. It's the army: "Behind him, the [American] gunners strafed the paddies, red tracers and white light, molded to their guns, part of the machinery, firing and firing, and Pederson was shot first in the legs" (161). The firing continues, and Pederson is shot again, this time in the lower stomach or groin. He will get his own licks by shooting through the bottom of the helicopter's "plastic belly." That is why soldiers riding in helicopters were advised to sit on, not wear, their flak jackets.

In part, this castration by friendly fire is an extension of the army's desire to obliterate the feminine. What these soldiers fight is not an implacable masculine enemy but the land. Once down the rabbit hole, the Third Squad meets Li Van Hgoc, a Viet Cong, who explains to them these things:

> "The soldier is but the representative of the land. The land is your true enemy." He paused. "There is an ancient ideograph—the word *Xa*. It means. . . . community, and soil, and home . . . earth and sky and even sacredness. Xa, it has many implications. But at heart it means that a man's spirit is in the land, where his ancestors rest and where the rice grows. The land is your enemy." . . .
> "So the land mines—"
> "The land defending itself." (107–108)

Unlike the Americans, the Vietnamese know why they fight. Paul Berlin is just a scared youth from Iowa who drifts into a war that existed for him as a "weird pretending." Why is he fighting this war—"I say why are we fightin' this fuckin-ass war? . . . To win it. . . . We fight this war to win it, that's why" (318)—a neat bit of solipsism that spins back on every soldier a "swingin' dick," an expression of a masculine desire to conquer by consuming and destroying not only the other but also itself:

> They did not know even the simple things: a sense of victory, or satisfaction, or necessary sacrifice. . . . They did not have targets. They did not have a cause. They did not know if it was a war of ideology or economics or hegemony or spite. On a given day they did not know where they were. . . . They did not know how to feel. . . . They did not know good from evil. (320–321)

To walk away from the war is to end it—"What if they gave a war and nobody came?"

But the issue is more complex because if it had been that simple, no one would have gone. Just outside of Zagreb, the Third Squad meets up with an antiwar student from San Diego State who had dropped out after her second year:[6]

> "Sometimes you've just got to separate yourself off from evil."
> Oscar stared at her. "You say it's same-same? Nam and fucking San Diego State?"
> "Not exactly, maybe. But I can empathize. . . . When you see evil you have to get away from it, right?"
> "Evil?" Oscar tapped Doc's shoulder. "You ever see evil in Nam?"
> "What's evil?" Doc said. (326)

The soldiers, exasperated with her superficial moralism, steal the van and leave her by the side of the road still smiling. Women can be wise, as is Sarkin Aung Wan, but since war is so foreign to their constructed nature (woman as myth) they can also be stupid, and even Sarkin Aung Wan, for all her feminine wisdom, cannot understand the web of obligations that keeps Paul Berlin in the war. She pleads with him:

> It is one thing to run from unhappiness; it is another to take action to realize those qualities of dignity and well-being that are the true standards of the human spirit. Spec Four Paul Berlin: I am asking for a break from violence. But I am also asking for a positive commitment. . . . Be happy. It is possible. It is within reach of a single decision. (374)

Berlin answers:

> I stress the importance of viewing obligations as a relationship between people, not between one person and some impersonal idea or principle. An idea, when violated, cannot make reprisals. A principle cannot refuse to shake my hand. Only people can do that. . . . The real issue is how to find felicity within limits. Within the context of our obligations to other people. (377–378)

That she speaks to him through a male translator indicates that he will have as much difficulty understanding her as she does him. They part, having stated their respective positions (hers containing within itself the unmistakable echo of Henry David Thoreau). Negotiation is not possible because for Sarkin Aung Wan to become a refugee is to go home, but for Paul Berlin to become a refugee is to go into exile. It is the tangle of obligations to his community and his people that keeps him in the war, as well as his inability to make that "single decision," to make an active commitment to peace and happiness, to "march proudly into [his] own dream." But the dream ends, and Berlin finds himself back in the war zone, the chase after Cacciato all the way to Paris a flick of the eye: "The war was still a war, and he was still a soldier. He hadn't run. The issue was courage, and courage was will power, and this was his failing" (379). If the constructed activist may be identified with the maimed (or castrated) soldier—Goodrich or, here, Pederson who shoots at those in the belly of the chopper who are killing him—Paul Berlin is not so much a maimed soldier as a defective human being, an unwilling cyborg—not a hero—who can't quite get control of his life.

Jack Fuller, in his novel *Fragments*, develops these same themes of choice and control. Like O'Brien and Webb, Fuller chooses a relatively passive protagonist who is swept into the war:

> It wasn't a matter of choice at all. It was something deeper, irresistible. When you came from where I did, when you'd been raised on certain tales . . . then you simply had no alternative when your number came up. You were swept along despite the arguments. And it wasn't the great historic ebbs and flows or even the coercive power of the state that did it. You were moved forward by

your own ineradicable past. . . . It had nothing to do with courage, moral or otherwise. It was simply who you were. (28–29)

Given that men writing of their own experiences in that war tend to
construct themselves, as did Ron Kovic in *Born on the Fourth of July*
and Philip Caputo in *A Rumor of War*, as youths whose decisions were
made for them—"We went overseas full of illusions, for which the intoxicating atmosphere of those years was as much to blame as our
youth" (*Rumor* xiv)—one can conclude that a passive narrator or main
character is as much a convention of Vietnam War fiction as the
trenches are of World War I literature. But to focus entirely on soldiers constructed as passive victims is to break other conventions in a
way that would render a war story sentimental and most probably
offensive. The role of passive victim was long ago assigned to women
and children. The essence of the hero is the ability to choose and, ironically, in these novels the ability to choose is given to the constructed
activist who, back then, when called did not go.

Fuller, however, has a problem. While he, of all the novelists considered thus far, has created the most fully realized constructed activist
in the character Jim Neumann (who, when we are first introduced to
him, is "dragging a bad leg" [19]), he has to get him into the war without denying him freedom of will. Thus, Neumann is not drafted. He
volunteers and shows up at the induction station with long hair, wearing beads and carrying a silver flute. However, he doesn't volunteer
because he's a militarist in drag. He does so to use the system to gain
control over what happens to him. He is described as one who refuses
"to accept that there was anything that would not shape itself to the
will." Bill Morgan, the narrator, takes a different course. He splits in
two, distancing himself from himself: "Somebody else submitted, not
me. I was just watching Morgan's progress. . . . Morgan just did what
he was told" (51).

The tension in the story rests on this contrast. Once in Vietnam,
Neumann joins the Blues, a team assigned to spring ambushes and
clear hot LZs. Morgan stays with the Greens, a more conventional
outfit, predictable, slow, "a beast of burden waiting to be whipped"
(93). When two of his friends are killed, Morgan snaps out of his passivity and makes a decision: "All at once it seemed to me that the
Green Machine was a lie. And you could not blame nature for what we

had done. . . . I had seen the way death wove its way in when you did not struggle against the binding. And now it was time to try Neumann's way" (99).

Neumann's way is odd, based as it is on values gleaned from older cultures. He used to hunt but quit after he realized that "you not only had to know how to kill, you had to know when and why, or else you were going to destroy yourself, too" (57). Neumann is not careless nor does he see the Vietnamese as "dinks" or "slopes" or anything other than human beings. He loves children. He respects the people he is fighting. When he kills an NVA outside the village of Xuan The he curses the man for moving where he could see him and guards the body so that his more bloody-minded company mate, Thompson, won't have a chance to cut off the dead man's ears. Then he adopts the village and wants to rebuild the medical dispensary.

He also adopts a family in the village: Le Van Tuyet, her mother, and her four-year-old Amerasian brother. It is at this point that the title of the novel comes into play because the story fragments and the pieces won't fit back together. Enemy troops attack the village. Neumann heads straight for Tuyet's hootch and finds a VC inside with the family. Neumann attempts to protect the family, the VC turns a gun on him, Neumann shoots him, and Tuyet goes mad, grabbing a weapon and screaming incoherently. When the smoke clears, Tuyet, her mother, and her brother are dead; Neumann is badly wounded. Morgan, under fire for the village is still under attack, drags him out. There will be an inquiry and Neumann will be cleared of war crimes but "not guilty is not the same thing as innocent" (206).

It is up to Morgan to try to put the pieces together. According to Apache, the unit's Kit Carson scout, the man in the hootch was Tuyet's older brother who had returned home to surrender, but Apache believes that the "Vietnamese never tell truth" (144). Neumann, however, balances this belief. They hedge on the truth because they have "suffered a lot of lies. . . . They're not fools. They have learned to distrust" (192). In the end, it is not clear who the man in the hootch was or where Tuyet's sympathies lay. Neumann blames himself: "If I hadn't known them . . . maybe I would have been more careful" (282). As it turns out, he didn't see any gun, he only saw the man move.

What Fuller intends by this story poses another problem. Neumann is a type, modeled after the kind of antiwar activist Todd Gitlin refers

to as a "prairie radical" (186). Taken allegorically, the story is a caution-
ary tale, warning us of the limits of New Left ideology, the faith that
human beings working in community can make a difference in what
happens to them. Neumann sides with the people antiwar activists saw
as victims of American imperialism. He tries to help them but in the
end does them far more harm than if he'd just left them alone. Or was
Neumann betrayed by people he had romanticized, as those who opposed the war had been taken in by the NLF in that they had seen
those people as far more gentle than they actually were? Or was Neumann himself the problem, thinking that by sheer force of will and
good intentions he could, like Graham Greene's dangerously innocent
quiet American, avoid evil?

Whatever the case, at the end of the novel Neumann settles in down-
state Illinois, living with a woman with faintly Oriental features and
trying to rebuild someone else's broken-down farm, in brief, living out
the quieter counterculture ideals of the 1970s as opposed to the more
active and participatory ones of the 1960s. But that's not quite it either. Neumann may not understand what happened—"nothing is
simple, nothing is true" (285)—but Morgan has an inkling, the sort of
intuitive understanding that can only be understood by those who have
it: "I understood Xuan The now. . . . The war was to blame, but we
were the war. Facts and forces drove us, but we gave them their mor-
tal shape. . . . Green and blue were not separate. The connection was
absolute" (287).

One of the problems with *Fragments* is that something doesn't quite
click. Neumann's transformation from latent pacifist GI Joe to moral
monster to broken recluse is too fast, perhaps too slick, although the
pattern of his disintegration certainly describes the process of what
happened to antiwar activists who slid, Raskolnikov style, from prin-
cipled opposition to self-serving underground terrorism to a fugitive
underground existence, sometimes within a matter of months.

Todd Gitlin, attempting to explain why many of his New Left friends
had gone around a collective crazy bend, writes:

> In the movement rhetoric of that hour, *we* were life and *they* were
> "the death culture." . . . The movement core were Manicheans as
> well as utopians; our sense of innocence required all-or-nothing

thinking, and innocence was the motor of our collective passion. . . . Whence the shock when it proved impossible to draw a
hard and fast line between the two. The revolutionary mood had
been fueled by the blindingly bright illusion that human history
was beginning afresh because a graced generation had willed it
so. Now there wasn't enough life left to mobilize against all the
death raining down. (408)

Though Neumann is not nearly as Manichean as that "graced generation," there is a sense that he can keep things together only so long as
he can maintain a balance of reciprocity. If he kills he must make restitution; thus the dispensary is an exchange for the dead NVA. The
circle breaks in that last battle because not only does he murder Tuyet,
a crime he cannot pay off, but the unfinished dispensary is leveled.
There is nothing left "to mobilize against all the death."

But Neumann's fall from grace is slick only in relation to, for example, Philip Caputo's description of his own fall in A Rumor of War.
Here Caputo meticulously chronicles his slide from clean-cut, all-
American marine lieutenant to a filthy wretch stinking of feces and
sweat and covered with pus-oozing sores, the physical decline a metaphor for spiritual and moral collapse. Toward the end of his tour Caputo was court-martialed for war crimes. He had sent five marines into
a village on a midnight raid to capture two suspected VC. The marines, punch-drunk from exhaustion, killed the two they were supposed to have captured, one of whom had been the wrong man. Though
Caputo was cleared in the ensuing investigation, as with the fictive
Neumann a verdict of innocent did not mean not guilty: "A verdict of
innocent . . . would prove what the others wanted to believe: that we
were virtuous American youths, incapable of the act of which we were
accused. And if we were incapable of it, then they were too, which is
what they wanted to believe themselves" (314). Even though Caputo
joined Vietnam Veterans Against the War after he got home, he was
torn between outrage over the war and nostalgia for it. He would later
explore this conflict and guilt through the vehicle of fiction in Indian
Country.

Lucius Starkmann, the activist in Indian Country, is not a soldier
but the father of one. This activist is not a hippie like Neumann but an

unbending Lutheran minister, a social crusader, a pacifist, dedicated, cold, and fanatic. His son, Christian, joins the army to get away from his father and to be with his friend, Bonny George, an Ojibwa Indian who had been drafted. "Go to war, go to jail, or go into exile—it seemed to him that his friend should have had more options than those. . . . [Chris] felt embarrassed by his divinity-school deferment, somehow less than a man for not having to face the hard decisions that had confronted his friend. He saw himself as a coddled, protected, middle-class white kid, and a fraud to boot" (24–25). Chris quits school, joins the army, and is sent to Vietnam. Halfway through his tour, caught in a firefight with a dead radio operator and a wounded CO, Chris has to call in an airstrike, but he calls it in too close and Bonny George is killed. Chris returns home to Chicago, finds himself unable to live there, and is drawn north to the Upper Peninsula. Twelve years later he goes mad.

The story line is simple enough. Chris rejects his own family to be with his friend—in effect, his brother—and then kills him, thus fulfilling the prophecy given the god Odin centuries before: "The Twilight of the Gods. There's war all over the world. Brothers killing brothers. Fathers kill their sons. Sons kill their fathers. And it all comes down when this giant wolf leaps up and swallows the moon and the sun. . . . Get the picture? When white people came over here, they brought all that baggage with them, and they wiped out the wolves because they were afraid of them" (32).

At this point the story shifts to larger issues: because the Indian is brother to the wolf, he as such had inspired in whites the same dread the wolf had. The action takes place in Indian Country, both in America and Vietnam. The term "Indian Country" had been used by American soldiers over there to "designate territory under enemy control or any terrain considered hostile and dangerous." In effect, the Vietnamese are Indians, a perception reflected in the soldiers' habit of calling their Vietnamese scouts Kit Carsons and their base camps Dodge City. Though in *A Rumor of War* Caputo dismisses the theory that the Vietnam War and its peculiar brutality grew out of American racism and the frontier heritage—a theory which fails to take into account the brutality of other peoples involved in that war— that theory is the core of *Indian Country*. This war is seen as a reenactment of all America's other wars and as the last Indian war. Or, as Philip Beidler puts it, all those wars conflate as "one endless 'Indian' war, waged by myth-haunted heroes out of date, waged in all the wrong ways for all the wrong reasons in a grand tragedy of mass cultural misperception. It is the tragic joke . . . of our whole collective experience as a people" (69).

In *Indian Country*, Indian victim, "myth-haunted heroes," and the totally other Vietnamese merge in the relationship between Christian Starkmann and Bonny George—the two as close as brothers or even closer, the same. That relationship also confers the status of brother on those people we traveled nine thousand miles to kill. Chris as survivor becomes Cain.

Caputo, emphasizing this connection, begins the novel with a quote from Homer: "God of the Sea, I beg you, punish Ulysses for this. . . . Let him wander many years before he reaches home, and when he gets there let him find himself forgotten, unwanted, a stranger." Chris represses the war. Though he is drawn to Bonny George's home territory and though he goes out of his way not to pass the town's war memorial, he can't remember why he is in that town or why he avoids certain places. Cut off from his own family, his father refusing to forgive him, Chris makes little effort to make new connections though he does marry. He cannot speak of his war experience, convinced that if people knew they would drive him out. He flees the war, but he can't run far enough or fast enough. Eventually, it comes in the night to get him. The nightmares commence on the twelfth anniversary of Bonny George's death.

On one level the story is a neo-Freudian thriller. If Chris can bring to the surface those memories causing his increasingly erratic behavior he can recover his sanity. On another level it is dark and uncanny, as if Chris's rigid father becomes God asking where is Abel. Thus it is not just a matter of confession but of absolution and from the father. But such is not possible. Chris's father dies but forgiveness comes from another quarter, Bonny George's grandfather, an Ojibwa shaman. Bonny George died not because Chris had made a terrible error but because the old man had. He'd misunderstood a dream and had advised his grandson wrongly. Both men need to learn to live with themselves, "how to live, period" (425). The problem becomes one of coming to terms. While the old man cannot forgive himself—there is no such word in his language and no such concept in his culture—Christian Starkmann, the son of a driven antiwar minister, must.

At the end of the novel, Chris heads into the woods to meditate beside the stream where, long ago, his dead friend had saved him from drowning: "He stood looking at his reflection in the smooth backwater and saw that the decision [to go to war] had not been made purely out of love and loyalty for his friend, but also out of hatred for his father. . . . His enlistment had been more than a liberating apostasy; it had been an act of vengeance as well. . . . He'd wanted to return. . . . a creature beyond forgiving and forgiveness, scorched and scarred by war" (432). Chris finds he doesn't need his father to forgive him. He forgives himself and then throws his uniform, Purple Heart and campaign badges pinned to the shirt, into the stream. It sinks and then he is free.

Like Webb's Goodrich, Caputo's Chris Starkmann is sick because he contains within himself two irreconcilable beings. Goodrich's problem is less severe because his conflict is with a "brother," Mark Solomon, who is returned to the correct path by Goodrich's father; the trace (not the actual) is then punished, enabling Goodrich to attain some sort of unity. Chris's problem is that he has internalized the code of his father who is himself split between pacifist and warrior: "The man had a warrior's soul. If he had been a general, he would have been like Patton; brave, brilliant, single-minded, and utterly intolerant" (29). Chris's problem is thus not with himself but in his enactment of the intolerable inner conflict that drives his father to the barricades to wage war on war in the name of peace. The son is driven by the father to commit the sin of the father and to have projected upon him those aspects of temperament the father cannot accept in himself. Chris becomes the warrior, at one point so completely that he nearly murders his wife and children; then he kills the warrior in himself so that he may return home.

Though the novel ends on a positive note—healing is possible—there are disturbing cross-currents. Chris has changed but the world has not. Though it appears new to him it is still "old and worn, full of death and pain" but also of "life, renewal, and hope" (433). But the renewal and hope are possible only because Chris "had been made a stranger in his own country. . . . the war had made him an outsider in the land of his birth" (427). There is something sad in this, something that echoes O'Brien's Sarkin Aung Wan's insistence that one becomes a refugee to go home.

Caputo's vision is fatalistic. In *A Rumor of War* he urges the reader not to see the book as a protest because protest "arises from a belief that one can change things" (xxi). *Indian Country* is equally fatalistic. Christian Starkmann goes to war to enact what his father had repressed, specifically, the desire to wage war. His father had repressed this desire because of what had happened to his own father: "It was war that outraged him the most. . . . His hatred of it arose from what had happened to his father in World War I: . . . he'd gone overseas a jaunty doughboy and returned horribly disfigured. . . . He'd spent the rest of his short life railing against the colossal butchery he'd seen in the trenches, the idiocy of generals, the monstrous indifference of governments that had wasted an entire generation of young men" (25–26). If the activist is identified with the maimed soldier, the maiming in *Indian Country* is displaced. His Purple Heart notwithstanding, Chris returns home whole of body if not of soul. His grandfather had not, and the wound takes three generations to work itself out, ironically enough, in a war that can be described in the same terms—the colossal butchery, the idiocy, the monstrous indifference—as the first one.

All of these writers—O'Brien, Caputo, Fuller, even Webb—rail against this war in those terms. It was a massive exercise in stupidity that left two and a half million people dead and the survivors damaged in ways difficult for those who did not live through that war to understand. The survivors are condemned to tell it to uncomprehending listeners just as Coleridge's Ancient Mariner was condemned to collar a horrified wedding guest. And what those who fought in that war have to say to those who opposed it is sobering. The protesters were cowards. They were stupid, shallow, unbending, moralistic, ignorant of the conditions over there, and they were right: "The chaplain's morally superior attitude had rankled me, but his sermon had managed to plant doubt. . . . I still believed in the cause for which we were supposed to be fighting, but what kind of men were we, and what kind of army was it that made exhibitions of the human beings it had butchered?" (Caputo, *Rumor* 170).

Perhaps the most sobering thought is the revelation that we who opposed the war were not fundamentally different from those who fought it. It was not a clean war, not on any level, with participants to be neatly divided between them and us, between the good and the bad. Such distinctions break down under the weight of the concrete particularities, and the role of the constructed activist as soldier is to show us that. If any of us had been transported from our collective Iowas and set down over there we would have broken in precisely the same ways the soldiers did. The moral, if any can be drawn, is that those who were sent to Vietnam could not be what those of us back home, opposed to the war or not, wanted them to be. But we could become as they were. And we did.

NOTES

1. Discussions of the antiwar movement (beyond those listed in the Works Cited) include Jacquelyn Estrada, *The University under Seige* (1971); Edgar Z. Friedenberg, *The Anti-American Generation* (1971); Erik Erickson, *Radicals in the Universities* (1974); Sandy Vogelsang, *The Long Dark Night of the Soul* (1974); Chuck Noell and Gary Woods, *We Are All POWs* (1975); Donald Light and John Spiegel, *The Dynamics of University Protest* (1977); Stephen Garrett, *Ideals and Reality* (1978); Peter Steinfels, *The Neo-Conservatives* (1979); Todd Gitlin, *The Whole World Is Watching* (1980); Geoffrey Ripps, *Un-American Activities* (1981); Judith and Stewart Albert, *The Sixties Papers* (1984); Nancy Zaroulis and Gerald Sullivan, *Who Spoke Up?* (1984); James Miller, *Democracy Is in the Streets* (1987); David Farber, *Chicago '68* (1988); and Tom Hayden, *Reunion* (1988).

2. Maurice Isserman, in *If I Had a Hammer*, dismisses this as ahistorical nonsense based largely on a speech by marginal SDSer Tom Kahn in 1962. Within a few years, Kahn became one of those "lapsed-radicals-turned-neoconservatives" (xv).

3. In *Long Time Passing*, Myra MacPherson reports that of the 1,200 students in the Harvard class of 1970, only 2 went to Vietnam and only 56 went into the military.

4. How "hot" this activity was is open to question. Harvard students, in general, were certainly opposed to the war but, as noted by Todd Gitlin in *The Sixties*, the politics of Harvard was that of "pragmatic maneuver." Nearby Brandeis, on the other hand, was genuinely radical (93). Privileged Harvard, with its embrace of counterculture values in the 1970s (a variation on the standard middle-class tendency to mind one's own garden in the face of crisis [429–430]), gives Webb an ideal metaphor.

5. Webb's dates are off. The My Lai massacre occurred March 16, 1968, but was not covered in the major papers until November 13, 1969, after Goodrich returns home.

6. The reference to San Diego State is no doubt a joke since the school was better known for its surfers than its radical politics even though Herbert Marcuse, a noted Marxist, was on the faculty.

WORKS CITED

Beidler, Philip. *American Literature and the Experience of Vietnam.* Athens: University of Georgia Press, 1982.

Caputo, Philip. *A Rumor of War.* 1977. New York: Ballantine, 1978.

————. *Indian Country.* 1987. Toronto: Bantam, 1988.

Fuller, Jack. *Fragments.* 1984. New York: Dell, 1987.

Gitlin, Todd. *The Sixties: Years of Hope, Days of Rage.* New York: Bantam, 1987.

Isserman, Maurice. *If I Had a Hammer.* New York: Basic, 1987.

Keniston, Kenneth. *Young Radicals: Notes on Committed Youth.* New York: Harcourt, 1968.

MacPherson, Myra. *Long Time Passing: Vietnam and the Haunted Generation.* Garden City, N.Y.: Doubleday, 1984.

Mailer, Norman. *The Armies of the Night.* New York: Signet, 1968.

O'Brien, Tim. *If I Die in a Combat Zone, Box Me Up and Ship Me Home.* 1973. New York: Dell, 1979.

————. *Going after Cacciato.* 1978. New York: Laurel-Dell, 1987.

Parenti, Michael. *Inventing Reality: The Politics of the Mass Media.* New York: St. Martin's, 1986.

Rosenberg, Milton J., Sidney Verba, and Philip E. Converse. *Vietnam and the Silent Majority: A Dove's Guide.* New York: Harper, 1970.

Rothman, Stanley, and Robert S. Lichter. *Roots of Radicalism: Jews, Christians, and the New Left.* New York: Oxford University Press, 1982.

Stone, Robert. *Dog Soldiers.* 1974. New York: Penguin, 1987.

Webb, James. *Fields of Fire.* Englewood Cliffs, N.J.: Prentice, 1978.

Wheeler, John. *Touched with Fire.* New York: Franklin Watts, 1984.

Wills, Garry. *Nixon Agonistes: The Crisis of the Self-Made Man.* New York: Signet, 1971.

Realism, Verisimilitude,

and the Depiction of Vietnam

Veterans in *In Country*

Matthew C. Stewart

Bobbie Ann Mason's 1985 novel *In Country* is the story of teenager Sam Hughes's remarkable desire to come to terms with the Vietnam War and of her maternal uncle Emmett Smith's equally remarkable inability to do the same. Sam's desire to know about Vietnam and to understand its consequences is striking because of her age and the intensity of her feelings. A war which ended when she was but a child is at the center of her life; as the narrator states: "She was feeling the delayed stress of the Vietnam War. It was her inheritance" (89). Sam has only just graduated from high school in the small, rural Kentucky town of Hopewell, but instead of concentrating seriously on college plans, summer work, or her future she is preoccupied with thoughts of her father, who was killed in Vietnam prior to Sam's first birthday without ever having seen her. She also finds herself attracted to Emmett's friend Tom, a Vietnam veteran who returned from the war sexually dysfunctional. Finally, she is beset with worries for her troubled uncle, whose health problems and difficulties integrating into the ordinary stream of Hopewell life Sam rightly attributes to his time as a soldier in Vietnam.

Since the subject of *In Country* is the aftereffects of Vietnam on individuals and communities, Emmett's story becomes inseparable from Sam's and is coequal in importance. He and his circle of friends form a microcosm of Vietnam veterans' feelings, complaints, and problems regarding reintegration into civilian society, and the symptoms and behavioral signs typical of these problems pervade the text. The novel is so complete in this regard that it seems as if Mason availed herself of the many psychological and sociological studies of Vietnam veterans and then managed to embody all that she learned in this one small group of fictional Kentucky veterans. This thorough depiction of the aftereffects of the Vietnam War on one family in particular and on one small Kentucky town resonates for all Americans who, like Sam, struggle to reckon the price and the lessons of U.S. military involvement in Southeast Asia. As a social document *In Country* is worthy of attention because of its comprehensive representation of troubled Vietnam veterans; as a novel it is praiseworthy for its unforced, suggestively condensed manner of depiction and its authenticity, although its ending sadly runs counter to these qualities. Indeed in part 3, the novel's final part, Mason seems to capitulate to wish-fulfillment and abandons the scrupulous verisimilitude which has marked her treatment of veterans until then.

Narrated in a terse, affectless manner, *In Country* is highly dependent upon the reader's powers of inference. Mason's narrator, while grammatically clear and simple, shows frequently and tells seldom. Because the narrative is tightly bound to Sam's point of view, her problems and puzzlements are occasionally given direct narratorial exploration. On the other hand, veterans' problems are always depicted, never analyzed or treated in narratorial discourse. In other respects, the novel's aesthetics are those of traditional realism with its concentration on surface details and mundane events. *In Country* presents everyday life as it is lived by a readily recognizable segment of the population, in this case a version of 1984 small-town America, complete with Pepsi, Bruce Springsteen, "M*A*S*H" reruns, and the general milieu of shopping-mall culture. *In Country* shuns the formalistic pyrotechnics of much modernist and postmodernist fiction, preferring to concentrate on old-fashioned storytelling, which Mason does in a style marked by allusiveness and a minimalistic spareness. Except for the obvious and uncomplicated framing device of the first and third parts, the plot is entirely chronological and is at all times easy to follow. The relationship between events is apparent and overt. In sum, to borrow Keith Opdahl's description of realism, the reader meets "with very little resistance, [and feels] the familiar patterns of actual experience" (4).

No doubt our society could well benefit from a literary work that enables it to come to terms with the Vietnam War, and presumably this is the project of *In Country*. For her title Mason has chosen a term used by soldiers to refer to time spent in active service in Southeast Asia. As the story develops we see the multiple levels of meaning and reference which this term accrues, and we come to realize that it is not only the fictitious characters of Hopewell who are still in country but to a greater or lesser extent each one of us. In content and effect, then, as well as in style the bulk of *In Country* fits Charles Newman's description of contemporary realism:

> The . . . energizing notion of this Neo-Realism is that there is *new* information which is not made redundant by other media, information which does not have to be "made up," but rather is shaped or *aimed*, because such substantive experience has been repressed, neglected or distorted. More importantly, this notion of literature often presupposes a receptive audience which has a special need for this information, a collective unconscious which in fact awaits collection. (174)

The existence of an audience in need of this novel is unquestionable, and for this reason the book's eventual lapses in verisimilitude and its culminating shift in style are lamentable on both an artistic and a social level, as we shall see.

Despite Emmett's status as a major character and despite the fact that veterans' problems are pervasive and should be apparent, his problems are never discussed at any length by the book's reviewers. And despite the fact that the novel's basic raison d'être is to examine the Vietnam War's legacy, they have scarcely mentioned the other troubled veterans who inhabit the novel. This inattention may be partially accounted for by the tendency to identify with a narrative point of view, critically to make this Sam's story because most of it is seen through her eyes. It is also possible that a lack of knowledge about troubled Vietnam veterans has prevented even well-informed, highly literate readers from giving this central topic its due attention.[1] Any such ignorance, to whatever extent it exists, is all the more troublesome precisely because Mason's allusive, show-don't-tell method depends upon a readership able to recognize her portraits of troubled veterans.[2]

Although it would be wrong to pretend that we can analyze fictional characters psychologically or sociologically as if they were real people, critical interpretation based on specialized knowledge of Vietnam veterans is particularly useful for *In Country*. This type of critical examination will help shed light on previously underexamined aspects of the novel and is called for by Mason's method, which in its reliance on uncommented-upon depiction entrusts much to the reader's powers of inference. By informing ourselves we may more thoroughly understand Emmett's odd behavior and better recognize the problems exhibited by various of Hopewell's Vietnam veterans. Most important, we are consequently able to judge the novel's level of verisimilitude and its relative success or failure as a piece of serious realism. Knowledge gained from sociological and psychological studies of Vietnam veterans is, then, not only a valid hermeneutic tool but also an indispensable one for the exegesis and evaluation of *In Country*. As Ernest Bramstedt has put the matter, "Only a person who has a knowledge of . . . a society from other sources than purely literary ones is able to find out if, and how far, certain social types and their behavior are reproduced in the novel in an adequate or inadequate manner. What is pure literary fancy, what realistic observation, and what only an expression of the desires of the author must be separated in each case in a subtle manner" (4). The differentiation of literary fancy and authorial desires from realistic observation is of primary importance in the present critique of *In Country*.

Any discussion of troubled veterans in *In Country* should begin with a consideration of posttraumatic stress disorder, the primary operative term governing the identification, diagnosis, and treatment of Vietnam veterans suffering from the psychic repercussions of their war experiences in southeast Asia. We can recognize a remarkable number of common manifestations of posttraumatic stress disorder in Emmett and his friends.[3] Indeed, the number is large enough to make a full discussion of each maladaptive behavior prohibitive here, but a fairly inclusive list can be made. Emmett has difficulty sleeping and has recurrent troubling dreams; he also clearly suffers from severe psychic numbing. Emmett's reluctance to attend the local veterans' commemorative party or to join in rap groups illustrates his deliberate avoidance of activities that dredge up specific memories of Vietnam, while his initial incident with Lonnie and Sam in Cawood's Pond demonstrates his susceptibility to flashbacks when confronted with a situation too strongly reminiscent of Vietnam. In Earl's childish fight with Pete and in Pete's own propensity for aimlessly firing his gun we see the sort of sporadic and unprovoked belligerence that sometimes marks those who suffer from posttraumatic stress disorder.

Besides these defining symptoms, other behaviors commonly found in troubled Vietnam veterans should be noted: Emmett's searing headaches and nervous tics, Tom's impotence, the overwhelming despair and distrust clearly evident in Emmett's refusal to acknowledge that any worthy jobs exist, Pete's irrational longing to return to Vietnam, Emmett's feeling old beyond his years, feelings that the war was an absurdity or meaningless joke, feelings of betrayal by elected officials and the citizenry of the United States. Sam even recognizes in Tom the by now famous thousand-yard stare. One cannot read any comprehensive account of troubled Vietnam veterans without encountering the prevalence of these traits, some of which are held even by those who are well-adjusted. As for Mason's novel, this is a remarkably inclusive list, a list woven into the text without seeming strain, yet (perhaps partly because of this effortlessness) a list which has so far received insufficient critical attention despite the magnitude of the issues it suggests.

Emmett's inability to cope with deep feelings typifies those troubled veterans who demonstrate a marked problem handling emotions associated with intimacy, tenderness, and sexuality. Emmett, whose appearance, habits, and personal history hardly qualify him as the most sought after of local bachelors, is nevertheless in a position to pursue a relationship with Anita Stevens, a local nurse who is pretty, shapely, kind, bright, and funny. Although we may find it difficult to credit Anita's interest in Emmett because it is insufficiently motivated in the novel, it is important to note that despite her efforts to interest Emmett and her obvious genuine fondness for him, his pattern of behavior with her, though it includes efforts toward friendship, is always marked by a series of eventual retreats. Emmett is fond of Anita, but he denies himself the opportunity of establishing anything lasting between them. Instead he pretends or has managed to convince himself that Anita has no interest in him. "Anita doesn't want a birdwatcher in a skirt," he says, alluding to his recent practice of wrapping himself in a skirt while working around the house (37). So incomprehensible to Sam is Emmett's seeming lack of interest in Anita that she wonders whether Emmett suffered some physical injury rendering him incapable of intimacies with women or uninterested in them. Eventually she brings up this subject with Emmett's mother, Grandma Smith, who has her own theory about mumps "falling" on Emmett in his youth, a theory decidedly more comic than Sam's but equally demonstrative of the lengths to which characters go in search of explanations for Emmett's oddities.

Emmett tries to justify his retreat from Anita by coupling it with an idea frequently voiced by Vietnam veterans, that unless someone experienced Vietnam for himself or herself, he or she cannot possibly understand what the veteran feels or thinks: "'Women weren't over there,' Emmett snapped. 'So they can't really understand'" (107). Of course the consequence of repeating and believing this phrase, besides frustrating those who wish to understand and help, is to keep the veterans' problems bottled-up indefinitely. Hence the daily "closed meetings" of Hopewell's veterans over breakfast at McDonald's both reflect and reinforce the belief that none but another veteran can understand veterans. The inclusion of "herself" is very important here for frequently it is the wife, girlfriend, or mother of the man who makes the initial and most dogged attempts to understand him.[4] *In Country* follows this pattern. The major female characters attempt to take care of men, to restore or rejuvenate them. Irene took care of Emmett; Anita wants to take care of Emmett; Sam is preoccupied with the problems of Emmett and Tom. When the men remain wounded and distant, this nurturing role can become wearing, entrapping, even embittering for the women, as we see with Irene, who has come to share her father's belief that "it's not too late [for Emmett] to pull himself up and be proud" (149).

Distressingly, it often seems that Sam is simply preparing to take her mother's place as Emmett's caretaker, as Irene herself fears: "The trouble is, I carried Emmett around on a pillow all those years when I should have made him take more responsibility, and now you're trying to do the same thing I did" (166–67). Sam's relationship to Emmett is really one of child-as-parent. She has taken on responsibilities that ought not be hers, and she frequently acts as parent and Emmett as child. Sam gives far more attention to solving Emmett's problems and giving him guidance than she does to her own future. She seeks no advice from him and he offers none, even though they are both aware that she is not involved in any meaningful activities for the summer and has no worthy plans for the coming fall.

Far from living the life of the average adult, Emmett spends much of his time in seemingly adolescent behavior as if to recover the typical late adolescence that he was never allowed to experience. He will not look for a job; he watches a lot of television; he plays video games; he spends much of his time with his teenage niece and her teenage boyfriend; he "runs away from home" with Jim; he even passes out in front of the high school after drinking to excess. In and of themselves these activities are not all intrinsically adolescent, but neither the amount of time Emmett spends at them nor the degree of interest he shows in them is normal, especially when put in relief by the scant hours he spends pursuing strictly or typically adult activities. Sam observes that Emmett and his veteran friends were "not allowed to grow up. That was it—they didn't get to grow up and become regular people. They had to stand outside, playing games, fooling around, acting like kids who couldn't get girlfriends. It was absurd" (140).[5]

Along with Emmett's conspicuously unadult life, we notice his unwillingness to communicate. The more important it is for Emmett to discuss something, the more Sam wants him to open up; the more pressure he feels to divulge something about Vietnam, the more evasive and uncommunicative he becomes. Emmett is not the only veteran who exhibits reticence about discussing Vietnam, as we see in various veterans' sometimes condescending refusals to talk to Sam about Vietnam. Even Tom, usually the veteran most forthcoming with Sam, puts her off: "Look, Sam. It's hard to talk about, and some people want to protect you, you know. They don't want to dump all this stuff on you. . . . You shouldn't think about this stuff too much" (95). Not only is this reticence about Vietnam a part of the previously discussed pattern of men distancing themselves from women and from unpleasant memories, it is a frequent source of exasperation for Sam, who not only wishes to help but also wishes to learn about Vietnam for her own sake.

Though Hopewell's Vietnam veterans are largely unwilling to talk at any length with Sam about Vietnam, she can still observe their behavior and puzzle over it. What may not be apparent to Sam but eventually become so to the reader are the destructive—usually self-destructive—urges that seem to underlie the veterans' oddities and aberrations. Pete may be taken as representative of veterans who have longings to return to combat in general or to Vietnam in particular, who have returned home with behaviors that were adaptive in a war zone but are maladaptive in ordinary civilian life. Emmett tells Sam about Pete shooting his gun at nothing in particular and conjectures that Pete would "rather be back in Nam" (50). Later Tom expresses a similar opinion, and eventually Pete himself tells Sam in the half-articulate fashion typical of Hopewell's veterans, "Hell yeah, I admit it. I enjoyed it. I felt good over there. I knew what I was doing. I knew certain things. There was a dividing line. Life and death" (134). To Sam, whose predisposition is antiwar and whose uncle decries his own Vietnam experiences, such a sentiment begs for further explanation. For despite Pete's assertions that his life is now as good as he could expect, we are privy to an accumulation of details which reveal that Pete's marriage is unstable and that many of its problems can be traced to his unresolved feelings about Vietnam.

The degree of self-punishment involved in the behavior of many troubled Vietnam veterans has been well discussed in professional literature. Emmett's behavior is often inexplicable and aggravating for those who have to deal with it, including at times the reader, and yet the extreme measure of self-destructiveness involved in the strange things he does (or, what is often the case, fails to do) seems to go unnoticed by all except Sam. Perhaps understandably, most of the other characters, Emmett's family included, have become fed up with him to the point that they see his problems primarily insofar as they affect their own lives, as we have seen with Irene. The problem is clearly that lives are more difficult to reconstruct than the dirt bikes which Tom likes so well because he can "put one together and wreck it and then . . . just put . . . another one together" again (80).

The denial and self-destructiveness under discussion here are very frequently bound up with guilt, and we eventually learn that such is the case with *In Country*. In the climactic scene at Cawood's Pond, for the first time Emmett openly articulates his sense of guilt to Sam. "You can't do what we did and then be happy about it," he says (222). It would seem, however, that Emmett's guilt involves something even more insidious than the pangs of regret he feels for his own actions. Robert Jay Lifton has shown that surviving as well as killing can cause guilt, and his concept of survivor's guilt is a valuable model for understanding Emmett, who eventually reveals that his own survival was made possible by the deaths of others. Indeed, in his case survival is not only a matter of symbolism or the product of a psychic construct, as is the case with many veterans, but it is also a literal truth. When Emmett finally opens up to Sam, we learn that he would very likely have been killed if it had not been for the corpses of his friends under which he hid after his unit was overrun in battle. He survived by lying hidden "for hours . . . until the next day" under the corpses of his fellow GIs, smelling their "warm blood in the jungle heat" while the enemy remained dangerously close by (223). Emmett's manner of telling this story coupled with his long history of posttraumatic stress disorder and his problems relating his experiences in Vietnam suggest

> the soldier-survivor's sense of having betrayed his buddies by letting them die while he stayed alive. . . . [He cannot] feel that it was logical or right for him and not others to survive. Rather, he becomes bound to an unconscious perception of organic social balance which makes him feel that his survival was made possible by others' deaths: if they had not died, he would have had to; if he had not survived, someone else would have. His transgression,

then, lies in having purchased his own life at the cost of another's. In a very real psychological sense he feels that he has killed that buddy. (Lifton 105–106)

It would seem that years after his harrowing experience Emmett remains tormented by his own survival, as he finally says to Sam: "I'm damaged. It's like something in the center of my heart is gone and I can't get it back" (225).

In this climactic memory, Emmett's literal position underneath his fellow soldiers' corpses suggests the figurative position of the people of the United States: the personal and the societal coalesce in one image. Burdened with yet sheltered by the corpses of young men sent to fight battles which many thought it wrong to fight, American society has seemingly called upon its veterans for what has been termed a "double sacrifice." First, veterans made many sacrifices in Vietnam, usually believing that they were serving their country; then they came home to a government and citizenry only too ready to sacrifice them again, this time "on the altar of shame and guilt in order to appease the national 'conscience' " (Brende and Parson 48).

Epitomizing images such as that of Emmett hiding under the corpses are often the most memorable aspects of a piece of fiction because they crystallize the efforts of long stretches of story to embody a central truth. This particular image is telling because of its vivid, affective quality; it is appropriate because it is consistent with and consummate of what has heretofore been narrated both in its verisimilar content and in its unadorned style.

We must read to the novel's conclusion before we encounter an equally memorable image. In the novel's final paragraph Emmett is reading names on the Vietnam Veterans Memorial in Washington, D.C.; he is "sitting there cross-legged in front of the wall, and slowly his face bursts into a smile like flames" (245). But whereas the image of Emmett hiding under his dead buddies is true to the novel this image is not, for the astonishing simile Mason has chosen is jarring in its departure from the simple language that has heretofore been inseparable from *In Country*'s style and its goals as a realistic work. At best one might try to make the case that this is an ambiguous image which appears abruptly in a novel that has not used unanchored symbols or highly abstracted metaphors.[6] In actuality the novel presses for an even more misleading and inappropriate reading since the bent of part 3 obliges us to conclude that this image is not merely ambiguous but optimistic to the point of sanguinity.

Put simply, the novel does nothing to suggest how Emmett has come to the point where he can sit in front of the Vietnam Veterans Memorial in the state of enlightened inner peace and harmony which this Buddha-like closing image invokes. It is clear that not very much time has passed between Emmett's dramatic breakdown at Cawood's Pond which ends part 2 and the trip to Washington, D.C., which begins part 3—probably only a few days. The novel would have us believe that some change has come over Emmett sufficient to make him suddenly ready to come to terms with his past and at once willing, able, and sufficiently insightful to do so.

After three initial paragraphs devoted to describing the confused and aimless inertia that has overwhelmed Sam, Mason continues part 3 by quickly completing Sam and Emmett's role reversal. The next paragraph begins thus: "Then Emmett announced a plan." And if this tersely stated turnabout in character is not enough to shock us, more follows immediately: "They were going to see the Vietnam Memorial in Washington. He was so definite about it. . . . He even insisted on bringing Mamaw along. . . . Emmett was so certain about everything that Sam felt powerless. Sam had never seen him swing into action like that" (230). In the space of one paragraph Emmett takes a job, plans to pay off an old debt to the federal government, and tells Sam that she will attend the University of Kentucky that fall.[7]

It is wrong even to suggest that any such sudden profound change could come over Emmett. As Robert Lifton has said in speaking of his experience helping troubled veterans to recover, "A veteran could never isolate all guilt around one or two particular actions and then be done with it—guilt is simply not manageable that way" (107). *In Country*'s strength and virtue are to be found in its realism, a realism which I have attempted to show is grounded in authentic depictions of the Vietnam War's damaging effects upon many of those who returned from fighting it and, by extension, upon a society which should deal with these returnees. But although Mason has succeeded in portraying a microcosm of veterans' problems and troubled behaviors in part 2, she has failed to finish the story properly. She simply wills it to end, apparently succumbing to "literary fancy" or to an "expression of her desires" rather than imaginatively fighting through to formulate a verisimilar ending based on "realistic observation," to return to Bramstedt's words.

This final failure of *In Country* should be seen in light of its three-part structure. The work gives the distinct appearance of having a long, novellike middle (part 2) sandwiched between two halves of a short story. The tone and events of parts 1 and 3, the parts which comprise the "short story," suggest an encouraging account of a healing family, of the reintegration of a troubled veteran into a once careless society, and of reconciliation on both a personal and a societal level. Taken on their own, parts 1 and 3 would comprise a gently comic, hopeful story. The trouble is that they do not meld with the material in the truly novelistic second part wherein we see the depth of Emmett's psychic wounds and the breadth of havoc which the war has played upon so many veterans' lives. The stuff of relatively hard-edged realism cannot be instantly and carelessly yoked to the sort of pat ending typical of a television movie.[8]

To retain the meticulous verisimilitude it has achieved in part 2, *In Country* needs at least to suggest that Emmett has only begun to solve his problems, that as difficult as his moment at Cawood's Pond was for him, he can expect to face more such moments, and that while keeping things bottled-up eventually creates a horrible numbness toward life, letting things out has its own set of difficulties to overcome and its own anguish to endure. Granted that Mason is by no means obligated to make the detailed depiction of Emmett's next stage of recovery a part of this novel, still she should not reverse her course by implying that instantaneous harmonious integration of self and society is somehow possible for a man like Emmett. The difficulties that Emmett is likely to face if he is truly to recover could be subtly suggested and left for the reader to explore; that is to say, there is no reason why part 3 cannot successfully retain the technique and style that made part 2 so effective. But in the end, alas, Hopewell becomes Fantasyland.

NOTES

1. Except for ignorance, it is difficult to explain, for example, why the reviewer for one highly regarded periodical chose to characterize Emmett as

"amiably weird," as if he were simply a little dotty (Boston). These are the only words used to describe Emmett, and hence they must stand as the predominant impression of him that the critic wishes to convey. Considered on its own, this inaccuracy simply bespeaks a particularly uninsightful reading, but considered in the context of the critical inadvertence I have described, it seems to suggest that even some of the most literate readers are oblivious to the problems of troubled veterans or at least to the seriousness of these problems.

2. I would like to draw deliberate attention here to my use of the adjective "troubled" to modify veterans. Nothing in this essay is meant to imply that all, or even most, veterans suffer debilitating psychosocial problems. The facts are quite otherwise. The depiction of those veterans who are troubled is the subject of discussion here.

3. For detailed studies of troubled Vietnam veterans, the reader should refer to the work of Brende and Parson, Figley and Leventman, Hendin and Haas, and Lifton. In 1980 the American Psychiatric Association for the first time delineated the term "posttraumatic stress disorder" in a detailed clinical definition and description in their revised *Diagnostic and Statistical Manual of Mental Disorders* (DSM-III). This definition is excerpted by Brende and Parson (77–78) and paraphrased by Hendin and Haas (30–31). See also Laufer et al.

4. The central role of women in Vietnam veteran recovery is especially well discussed in Brende and Parson's sixth chapter.

5. In his article, "Conflict, Stress, and Growth: The Effects of War on Psychosocial Development among Vietnam Veterans," John P. Wilson uses an Eriksonian model of psychosocial growth to discuss the fact that nearly all combat GIs were deprived of the opportunity to develop along normal lines during the critical period of late adolescence, a stage of especially difficult psychosocial tasks even under normal circumstances. He writes: "Where the stress overpowers the individual's ability to meet the demands confronting him, a retrogression to earlier modes of conflict resolution may occur" (137). Although Wilson does not specifically discuss turning toward typically adolescent behavior at inappropriate times, he does discuss the immaturity and inability to resolve problems in an adult fashion characteristic of many troubled Vietnam veterans.

6. The important exception to this lack of highly allusive symbolism is the egret that Emmett periodically hopes to see.

7. It might be objected here that Emmett's newfound energy and purposefulness are simply a product of the narration being filtered through Sam's dazed point of view, that it is she alone who regards Emmett as "definite" and "certain." This argument does not bear out, however. Regardless of Sam's condition and of the narrative focus, Emmett is unquestionably presented as undertaking these various activities all at once. A man who hasn't worked,

traveled, or taken responsibility for years is presented as suddenly, "confidently" venturing to do all three.

8. It is sadly ironic that a novel which has frequently pointed out the gross inadequacies of television as a model of the world and as a helpful shaper of psyches should itself succumb to the sort of facile, Pollyanna ending characteristic of television. Sam frequently refers to television in order to judge her own behavior and make sense of her situations. She herself thinks at one point that Emmett's problems cannot be resolved in the manner that problems are so quickly resolved on her own favorite show, "M*A*S*H."

WORKS CITED

Boston, Anne. "With the Vets in Hopewell." *Times Literary Supplement*, April 18, 1986, 416.

Bramstedt, Ernest K. *Aristocracy and the Middle Classes in Germany: Social Types in German Literature*. 2d ed. Chicago: University of Chicago Press, 1964.

Brende, Joel Osler, and Erwin Randolph Parson. *Vietnam Veterans: The Road to Recovery*. New York: Plenum, 1985.

Figley, Charles R., and Seymour Leventman, eds. *Strangers at Home: Vietnam Veterans since the War*. New York: Praeger, 1980.

Hendin, Herbert, and Ann Pollinger Haas. *Wounds of War: The Psychological Aftermath of Combat in Vietnam*. New York: Basic, 1984.

Laufer, Robert S., Ellen Frey-Wouters, and Mark S. Gallops. "Traumatic Stressors in the Vietnam War and Post-traumatic Stress Disorders." *Trauma and Its Wake: The Study and Treatment of Post-traumatic Stress Disorder*. Ed. Charles R. Figley. New York: Brunner, Mazel, 1985.

Lifton, Robert Jay. *Home from the War: Vietnam Veterans, neither Victims nor Executioners*. New York: Simon, 1973.

Mason, Bobbie Ann. *In Country*. New York: Harper, 1985.

Newman, Charles. *The Post-Modern Aura: The Act of Fiction in an Age of Inflation*. Evanston: Northwestern University Press, 1985.

Opdahl, Keith. "The Nine Lives of Literary Realism." *Contemporary American Fiction*. Ed. Malcolm Bradbury and Sigmund Ro. London: Edward Arnold, 1987.

Wilson, John P. "Conflict, Stress, and Growth: The Effect of War on Psychosocial Development among Vietnam Veterans." In *Strangers at Home*.

"A Hard Story to Tell"

The Vietnam War in Joan Didion's

Democracy

○ ○ ○ ○ ○ ○ ○ ○ ○ ○ ○ ○ ○ ○ ○

Stuart Ching

In "Slouching towards Bethlehem," Joan Didion describes the fragmentation of the nation's youth in the 1960s. The essay's title, which is also the title of the collection in which it appears, is from the last line of Yeats's "The Second Coming." Didion claims in the preface to her collection that certain lines from the Yeats poem have "reverberated" in her "inner ear": "the widening gyre, the falcon which does not hear the falconer, the gaze blank and pitiless as the sun" (xi). These images are Didion's only points of reference, the only pattern that makes sense of what she is observing in the world.

The falling apart, the collapsing center, the spiraling gyre—the falcon out of control, unable to hear the falconer—are recurrent motifs in *Democracy*. The internal drama of the novel, the love story of Inez Victor and Jack Lovett, is set against the historicity of the Vietnam War, and Didion uses the pattern of the gyre to illustrate the simultaneous collapse into disorder of both the internal fictive world and the external factual world which impinges on the novel.

In his annotation to "The Second Coming," Yeats claims that history, like the mind, takes the form of two vertical intersecting cones which spin in opposite directions: one narrowing, one widening. The end of an age is marked by one gyre reaching its greatest expansion and the other its greatest contraction (*Robartes* 30–34). The revelation that approaches takes its shape from the movement of the inward gyre and begins its spiral outward, unraveling the "thread" of the previous age, "all things dying each other's life, living each other's death" (*Vision* B 270–271). As Thomas Whitaker suggests, the apocalypse for Yeats is nothing more than "a full rendering of the opposites" within the world and the self (54). The revelation will be a "lightning flash" but paradoxically will strike in more than one place and occur for some time as the next era succeeds its antecedent. The next age, while reversing the previous age, still repeats past eras within itself (*Vision* B 263). History, then, is cyclical. Yeats claims that in the present day the gyre is nearing its widest expansion (*Robartes* 30–34).

The gyre as a pattern in *Democracy* becomes clear when one establishes the novel's time frame. The novel begins during the last weeks before the fall of Saigon in March 1975 and ends at an unspecified time after March 1976. Within this span, the novel moves back and forth between 1952 and 1975—although it does leap as far back as 1934 in another story that begins, "Imagine my mother dancing" (21). The novel, however, does not operate by the standard use of flashback. Didion once claimed that in her first novel, *Run River*, she wanted to have "the past and present operating simultaneously," but she wasn't "accomplished enough to do that with any clarity" (*Writers at Work* 347). In *Democracy*, she succeeds in creating the illusion of simultaneity, and this technique adds to the elusiveness of the novel, thus heightening the reader's sense of disorder.

Within this elusive world, however, Didion hints that there might be "tenuous connections" (219), cycles in which the past is relived in the present time of the novel. In 1952 Jack catches lobsters in the lagoon off Johnston; in 1975 Inez washes her bandana in the same lagoon. In 1969 her children, Jessie and Adlai, play Marco Polo in the pool at Borobudur; in 1975 Jack drowns in the same pool. In 1952 Inez walks through the graveyard at Schofield; in 1975 she buries Jack in the same graveyard. In 1946 Carol Christian's marriage deteriorates, and she later departs for San Francisco on the SS *Lurline*; in 1975 Inez's family collapses, and she leaves for Hong Kong. Finally, the Pacific tests of 1952 are "another dawn in another year" (177); in 1975 Inez's flight to Hong Kong is an "eleven-hour dawn."

Didion also suggests a cyclical history by alluding to the 442nd Regimental Combat Team and Vonnegut's *Slaughterhouse-Five* ("aloha oe" or "so it goes"), both of which link the Vietnam War to World War II. The Hawaiian setting of the novel is also significant to this connection, for Didion claims that "war is the very fabric of Hawaii's life" (*Slouching* 196), and in both of her essay collections, *Slouching towards Bethlehem* and *The White Album*, Punchbowl Cemetery joins the two wars, where graves from World War II share the same dormant crater with fresh graves for bodies arriving from Vietnam.

Didion establishes this cyclical history in the opening sentences of the novel—for here we see the syncretism of the creation myth, the resurrection, and the prophecy (by Yeats) of the Second Coming. It is March 30, 1975, Easter Sunday, when Jack says to Inez in the lounge of the Happy Talk:

> The light at dawn during those Pacific tests was something to see.
> Something to behold.
> Something that could almost make you think you saw God, he said. (11)

As in the creation myth, there is light. The allusion to Christ's resurrection (Easter Sunday) emphasizes the succession of eras from the Old to the New Testament; the latter rewrites the first. The allusion to the resurrection also marks approximately A.D. 30, near the birth of Christ, which Yeats designates both in *A Vision* and in his annotation to "The Second Coming" as the end of Greco-Roman civilization and the beginning of the Christian era. Similar to Yeats's vision of the Second Coming, the gyre is now at its widest expansion, and anarchy is let loose upon the world with the impending fall of Saigon.

The circular pattern of the gyre also appears in the imagery of islands. In the opening chapter, Jack mentions the Philippines and Johnston Island, the Aleutians and Jakarta, "ass end[s] of the universe"

(13, 14). The islands are points of reference without a center. As the narrator suggests, "At the end of the known world there is only water, water as a definite presence" (82).

Yet if the islands are considered central locations, they also become part of the imagery of disappearing centers. Islands, the narrator suggests, are mutable and subject to erosion: "When a hill slumps into the ocean I see the order in it" (18). When an island erodes an atoll remains, a circle of reef without a center. Hence, a phrase from the last line of the novel, "where islands once were," again signifies the vanishing center. In addition, there are other references to disappearing centers. During 1975, for the narrator (the fictive Didion) time quickens and collapses into itself the way a "disintegrating star contracts into a black hole" (69), and she can remember only splinters of poems by Housman, Eliot, and Schwartz. The news clips she reads in March and April are mere "dislocations," fragments of an incomplete picture, and when she reads the breaking news of "falling capitals" in Southeast Asia she calls them instances of the "black hole effect" (70–71).

The lives of the characters also evidence this collapse. The two central characters, Inez and Jack, are not a fixed center for the novel. They are "evanescent," "emotionally invisible," "unattached," "wary to the point of opacity, and finally elusive" (81–82). For the narrator, they become indefinable and seem "not to belong anywhere at all" except together (82). Neither the narrator nor Inez discovers Jack's real identity. The narrator suggests that a record of Jack's life would reveal "overlapping dates" and "blank spots" (39). Equally elusive is Inez. Temporarily obliterated from the narrator's memory, at one point she loses her individuality, developing the mechanical characteristics of media personalities: the fixed gaze, the reposeful countenance, the "frequent blink" (48).

Inez is part of a society of homeless jetsetters. The setting of the novel, then, appropriately sprawls across the globe from Jakarta to the mainland United States. The Victor and Christian families disintegrate. Carol Christian leaves for San Francisco. Paul Christian probably murders his daughter Janet. Adlai organizes a rally for the liberation of Saigon, while Jessie undergoes drug rehabilitation and later boards a C-5A transport to Saigon. Inez leaves Harry Victor and flies to Hong Kong with Jack. At the end of the novel the members of the Victor family are detached from each other, and the reader senses that this separation is more than geographic: Inez is in Kuala Lumpur indefinitely; Harry is in Brussels; Jessie is in Mexico; and Adlai is in San Francisco.

Beyond this domestic world, the historical world is fragmenting just as fast if not faster. In his paper "Internal and External Historicity in Joan Didion's *Democracy*," James Wohlpart cites four major historical events that Didion uses in her novel. As Wohlpart observes, through the description of these events—the fall of Da Nang, Phnom Penh, and Saigon, along with the evacuation of a flight of orphans—Didion adds a "dimension of reality" to her novel, thereby meshing the internal fictive world with the external historical world. In addition, however, this fusion allows Didion to underscore the simultaneous collapse of both worlds. Thus, while teaching at Berkeley the narrator refers to the cities that were "falling" in Southeast Asia during the major offensive launched by the North Vietnamese. In the months of March and April the following South Vietnamese cities and American military bases fell (many without resistance): Ban Me Thuot, March 12; Pleiku, March 16; Quang Ngai, Chu Lai, and Tam Ky, March 24; Hue, March 25; Da Nang, March 29; Nha Trang and Qui Nhon, April 1; Bien Hoa, April 19; Xuan Loc and Ham Tan, April 21; Saigon, April 29–30 (Dawson xi-xvi, 54, 71, 142, 195). In addition, the narrator refers to Ken Healy, the pilot who on March 29 made an unauthorized flight to evacuate people from the Da Nang airport. In a mad scramble women, children, and South Vietnamese soldiers mobbed the plane, crawling into the baggage compartments and wheel wells and clinging to the undercarriage. Others who could not hang on after take-off plummeted into the South China Sea (Vogle).

Both Eagle Pull and Frequent Wind, which the narrator refers to in *Democracy* (70), were real operations: Eagle Pull the evacuation of the American embassy in Cambodia on April 12 and Frequent Wind the evacuation of Saigon on April 29–30 (Benjamin 24; Olson 331, 333). The photo of John Gunther Dean leaving the American embassy in Cambodia actually appeared on the cover of *Newsweek*. In the background are two shadowy figures, one of whom the narrator of *Democracy* believes is Jack Lovett (104).

Furthermore, Jessie's flight to Vietnam on "that March night" (176) corresponds with the evacuation of Da Nang (March 28–29) in which uncontrolled rioting broke out everywhere in the city. Women were raped, cars stolen, jeeps blown up, houses looted. General Truong ordered the tanks of the South Vietnamese army onto the streets to restore order, but the soldiers joined in the looting or were afraid to face the rioters (Dawson 169).

In *Democracy* the telecast of helicopters vanishing into fireballs and ditching in oil slicks off the *Pioneer Contender* (176) corresponds with the *Pioneer Contender*'s role in the evacuation of Da Nang from March 28 to April 1 (Dawson 170, 196). The reference to "orphan" escorts (192) corresponds with Operation Babylift, which occurred on April 5 and 6 when U.S. officials escorted orphans onto airlifts out of Southeast Asia (Dawson xiv, 212–216). And Jessie's flight to Vietnam illustrates the confusion in Southeast Asia during the last few weeks before the final evacuation of Saigon. For example, between April 15 and April 28, 277 whites and blacks without identification or passports who spoke English and presented themselves as Americans at evacuation sites were evacuated without question (Dawson 260–261).

The narrator describes the situation in South Vietnam as one of growing hysteria and confusion, and the collapse of the moral center heightens this rapid disintegration. The Americans were pulling out, or as Didion defines morality in one of her essays, they were leaving the body on the highway for coyotes (*Slouching* 158). For example, during the evacuation of Nha Trang, Americans armed with guns prevented Vietnamese employees from boarding evacuation aircrafts ("Americans" 15), and after the United States evacuated the American embassy in Phnom Penh, President Sokham Koy stated: "The United States led Cambodia into this war . . . but when the war became difficult, the United States pulled out" (Benjamin 29). Finally, after the last American helicopter left Saigon, hundreds of civilians huddled on the roof of one of the buildings, an emergency helipad, and waited for more helicopters to appear (Esper 16).

Thus, the fragmentation of the fictive world—Inez's flight to Hong Kong—concurs with the collapse of the external world—the fall of Saigon. For the first time, Inez feels detached from her entire family. She is "not interested in them," unable to grasp "her own or their uniqueness" (196–197). While listening to the radio in mid-April, she thinks about Jack and wonders when "it" (the final evacuation) will occur: "The world that night was full of people flying from place to place and fading in and out" (197). Didion's time frame remains ambiguous, leaving the reader uncertain whether "that" night is the night in mid-April or the night of the final evacuation, April 29. Here the gyre is at its widest expansion in both worlds, the fictive and the historical, and no persons, not even those who believe they have a "home to call" (197), are excluded from the continual movement, the shuttling back and forth, the falling apart.

Rightfully, then, the novel is told in "fitful glimpses" (220), for it is shaped by the external world of fragments, clippings, and repetitions (in which the chronology is obscured because of lapses in memory), as well as by the international dateline and the mutability of islands. It is not the novel that begins "Imagine my mother dancing," though Didion as character says such was her intention (21). In this case, life shapes art. Didion gives shape to disorder, while disorder shapes her novel. In the end, the options do not "decrease to zero" (220); instead, the scope of the novel widens, and the gaps in the text multiply. Didion finds a pattern, a falling away.

Some of these textual gaps are startling. Who is Jack Lovett? A certain "gray" area, a corpse in a body bag (209). How does Wendell Omura get on Janet Christian's lanai? How does the paperboy see the .357 Magnum tucked in Paul Christian's beachroll (112)? Why does Inez agree to talk with Joan Didion (205)? Are Inez and Jack's meetings purely circumstantial? Inez has to have a passport when she leaves for Hong Kong, doesn't she? As Didion asks, "What does that suggest? You tell me" (177).

Didion observes, reveals, and records, but she does not explain. Nor does she provide an answer to the questions raised by the Vietnam War. Yeats prophesies the future; Didion seeks the answer in the past. In the future, for Didion, anything can happen: "The options remain open here" (221).

Was there a cause for the Vietnam War? Has history turned full circle, the "past" serving as "prologue to the present" (221)? And if history has completed a cycle, will it do so again? Does the individual affect history—"the long view" (201)—or have people, as Harold Bloom suggests in his interpretation of Yeats, like the falconer lost control of nature (321)? Are people, as A. Norman Jeffares argues, like the falcon being swept beyond their control away from Christ (203)? Or are people falling beyond the mute voice of their homeland? None of these uncertainties is resolved.

Yeats attempted to account for some of the enigmas facing twentieth-century humankind. On the one hand, "The Second Coming" predicts the coming era: "Surely some revelation is at hand." Yet it is not clear exactly what will come, for the beast—a "shape," its gaze "blank and pitiless as the sun"—is not clearly defined. However, as Thomas Whitaker suggests, this paradox does not leave the reader uncertain, for the final lines of the poem, in which the rough beast "slouches towards Bethlehem to be born," are spoken by one "who can maintain his questioning stance even when nearly overpowered by that image erupting from the abyss of himself and of his time" (74).

Similar to Yeats, faced with the inexplicability of chaos, the narrator of *Democracy* finds a pattern within history, but dissimilar to Yeats, the narrator of *Democracy* is not expectant. For the narrator as well as for Inez, there is "no revelation, no instant of epiphany" (202). When the reader anticipates resolution, or in the Yeatsian sense an apocalyptic "dawn" (177), the narrator leaves the reader without an answer. The novel is inconclusive, as the narrator indicates: "Last look through more than one door. This is a hard story to tell" (15).

At the end of *Democracy*, Didion conveys a feeling—not an answer but a "sudden sense" of flying into those "dense greens and translucent blues" (222). She leaves the reader with the image of the fallen center, the vanishing island. The narrator has "not been back" (222). As in many postmodern novels, it is the reader's prerogative to fill the space.

In summarizing John Clark Pratt's analysis of Vietnam literature, Timothy Lomperis notes that the literature of the Vietnam War does not add up to a totality. Instead, this literature consists of fragments that illustrate the multiplicity of the war: "Such a literature cannot divine the truth, but it can present fragments of it and get the reader involved in the quest" (8).

Given the method and mood of *Democracy*, I believe Didion would agree.

WORKS CITED

"Americans Failed to Help Nha Trang Staff Escape." *New York Times*, April 3, 1975.

Benjamin, Milton R., and Paul Brinkley Rogers. "Farewell to Cambodia." *Newsweek*, April 21, 1975, 23ff.

Bloom, Harold. *Yeats*. New York: Oxford University Press, 1970.

Dawson, Alan. *55 Days: The Fall of South Vietnam*. Englewood Cliffs, N.J.: Prentice-Hall, 1977.

Didion, Joan. *Democracy*. Pocket, 1985.

——. *Slouching towards Bethlehem*. New York: Dell, 1968.

——. *Writers at Work: The Paris Review Interviews 5*. Ed. George Plimpton. New York: Viking, 1981.

Esper, George. "Evacuation from Saigon Tumultuous at the End." *New York Times*, April 30, 1975.

Jeffares, A. Norman. *A New Commentary on the Poems of W. B. Yeats*. Stanford: Stanford University Press, 1984.

Lomperis, Timothy J. *"Reading the Wind": The Literature of the Vietnam War*. Durham: Duke University Press, 1987.

Olson, James S., ed. *Dictionary of the Vietnam War*. Westport, Conn.: Greenwood, 1988.

Vogle, Paul. "Troops Beat out Civilians in Rush for Da Nang Plane." *New York Times*, March 30, 1975.

Whitaker, Thomas R. *Swan and Shadow: Yeats's Dialogue with History*. Chapel Hill: University of North Carolina Press, 1964.

Wohlpart, A. James. "Internal and External Historicity in Joan Didion's *Democracy*." Popular Culture Association Eighteenth Annual Meeting. New Orleans, March 23, 1988.

Yeats, W. B. *Michael Robartes and the Dancer*. 1920. Shannon: Irish University Press, 1970.

——. *A Vision*. A Reissue with the Author's Final Revisions. 1956. New York: Macmillan, 1961.

Darkness in the East

The Vietnam Novels of

Takeshi Kaiko

⊃ ○ ○ ○ ○ ○ ○ ○ ○ ○

Mark A. Heberle

Since its publication in English in 1980, Takeshi Kaiko's *Into a Black Sun* has been admired by American readers and critics of Vietnam War literature as a powerful and uniquely Asian perspective on the war (Tuohy; Pratt 152–154). Less familiar is its sequel, *Darkness in Summer*. Although the setting of the latter novel is western Europe, its central character is the protagonist of *Into a Black Sun* and its ultimate subject is Vietnam, though the war is presented obliquely rather than directly. While each book handles Vietnam very differently, each providing a complex and occasionally somewhat opaque meditation on the war, the thematic focus of both is a darkness that lies at the heart of the Vietnam experience for Kaiko's protagonist. Moreover, this theme of darkness, which is reflected in the title of each book, reflects the author's own Vietnam experience.

Takeshi Kaiko covered the war as a special correspondent for the

Japanese newspaper *Asahi Shimbun* from 1964 to 1965, contributing weekly reports to the magazine *Shukan Asahi* and completing a Vietnam War journal upon his return to Japan. He came back to Vietnam in 1968 and later in 1973, impelled by his own interest in seeing a final resolution of this seemingly endless tragedy. An early fictional attempt to present his views on Asian revolution appeared in the *Asahi Journal* in 1966, a fantasy narrative called "From the Shore," which took place in an imaginary country called Agonesia. After deciding against publishing this allegory in book form, he determined to present his own experiences more directly in a first-person narrative that became *Into a Black Sun*. In an essay included in the 1974 edition of his *Complete Works*, Kaiko explained his motivations for writing the novel:

> I felt like starting from the very beginning, as if I had written nothing about Vietnam up to that point. Thus, with a desire to begin from the very basics, I resolved to start on an entirely new work. Somewhere behind my resolution smoldered an irrepressible dissatisfaction with the controversy and reporting on Vietnam in Japan at that time. It took me approximately one year to complete the book. (Tokumoto 291)

The novel was published in Japan in 1968, the year that Kaiko returned to Vietnam, and that return concludes *Darkness in Summer*, which was published in 1972. The relationship between the two books has been obscured in the United States because Cecilia Segawa Seigle's translation of *Darkness in Summer* was published in 1973 while her translation of the earlier novel did not appear until seven years later. Partly as a result, most reviewers of *Darkness in Summer* praised its graphic eroticism and dramatization of spiritual exhaustion or condemned it for its slack plot and concentration on sordid or trivial details of lovemaking, eating, or flycasting without recognizing that the protagonist's experiences in Vietnam lay behind his apparent paralysis.

Both works seem to be autobiographical first-person narratives in which there is little or no distinction between the author and the central character, a traditional Japanese narrative form known as *shishosetsu* or "I-novel" (Fowler 4). Instead of a fictional presentation of the war structured according to a significant plot, Kaiko's "I-novels" present the author's direct testimony or confessions, exploring the self by means of the war and the war by means of the self. As a result, both works appear to be unmediated and completely authentic reactions to Vietnam rather than fabricated fictions or reified historical or ideological analyses. In both novels the protagonist is a correspondent whose experiences in Vietnam mirror Kaiko's. Such experiences have not made the war clearer to this correspondent, however; instead of achieving enlightenment, he is left in darkness. Unable to fully understand or accept the motivations or actions of those who are fighting the war or trying to survive it, he is likewise dissatisfied with his own lack of involvement. The experiential, cognitive, and moral darkness that lies at the heart of Vietnam for Kaiko evades his understanding in the first novel yet cannot be effaced in the second, as its title, *Natsu no Yami* (Darkness in Summer) indicates.

The title *Into a Black Sun* is haunting and appropriate as well but obscures the actual Japanese title, *Kagayakeru Yami*, that obviously links the two works thematically. *Kagayakeru Yami* (Shining Darkness) reflects the novel's epigraph from 1 Corinthians 13.12: "We see now through a mirror in an obscure manner, but then face to face. Now I know in part, but then I shall know even as I have been known." As he goes about his job of observing the war, Kaiko's correspondent catches only glimpses of some final "truth," and they increase his moral repulsion. To an American who feels that only the U.S. presence is immoral, Kaiko offers a less easy conclusion near the end of the book: "In terms of casualties, guerrilla warfare is horrible but almost humane. Yet it's a mistake to count, I feel. The point is, it's brothers that are killing each other. That's the crime of it" (167). The Viet Cong fighters are revolutionary heroes, while those in the ARVN lack any purpose beyond personal enrichment or survival; yet

> though they went by different names—the Can Lao Party in the South and the Lao Dong Party in the North—they both deceived their people. An unqualified, uninformed, and unprincipled bunch they were; and their citizens were probed, examined, spied on, commanded, legislated, ruled, classified, educated, lectured, scrutinized, evaluated, judged, reprimanded, and convicted. (101)

Into a Black Sun is set in South Vietnam and formally imitates a reporter's journal, dividing its narrative into two main sections headed "1964" and "1965" and recording the correspondent's conversations with and observations of a wide array of Vietnamese and Americans, as well as Japanese journalists. Descriptions of his daily life and actions and his interviews and conversations with others build a richly detailed picture of life within the war as he moves from an American-advised ARVN camp to Saigon and Cholon, then back to the camp and a disastrous jungle operation against the Viet Cong.

The novel is reminiscent of Graham Greene's *The Quiet American*, which also employs a first-person narrative viewpoint focused upon the internal struggle of a journalist-protagonist who has tried to understand the catastrophe unfolding all about him. Fowler, Greene's cynical British journalist, is not as direct a presentation of the author's self as is Kaiko's unnamed correspondent, but he clearly represents Greene's own political viewpoint about the war. Kaiko's correspondent resembles Fowler in several important ways: he is distressed by the war and is professionally detached from the ideological claims of either side, nonetheless he finds the American cause wrong and anticipates an eventual Communist victory; he is attracted to and repulsed by the chief spokesperson for American policy, an ARVN adviser named Captain Wain, whose name may be a homonym for John Wayne, as John Clark Pratt has suggested (134); and his passionate relationship with a Vietnamese mistress (To-Nga) helps him forget the war. Indeed, Kaiko explicitly includes Greene's novel within his own book during the correspondent's conversation with a former Viet Minh commander turned novelist who knew Greene and finds that his work is untrue:

> I gave him the material for the novel. After it came out, I realized that Greene didn't understand anything about this country. It's a novel written to please European readers. I was very disappointed with it. There's a young woman who smokes opium in the book. I know her, too. I hear she's in Paris now. (87)

Here as elsewhere Kaiko plays strikingly with the boundary between fiction and nonfiction, and one of the effects is to convince the reader that Greene's novel is inaccurate and that his own less dogmatically secure testimony is more honest.

Kaiko's reference to his generic source cleverly combines praise with criticism, defining Greene's ethnocentric limitations. His Asian perspective frequently allows him startling understanding of and empathy with the Vietnamese. Recalling his terror as a boy as he watched the American soldiers occupying Osaka, the correspondent reflects that "it wasn't hard, now—twenty years later—to understand the fear with which Vietnam's peasants reacted to their first sight of those same blue eyes and flaming cheeks" (173). This war occasionally stirs memories of his childhood during those terrible years of devastation and defeat at the hands of the Americans, a period still recalled as a "dark valley" by the Japanese who survived it (Havens, *Valley* 6).

Nonetheless, the correspondent's position is not comfortably Asian either—he finds Japanese chess different from both Vietnamese and Western versions and reflects that Tokyo is the least Asian of non-Western capitals. His critical detachment from American cold warriors as well as Communist patriots reflects the uneasy lack of consensus that characterized Japan's response to the Vietnam War. While the Sato government unenthusiastically supported the United States logistically, socialists, some workers, and many students and intellectuals loudly but vainly supported the Vietnamese nationalist revolution, as Thomas Havens points out in his recent history of Japan's involvement in the Vietnam War, *Fire across the Sea*. The correspondent's ethnic identity ultimately reinforces his professional identity as a Vietnam War correspondent—an observer, a man in the middle who can only record or observe the words or actions of those directly involved on either side but cannot genuinely enter into their experience.

Thus, *Into a Black Sun* does not simply question Greene's version of the truth, it denies the validity of any such external perspective including its own, which is not simply "Asian" but Japanese. The amount of information and variety of perspectives reported resist any simple truths or moral judgments, and Kaiko's picture of the Vietnamese situation is filled with striking ironies in virtually every scene. For example, Tran, To-Nga's brother, admires Ho Chi Minh as Vietnam's greatest leader but deplores the brutal record of the North Vietnamese regime, which he details to the correspondent; he fears a Communist victory yet he cuts off two fingers to avoid induction into the South Vietnamese army. In the end, he is drafted anyway into an army of unfortunates who abuse the people they are supposed to defend. The Americans are viewed with comparable complexity. Walt Rostow's arrogant and misguided theories of guerrilla warfare are balanced by

Mark Twain's prophetic vision of American failure in *A Connecticut Yankee in King Arthur's Court*:

> Good will, he showed us, couldn't forestall *it*. The Caucasian fraternity couldn't prevent *it*. Anglo-Saxon kinship couldn't stop *it*. The absence of communism couldn't hinder *it*. And King Arthur died, Sir Lancelot died, the Knights of the Round Table died, Merlin died. And the American died. The war died seventy-five years ago. (48)

The correspondent both regrets and admires the violent energy of Captain Wain; and he finds more similarities than differences between Wain and his passionately antiwar countryman: "Wain flew ten thousand miles to fight; and this old man had journeyed just as far to do penance. They were all descendants of Captain Ahab, a strange, obsessive species, driven to fill their tormented souls with purpose and action" (165).

As a man privileged by profession and nationality to maintain a neutral position that is denied to any Vietnamese and as a mere observer of the tragedy of other Asians, Kaiko's correspondent comes to condemn himself and the place he occupies: "I was paid, had the money credited to my account in a Saigon bank, ate Cantonese food, and inexorably gained weight. The more havoc I saw, the keener my reports became—a hyena feasting on carrion" (61). The two episodes that lie behind the translator's title for "Shining Darkness" both involve attempts to withdraw from or forget the darkness on which he feeds. After witnessing the brutal predawn execution of a teenage terrorist in the Saigon central market square, the stunned observer returns to his room but cannot easily sleep off what he has seen: "When I got back I reeled into bed. My sleep was shallow; there were flashes of light and blood and my limbs twitched uncontrollably. I had blocked out the windows with the blackout curtains, but I felt I was looking at the sun behind eyelids that were almost clear" (135). More emphatically than his disturbed sleep, Kaiko's desperate appetite for food and sex graphically dramatizes his need to repress or obliterate the darkness of the war, yet even sexual orgasm recalls the earlier unwelcome illumination: "The darkness exploded and, for a second, opened its glittering core and then was gone. It was exactly like the clear, blinding void that had appeared behind my eyelids that morning of the execution" (187).

In the final two chapters, however, he abandons his own inertia and the moral decay of Saigon, returning to the ARVN camp. His subsequent decision to go on a search-and-destroy mission with Wain and the South Vietnamese battalion engages him directly in the war. By moving into the jungle, which is associated throughout the novel with the revolution and its uncertain moral outcome, he hopes to encounter directly the ultimate reality of the war that transcends the moral blackness at its center: the obligation to kill or be killed. Even before actual contact with the Viet Cong, however, in the middle of the jungle Kaiko's correspondent recognizes the meaningless darkness of the war for him, whether in the jungle or in Saigon, whether he is a participant risking his own life too or simply a spectator: "Everything seemed futile in that corroding quiet, among those glaring shafts of light. . . . I might return alive and weave some words together that shed some light on my motives and ambitions, but the effort would be as meaningful as froth churned out behind a ship" (193–194). The outcome is both meaningless and prophetic: the South Vietnamese battalion simply disintegrates under the fire of the unseen enemy, and correspondent, South Vietnamese commander, and American adviser flee deeper and deeper into the jungle as the novel ends.

In *Darkness in Summer* Kaiko's persona again engages himself in the war after finding ironically that the world outside Vietnam is now also meaningless for him. He renews an affair with a former lover ten years after she had left Japan to study in Europe and he had begun traveling throughout the world as a correspondent. Spiritually exiled from Japan, the unnamed hero and heroine are also alienated from the Western societies through which they pass, a condition indicated by the vagueness of the setting: they meet in what may be Paris, move to her apartment probably in Bonn, go on a fishing trip somewhere else, and end up in what appears to be Berlin—but none of the cities or countries through which they move is ever named. Except for the fishing expedition—Kaiko is an expert angler and has written articles and a book about flycasting—the correspondent spends most of his time in bed, his activities alternating between sleeping, eating, and sexual intercourse, all of which are given detailed descriptions that contrast strikingly with the vagueness of external circumstances. Until the fishing trip Kaiko's character never leaves his various rooms except to eat, and the only person he has any contact with is his lover. In some ways the first two-thirds of the novel seems a cross between *Naked Lunch* and *Last Tango—Somewhere in the West*.

An early reviewer found the novel "crushingly vacuous and uninteresting," but he apparently didn't read it very closely for he claimed that it is set in "contemporary, conflict-torn Saigon" (Allen 66). His mistake is unintentionally acute, however, for as the protagonist moves from one kind of meal to another his dreams and his memories are increasingly absorbed by his experiences in Vietnam, which are largely responsible for his present paralysis, as an early reflection during the trip to Bonn suggests:

> Each time I saw deep gorges and shallow streams, pools, falls, and whirlpools, my eyes forced me to stop and wonder and ponder on where and how I should throw my hook and how I should let it drift. The scenes of blood and devastation receded and became nothing but a dull pain like a toothache; I put my face against the window and, sipping wine in the sparkling sunshine, kept thinking about sharp fishing hooks . . . and the spots that were like powdered gemstones glistening in the sunshine. (47)

As we discover only toward the end, the novel is taking place in 1968, after the Tet offensive and its brief resumption in May, and the darkness that invades this brief summer is the war, still continuing both outside and inside the narrator's consciousness more than three years after his escape from the jungle that had enveloped him at the end of *Into the Black Sun*. His regressive attempt to escape that darkness is ultimately destructive and contemptible, and his mistress comes to reject his behavior as well, feeling that she has been nothing more than a "station restaurant, a pizza snack" (190) for the Kaiko figure.

Their separation from each other begins in the last third of the novel, when she informs him of a newspaper report discussing a possible Vietnamese Communist offensive in the fall. The news from Vietnam suddenly and radically transforms and energizes his life. He leaves bed and bedroom, consults all the local news sources for further information, describes his war experiences in 1964 and 1965 to his mistress, outlines what he has learned of the large Viet Cong offensives earlier in the year, and reveals his hope that the war is coming to a climax and conclusion as well as his own desire to experience it. Ultimately, he returns to the very catastrophe that has evidently crippled him emotionally in the first place. The correspondent's return to Vietnam repeats his movement into the jungle at the end of *Into a Black Sun* but on a larger scale: just as the jungle promised an encounter with the heart of the Vietnam War and a rejection of the meaningless moral chaos surrounding it, so the war as a whole now promises an escape from the meaninglessness of his life in the West. Nonetheless, as he prepares to leave to resume his correspondent's role he recognizes again in a startling outburst that he can never be more than an anguished observer of the darkness:

> This is not Japan's war—the simple, barren thought dawns on me in all its immensity and settles on my heart. The fact that I, who am supposed to be an absolutely free spirit and a liberal, should lean on blood and geographical ties is laughable, but it is true. I want it to be the coercion of the state, an absolute command, a mandate. I want my hatred and despair to be given roots. (207–208)

Only then could he understand the war in a way that *is* directly meaningful, a way that only the Vietnamese themselves can experience:

> It seemed to me that I had no right to criticize blood in a loud voice unless I was prepared to kill or be killed. And making either preparation meant to write, not in sentences, but in my guts: To kill or be killed. The preparation to be made depended for the most part on one's attitude as to whether one expected anything after the revolution or not; but I was too detached for either. All I could do was watch. (99–100)

The lack of strong commitment to something beyond the self is epitomized in another biblical epigraph that introduces *Darkness in Summer*, the preapocalyptic warning of Christ in Revelation 3:15 to the Laodiceans, accusing them of lukewarm faith: "I would know thy works, that thou art neither cold nor hot: I would thou wert cold or hot." As the two Japanese lovers ride the circular tramline from West to East Berlin over and over again on the correspondent's last evening in Europe, however, he remains unable to be either; detached from both ideologies, uncommitted and unengaged: "East and West ceased to be distinguishable. I could not tell 'Over there' from 'Over here.' I no longer knew whether the train was running or standing still" (210).

Ultimately, confronting the war again is preferable to rotting away in peace, which he identifies with syphilis, a particularly significant metaphor for this previously bedridden narrator. The last paragraph of the book is a single sentence fragment: "Ten o'clock . . . tomorrow morning the plane to Vietnam" (210)—the final word of the novel's final sentence is the only non-Japanese city or country named in Kaiko's novel, the only place in the world that now has any meaning to the correspondent. He travels east to Vietnam to *observe* the apocalypse in which he cannot participate. The trip seems both inevitable and futile: there was no third offensive in 1968, no conclusive resolution to the darkness that continued to engage Kaiko morally and to resist any final truth. His own later explanation of his journeys to Vietnam suggests the mythic importance of the war as a site of significance which his two dark visions attempt to fathom: "I felt strongly that whether at home or abroad, somewhere, sometime, at least once in his life, a writer must be present at the site of reality in the making. So that's why I went and that's why I even dared to enter into the jungle war" (Tokumoto 292).

Kaiko's inability to choose one side or the other without reservations derives from his outsider status both as a noncombatant and as a Japanese. As he tells his lover, "There's only one or the other over there; they are either pro-government or antigovernment; that means kill or be killed. If you keep silent, it may mean that you don't care who wins, but, in effect, it means you are supporting one or the other" (178). As one of the founders of Beheiren in 1965, the largest Japanese antiwar movement in history (Havens, *Fire* 46), Kaiko might be expected to be more prorevolution than he is in these two novels. He is certainly not silent, however, and their very power derives from the novelist's ability to suspend or complicate judgments that the journalist or the opponent of Japanese government policy might have to make. By presenting himself as perplexed and appalled, unable to fully understand or accept the war, he registers its darkness all the more truthfully.

Kaiko's detachment may be parasitical, but it is also morally acute: both novels suggest that those who claim to see through the darkness clearly, hot with ideological fervor, are also responsible for the catastrophe. The insight afforded his own perspective is suggested by the correspondent's reflections on the Berlin Wall near the end of *Darkness in Summer*: "My position is neither east nor west of the wall. . . . There must be facts that only the people in the East can grasp, and other facts that only the Westerners can discover. Both sides claim to know the whole truth. But there must be other facts that only the men on the wall itself can understand" (190–191). The "darkness novels" present the precarious, uncertain, and yet indispensable viewpoint of someone looking at the tragedy of Vietnam while attempting to stand on the wall.

WORKS CITED

Allen, Bruce. Review of *Darkness in Summer*, by Takeshi Kaiko. *Library Journal*, Jan. 1, 1974, 66.

Fowler, Edward. *The Rhetoric of Confession: "Shishosetsu" in Early Twentieth-Century Japanese Fiction*. Berkeley: University of California Press, 1988.

Havens, Thomas R. H. *Fire across the Sea: The Vietnam War and Japan, 1965–1975*. Princeton: Princeton University Press, 1985.

———. *Valley of Darkness: The Japanese People and World War Two*. New York: Norton, 1978.

Kaiko, Takeshi. *Darkness in Summer*. Trans. Cecilia Segawa Seigle. New York: Knopf, 1973.

———. *Into a Black Sun*. Trans. Cecilia Segawa Seigle. 1980. Tokyo: Kodansha, 1983.

Pratt, John Clark. "Bibliographic Commentary: 'From the Fiction, Some Truths.'" *"Reading the Wind": The Literature of the Vietnam War*. Timothy J. Lomperis. Durham, N.C.: Duke University Press, 1987.

Tokumoto, Mitsumasa. Review of *Into a Black Sun*, by Kaiko Ken. *Japan Quarterly* 28 (1981): 290–292.

Tuohy, Frank. "A Nose for War." Review of *Into a Black Sun*, by Takeshi Kaiko. *Times Literary Supplement*, Oct. 10, 1981, 1270.

Line of Departure

The Atrocity in Vietnam

War Literature

⊃ ○ ○ ○ ○ ○ ○ ○ ○ ○ ○ ○ ○

Cornelius A. Cronin

One of the most agonizing moments in Larry Heinemann's harrowing first novel, *Close Quarters*, occurs when the reconnaissance platoon, accompanied by an engineer detachment to sweep the road for mines, is ambushed by two hidden VC operating command-detonated mines. The first mine kills one of the engineers and the second almost destroys Philip Dosier's track (an armored personnel carrier) and nearly kills the crew. The two VC, an old man and a teenage boy, are captured. While guarding the boy, Dosier looks for an opportune moment to kill him. He gives his shotgun to his friend Quinn in the hopes that Quinn will kill the boy; when Quinn does not, Dosier takes the gun back and, "picking a time when no one was looking, when even Quinn was fooling with his M-60, I clicked off the safety, looked again, and blew the top of his head off. The fucking round hit him right in the forehead and he flew back over the berm ass over teakettle as though somebody had dropkicked him under the chin. I hated him when he was alive and I hated his corpse" (219–220). There is a furor, and the shotgun is taken away from Dosier. When several of his platoon mates and his lieutenant back up his story that the prisoner made a grab for the gun the incident is settled. The shotgun is returned to him along with a stern look from the colonel, but, Dosier reflects, "I could have cared less what he thought, the dink was dead" (220).

This narrative describes an atrocity—in this case the murder of a prisoner of war—and as such it is central to our understanding of the experience of the Vietnam War. This war abounds with atrocities. My Lai is one of the most enduring memories of the war, and the Winter Soldier hearings document an apparently endless string of atrocities. The public perception of the American soldier in Vietnam as an out-of-control killer is well established, and most attempts to rehabilitate this image have turned on re-creating the soldier in the image of a hapless victim or portraying the VC and NVA as devil-figures. I will argue that the reality is infinitely more complex than either of these views. A great many atrocities were committed in Vietnam—on both sides. Many of these atrocities can be attributed to the interracial nature of the war; many were of the kind that occur in all wars. What is different about the representations of personal experience in this war is not so much the nature and number of the atrocities but rather the self-awareness of those writing about them.

Atrocities are always a part of war. The taking of prisoners of war alone is a complex enough topic to be the subject of a book. In early warfare the entire losing army, or at least that part which did not escape, was often killed. In medieval warfare surrender was often accepted based on the ransomability of the person trying to surrender; common soldiers trying to surrender were likely to be killed. (Of course, in the small battlefields of the time such soldiers could often just slip away.) John Keegan points out that in the Napoleonic wars, infantry-to-infantry and cavalry-to-cavalry surrenders were fairly routine and easy to work out, but surrenders between infantry and cavalry were tricky at best. In modern industrial warfare the unwritten rules are even more complex. In theory soldiers who want to surrender must have their surrender accepted and must then be treated according to the rules of the Geneva convention. However, in the heat of battle this "right" of surrender can be difficult to exercise. In World War I, for example, the British insisted on challenging large numbers of well-entrenched machine guns with lines of infantry. Naturally, the machine guns mowed the soldiers down in great numbers. Often the attack faltered, but when it did not machine gunners in overrun trenches found that backing away from their machine guns with their hands up usually did not produce the desired results. The attacking infantry were in no frame of mind to accept the surrender of those who had been killing their friends in wholesale lots just seconds before, and these soldiers were usually killed instantly. In World War II the issue of surrender became very complex, and the rules varied from front to front. In Vietnam being taken prisoner was every soldier's worst nightmare. The vast majority of American POWs were aircrew, while the nature of the war itself meant that many of those taken prisoner by American troops were guerrillas rather than regular soldiers and often were only marginal participants in the conflict.

I am going to compare three books, one about World War II and two about Vietnam, each of which portrays the experience of a soldier in war. I have chosen these books because they are representative of the literature of their respective wars. The first, *Company Commander*, is a memoir by Charles B. MacDonald of his experience commanding two infantry companies across Europe in World War II. The second, already mentioned, is *Close Quarters*, an autobiographical novel by Larry Heinemann, based on his experience as a soldier in a mechanized infantry battalion in Vietnam. The third is Philip Caputo's *A Rumor of War*, a memoir of Caputo's experience with the first American ground combat unit in Vietnam. All three books are built around a central consciousness; all three show how that central consciousness responds to combat. And all three tell stories of the killing of prisoners of war. But the stories are told for different reasons and to different effect, and an examination of the differences will tell us a lot about how MacDonald sees himself as a soldier in comparison to how Heinemann (through his narrator, Dosier) and Caputo see themselves.

A significant reason for the differences between these writers can be revealed through an analysis of the military environments they experienced. This approach allows us to remain cognizant of the many points of connection between the Vietnam War writers and their pre-decessors in earlier modern wars, particularly the two world wars, while noting the significant differences. I am not claiming that this method provides a complete explanation; obviously, the larger culture influences the military establishment and those in it. The young men and women who went to World War II and Vietnam were the products of particular cultures that had a lot to do with determining how they would behave as soldiers or sailors. Indeed, virtually all the work that has been published so far on Vietnam War literature tends to locate the uniqueness of that literature either in the contemporary culture or in some larger American myth.

But becoming a soldier or sailor is in itself a transforming experi-ence. The training is designed to break down the trainee's identity and replace it with a group identity. It is designed to replace preexisting social ties with much more intense, if shallower, ties to the immediate group—the fire team, the squad, the platoon. The trainees do not cease to be who they were before training, but they do, willy-nilly, acquire new identities that function within the group. In addition to understanding how the political culture of the 1950s and 1960s helped shape the experiences of soldiers in Vietnam, we must also be aware of how the specific military culture of the time helped shape those experiences.

While all soldiers are significantly transformed by training and while there are common elements to this transformation, military experi-ence is not the same everywhere. The specific military culture soldiers find themselves in influences the way they will react in combat. For one thing, armies have a national style. The British army is built around regimental loyalties; soldiers remain with the same regiment usually for their whole careers. The Israeli army is dogmatically egali-tarian. The American army, too, has its own identity. It tends to be machine-dependent and roadbound. In contrast to most armies it his-torically puts its weakest recruits in the combat arms, and it has tra-ditionally resisted the establishment of elite units like Rangers and Special Forces.

American military culture changed markedly between World War II and Vietnam. Prior to World War II the American army had spent most of its existence as a border constabulary, presenting itself in battalion-sized or smaller units on frontier posts. A military career carried low prestige, even for officers, and the military budget was regularly the first thing cut. The Civil War and World War I represented the country's only experience with mass armies, and those armies were disbanded as quickly as possible after the wars were over. The Cold War changed all that. America demobilized as precipitously as usual after World War II, but the Berlin crisis and the Korean War resulted in the reinstitution of the draft and the first large peacetime military establishment in the nation's history. This large conscript army required a substantial permanent training establishment which resulted in the first serious thought given to training doctrine.

As a result of these changes, the military experience for soldiers in Vietnam was very different from that of their World War II counterparts. All riflemen had fully automatic weapons, and training now emphasized bursts of fire at area targets rather than aimed fire at clearly identifiable targets. NCOs were trained to make sure that all their men were firing; thus, many who in World War II would have merely been inactive observers became active participants in Vietnam.

Another difference between these wars is that many political decisions affected military conditions in Vietnam. The decision not to mobilize the National Guard and the reserves meant that the Vietnam War would be led by career-minded field and general-grade officers, a cadre unleavened by reserve counterparts who would have a greater interest in getting the war over with. Further, Selective Service policies created conditions in which those who were drafted came disproportionately from the least influential groups in the society. Many of these draftees felt more like victims than like contributors to a common goal.

Of all the conditions under which the Vietnam War was fought, two had the greatest influence on individual experience. The first was the one-year tour of duty (thirteen months for marines). This practice was the logical culmination of an individual rotation policy experimentally employed in World War II and established in the form of a point system during the Korean War. In Vietnam, the army policy was that a soldier would be returned home 365 days after leaving the continental United States (actually 364 days since a day was lost because of the international date line). The effect of this policy was to destroy unit cohesion by guaranteeing that each unit would have a 100 percent turnover each year, without figuring casualties. A soldier's status as a member of a group was thus weakened while status as an individual enhanced. Except for those in a unit when it first arrived in Vietnam, each soldier arrived alone and left alone, and each counted the days in between on a short-timer's calendar. It is not that units in Vietnam had no coherence but that insofar as they did it was something arrived at self-consciously—not a given. Because soldiers returned home singly, the shedding of military identity was performed alone and without meaningful ceremony. This lack of clear boundaries between one phase of life and another caused many incomplete transitions.

The second condition was the decision to fight the war as a war of attrition. Since the Civil War, American military doctrine had consistently emphasized the destruction of the enemy's army in the field. But Vietnam was different. The establishment and relentless publicizing of such indexes as the body count and the kill ratio made certain that these soldiers would be more aware than their predecessors of their status as socialized warriors, as killers. Some units gave extra furlough to soldiers with a large number of certified kills, and units were pitted against each other to see which could produce the highest body count, with cold beer or extra time at the base camp as a reward (Cincinnatus 92–98). If we are to understand the experiences of writers of participant literature we must understand them, among other ways, in the context of the specific military culture that shaped them. We begin this inquiry with a look at a soldier whose experience reflects the military culture of World War II.

Charles MacDonald's *Company Commander* is the memoir of a World War II infantry commander who commanded first I and then G companies of the 28th Infantry, 2d Infantry Division, in Europe. He participated in more famous and larger battles than anything that appears in *Close Quarters*, including the battle at Elsenborn Ridge at the start of the Battle of the Bulge. Yet while the book is filled with a sense of the historical significance of the events it portrays, the writer seems to have trouble clarifying the impact of these events on himself. Before we look at the episodes dealing with prisoners of war, we need to see how MacDonald's tendency to determine his own self-worth by what others say about him leaves him unwilling to make moral judgments about himself or his associates.

In his first action, a series of defensive battles among the pillboxes of the Siegfried Line near Kesfeld in Germany, MacDonald is worried whether he will perform adequately in combat. Recalling a major nighttime counterattack he writes:

> I was suddenly more afraid than I had ever been before. My body seemed weak all over, and I wondered if I had the strength to stand up. I opened my mouth to sound the alarm, and I wondered if anything would come out. (59)

His thoughts after that battle show that his self-definition depends on the approval of those around him:

> It was five o'clock when I finally climbed into my bunk. I wondered what the men of my headquarters group thought of me as a company commander now. Had I been a complete failure? Had I done anything correctly? Was my fear as noticeable as I imagined it must have been? But perhaps they thought of me as one of them now that we had experienced our first action.
>
> That was how I wanted it to be. (64)

A more dramatic illustration of MacDonald's emphasis on approval from without comes after his company has been decimated at the Monschau Corridor. MacDonald and his men straggle in confusion to the rear and stumble upon their battalion command post, where MacDonald breaks down in shame, feeling that he has performed inadequately. When the colonel informs him of the size and extent of the German attack and assures him that he and his men performed superbly, MacDonald is overjoyed.

> So I had not failed! And I Company had not failed! I was almost happy that the German offensive *was* on a large scale. My men had done an excellent job against heavy odds, and those who had died were not dead because of some personal failing of mine. The realization made me want to cry again. (138)

MacDonald raises no question about the rightness of the war; that is taken for granted. His concept of evil has less to do with individual responsibility than with how well things are going: "I still could find no glory in war, but there was much less evil in a successful attack than in a perpetual defense or retreat. It made you feel elated, some way" (215).

The clearest sense of MacDonald's understanding of individual responsibility and the nature of evil can be seen in the incidents in which his men capture prisoners. The first one occurs when MacDonald and his reconstituted company are patrolling shortly after the battle at Elsenborn Ridge. When a German soldier tries to surrender they tell him to come out. When he says that he is blind and they must come to get him, MacDonald reports their natural response: "The same thought must have entered each of our minds. This was a German trick to lure us into the open firebreak. I ran forward to the head of the column, apprehensive lest someone should decide to go out into the open toward the voice" (172). When the man comes out with a "dirty, blood-stained bandage stretched across his forehead" he is taken in custody, and when the company reaches its objective MacDonald sends two men to accompany him back to A Company. The men who were accompanying him soon return.

"Did you get him back OK?" I asked.

"Yessir," they answered and turned quickly toward their platoons.

"Wait a minute," I said. "Did you find A Company? What did Lieutenant Smith say?"

The men hesitated. One spoke out suddenly. "To tell you the truth, Cap'n, we didn't get to A Company. The sonofabitch tried to make a run for it. Know what I mean?"

"Oh, I see," I said slowly, nodding my head. "I see." (173)

That "I see" is the extent of MacDonald's response. He nowhere explicitly acknowledges that his men have killed a prisoner. Later, almost the same thing happens when he is commanding G Company, 28th Infantry, as they are rolling across Germany, and his response is even more startling:

Sergeant Patton's platoon arrived, tired and dusty from the tiring uphill walk from Bendorf-Sayn. The prisoners were not with them.

Company G committed a war crime. They are going to win the war, however, so I don't suppose it really matters. (215)

The quick raising of the moral issue and the almost instantaneous dismissal of it are remarkable; they seem even more remarkable since he is able to work up a good deal more indignation about the fact that the regimental staff sits down to breakfast in buildings captured by his men who must march off to combat after a breakfast of cold C-rations. In a sense, MacDonald's acknowledgment that his men's action in killing the prisoners constitutes a war crime underscores the fact that he is writing in a rhetorical world in which Americans cannot commit war crimes. Everyone knows that the Germans are the war criminals; it is not really a war crime to kill Nazis.

In the light of these POW incidents, let us reexamine the incident related at the beginning of this essay. A soldier is taken prisoner, but before he can be turned over to the proper authorities he is killed by the troops who captured him. Seen purely as a series of events, there is no difference between I Company's killing of the blind German soldier and Dosier's killing of the young VC. But a closer examination will reveal profound differences.

MacDonald tells the two stories of the killing of the POWs without blinking, but he tells them with as few details as possible. He makes it easy for his audience to brush by them and file them away as he clearly has done. Dosier will give his reader no such chance. He draws the narrative out and tells it in as much detail as possible, being not merely honest or unsparing but downright gruesome. He is not delicate as he describes his feelings—"I wanted that smooth, smug, slant-eyed face ground into meat, transformed into spray" (219)—and his description of the shooting itself is nothing if not graphic. In short, he draws a picture of himself as a homicidal monster, no better than Sgt. Barnes in *Platoon*.

But Dosier explains a good deal more. He is far more self-conscious about his situation than MacDonald is. He arrives in Vietnam totally ignorant of the reality of combat, not even knowing that KIA means "killed in action," but he learns fast and re-creates his learning experience for the reader. All through the book his descriptions of his actions are painfully detailed and make clear his self-consciousness about his capacity for evil. In *Dispatches*, Michael Herr says that the grunts' story was always the same: "Put yourself in my place" (31). One of the characteristic modes of writing about the Vietnam War is just what Heinemann has Dosier provide—an extremely detailed, unsparing narrative which creates moments of easy judgment for the reader and then overwhelms those easy judgments with a mass of details which qualify and undercut them, until the reader is left as brutalized and confused as Dosier.

Historians can explain a lot about the kinds of atrocities described above. The first of MacDonald's two atrocities occurs late in the Battle of the Bulge. Kampfgruppe Peiper, an armored SS task force under Lt. Col. Joachim Peiper, had driven into the Ambleve valley searching for a route to the Meuse River. Along the way they had killed a number of American POWs, most notably at Malmédy where more than eighty were taken to a field and machine-gunned. Word of this atrocity spread, and American troops were less than scrupulous about accepting surrenders and properly treating prisoners for the rest of the Ardennes campaign and beyond (Weigley 695). This response is understandable; on one level it explains why MacDonald's men deal with prisoners the way they do and why MacDonald acquiesces. But it does not explain why his personal response is so much less aware than either Heinemann's or Caputo's. There are circumstances in both the latter two cases which explain their behavior. Dosier confronts a person who just tried to kill him, and Caputo's unit has been taking casualties around the village from which the two young men are kidnapped. The point is that MacDonald does not see what he has acquiesced in as an atrocity while the two Vietnam War writers do. In other words, an examination of the events surrounding these incidents does not explain away the huge difference in the writers' responses.

In Heinemann's novel, the reader perceives the atrocity because of the way the incident is described. Dosier's narrative calls attention to the act and captures the barbarity of it. The act itself does not differ fundamentally from the killing of the blind German by the soldiers of MacDonald's I Company, but a radically different perception of it is created by the way it is told. MacDonald encourages us to pass over his incident, after perhaps noting sympathetically the terrible things wars make people do. Dosier insists we look at what he has done and at how he felt doing it. But he also immediately begins to undercut the morally simple situation he has set up.

MacDonald clearly understands that there is a different set of rules in war, different even from the formally defined laws of war. His dismissal of the unimportance of G Company's "war crime" speaks to his awareness of the existence of such a code, but he does not refer to it explicitly. Dosier spells out his understanding in full detail, as he speaks of the rage he feels standing guard over the boy who has killed one of his compatriots and has come very close to killing him:

> No kid could watch a man die. You goddamn skinny gook punk. I should just go ahead and blow your fucking brains out. By the rule he was a man, and the rule says to the hilt with your fucking anger, to the fucking hilt. My jaws would ache later, that thought would grind so hard. (218)

Dosier understands that the rules that apply here are not the rules of the Geneva convention. The rage he experiences and which the reader is invited to experience is precisely what the reader of *Catch-22* is defended from by comedy when Yossarian insists that "they" are trying to kill him personally. The Vietnam soldier, who arrives alone and leaves alone, realizes that Yossarian was right, that war is personal and that they are trying to kill him.

Dosier's time in Vietnam is an education in these unwritten rules. Early in his tour, when the moaning of a wounded prisoner threatens to expose their position, Cross, one of his platoon mates, deliberately administers a fatal overdose of morphine to the prisoner. Dosier is appalled and says to him, "Cross . . . you've killed him." Cross replies, "So?" and Dosier says, "But he was wounded. He was a prisoner." Cross then gives Dosier, who has been in country only a short time at this point, his first lesson in the rules:

> "Look, Dosier," said Cross. "He was giving away our position. . . . He was dying anyway. . . . And besides, it was a gook. You give gooks a break like that and you ain't gonna last. Listen, I took a chance for Murphy, I'll take a chance for Atevo, and I'll take a chance for you, but don't ask me to take a chance for gooks. Dosier, look: the only thing more fucked up than being here, is getting killed here. Savvy?" (63)

By the time Dosier kills the prisoner he is a master of the rules.

The contrast between the rules in the field and the rules back home is made clear when in the second paragraph after this incident Dosier reports that Rayburn, a mechanic who has gone home, is in jail for killing his unfaithful wife. The difficulty of adjusting to the change in rules is just as explicit.

But Dosier's sophisticated understanding of the true code is not without its price. He is aware that in killing the boy he is killing himself: "The day after Christmas I stood over a weak, wounded kid and saw his grave and my grave, and the grave of those around me—a deep smooth-sided shaft and you will never fill it" (220). The night before he is to return home, he contemplates what has happened to him. "Nobody goes home from here" (278), he says, and he questions how he has changed: "How did I come to love it so? . . . I can never go home. I just want to see it. . . . I have not been getting closer, only farther away." And finally, "I have lost a great deal" (279–280).

MacDonald's return home is described differently: "A month later we were loaded on a big boat at Le Havre, and on July 20, 1945, we sailed into New York Harbor and received the cheers of grateful America and saw a tall lady with a torch that brought tears to our eyes" (370). The very availability of that rhetoric suggests something of the psychic distance between World War II and the Vietnam War. These visions of home underscore the point that our perception of the atrocities in the two books is largely determined by the way they are narrated. MacDonald wants the atrocities he was indirectly involved in to be seen as unfortunate but routine events in war, which they are. Dosier wants his actions to be seen as atrocious, which they are. However, as events, Dosier's actions are also unfortunate but routine happenings in war, and the killings of prisoners in MacDonald's narrative are also atrocities. What has changed is not the nature of the actions but the way they are perceived by those performing them.

What is at issue here is the kind of knowledge represented by war literature. As James William Gibson says:

The warrior's knowledge as expressed in memoirs, novels, poems and plays by the soldiers, together with reports by oral historians and essay journalists, posits a literature about the war that contradicts the war-managers at virtually every level. . . . How can a major war like Vietnam be absorbed into the historical record without listening to those who fought the war, especially when over 200 books have been written by soldiers and close observers? What are the tacit rules governing legitimate knowledge about the war, and how have they marginalized and discredited the warrior's knowledge? (461)

Philip Caputo's treatment of his own atrocity in *A Rumor of War* illuminates the issue of what kind of knowledge is represented by participant literature. Caputo makes explicit what is only implicit in most participant books about war—what these authors are doing is nothing less than creating their war's soldiers. Thus, Audie Murphy in *To Hell and Back* creates the typical American World War II soldier—one who hates war but who, when given no choice, squares his shoulders and gets on with the job, trading wisecracks with his buddies when they are alive and grieving for them when they are dead. This pattern of creating an identity for the soldiers of a particular war continues in Vietnam participant literature but, typically, in a much more self-conscious form.

Caputo begins his book by insisting on its status as participant literature:

This book does not pretend to be history. It has nothing to do with politics, power, strategy, influence, national interests or foreign policy; nor is it an indictment of the great men who led us into Indochina and whose mistakes were paid for with the blood of some quite ordinary men. In a general sense, it is simply a story about war, about the things men do in war and the things war does to them. More strictly, it is a soldier's account of our longest conflict, the only one we have ever lost, as well as the record of a long and sometimes painful personal experience.

. . . I have tried to describe accurately what the dominant event in the life of my generation, the Vietnam War, was like for the men who fought in it. Toward that end I have made a great effort to resist the veteran's inclination to remember things the way he would like them to have been rather than the way they were. (xi, xix)

The second passage provides a useful counterpoint to the first, for Caputo moves from writing a book about "a soldier's account of our longest conflict" and "the record of a long and sometimes painful personal experience" to describing what the war was like "for the men who fought in it." He thus states explicitly that he is going to be creating the Vietnam soldier, and he gives us a clue when he says that he will stick to the facts and will remember things "the way they were," not as he "would like them to have been." Throughout the book he positions himself very self-consciously in relation to his predecessor soldier-writers, particularly the British World War I soldier-poets, and he makes himself the typical Vietnam soldier. As such, he has his atrocity to deal with.

Caputo's atrocity occurs near the end of his book, and it culminates a series of reflections on the evils that people do in war. Early in his tour in Vietnam Caputo watches other units burn Vietnamese villages, and he reflects that soldiers do evil things which are caused by the war but for which the soldiers are individually responsible. Much later his men torch several huts containing a VC arms cache, and Caputo feels neither vengeance nor remorse. Soon after, however, when his men go completely out of control and burn down the village of Ha Na, he is wracked with guilt:

> I could analyze myself all I wanted, but the fact was we had needlessly destroyed the homes of perhaps two hundred people. All the analysis in the world would not make a new village rise from the ashes. It could not answer the question that kept repeating itself in my mind nor lighten the burden of my guilt. The usual arguments and rationalizations did not help, either. Yes, the village had obviously been under enemy control; it had been a VC supply dump as much as it had been a village. Yes, burning the cache was a legitimate act of war and the fire resulting from it had been accidental. Yes, the later deliberate destruction had been committed by men *in extremis*; war was a state of extremes and men often did extreme things in it. But none of that conventional wisdom relieved my guilt or answered the question: "Tai Sao?" Why? (306)

The contrast between Caputo and MacDonald (or virtually any other World War II writer) is clear. The World War II writers almost never ask the questions that Caputo asks. They almost never question the rightness of what they are doing—even the excesses are the fault of a series of impersonal agencies known collectively as "the war." In contrast, Caputo has been questioning what he is doing in Vietnam from the beginning. He joins the Marine Corps in order to prove himself to himself, "to find, in a commonplace world, a chance to live heroically" (5). The Marine Corps seems to be the place to fulfill that desire, and so he and fellow marines fly to Vietnam carrying "along with our packs and rifles the implicit convictions that the Viet Cong would be quickly beaten and that we were doing something noble and good. We kept the packs and rifles, the convictions we lost" (xii). Later he characterizes the gulf between his heroic fantasies and mundane reality: "And then there was that inspiring order issued by General Greene: kill VC. In the patriotic fervor of the Kennedy years, we had asked, "What can we do for our country?" and our country answered, "Kill VC" (230). Finally, when he requests a transfer to a line company after his stint on the regimental staff, he gives a number of reasons and says, "Revenge was one of the reasons I volunteered for a line company. I wanted a chance to kill somebody" (231).

Caputo already sees himself as what Robert Jay Lifton calls a "socialized warrior." The socialized warrior, a perversion of the myth of the warrior-hero, is one whose worth is "measured by concrete acts of killing, and by a still more concrete body-count," and in whom "the larger purpose of the heroic quest gives way to a cultivation of skill in killing and surviving" (Lifton 27). What is important is not that Caputo is a socialized warrior; all soldiers at least since the Renaissance have been. The point is that he is aware that he is a socialized warrior. Thus, when he is involved in an atrocity the event is secondary to his response to it.

The event is small enough. Caputo sanctions an unauthorized raid on a nearby "ville" to capture two alleged VC. The wrong men are taken and killed—one of them being their own informer. Caputo is devastated by the realization of what he has caused.

> They walked off. I stayed for a while, looking at the corpse. The wide, glowing, glassy eyes stared at me in accusation. The dead boy's open mouth screamed silently his innocence and our guilt. In the darkness and confusion, out of fear, exhaustion, and the brutal instincts acquired in war, the marines had made a mistake. An awful mistake. They had killed the wrong man. No, not they, *we.* *We* had killed the wrong man. That boy's innocent blood was on my hands as much as it was on theirs. I had sent them out there.

My God, what have we done? I thought. I could think of nothing else. My God, what have we done. Please God, forgive us. What have we done? (321)

What Caputo has done is only marginally more serious than what Mac-Donald has done by ignoring his men's killing of the POWs. He feels guilty because he wanted the VC killed. "It was my secret and savage desire that the two men die. In my heart I hoped Allen would find some excuse for killing them, and Allen had read my heart. He smiled, I smiled back, and we both knew in that moment what was going to happen" (317).

Caputo has seen clearly the dark underside of comradeship which redeems the experience of combat for many soldiers. Earlier in the book he speaks of "the intimacy of life in infantry battalions, where the communion between men is as profound as any between lovers" (xv), but just two pages later he states that "at times, the comradeship that was the war's only redeeming quality caused some of its worst crimes— acts of retribution for friends who had been killed" (xvii). What separates Caputo's Vietnam soldiers from the soldiers of World War II is this doubleness, this clear sense that evil and good are inextricably mixed in war, and that the soldiers must see themselves as individuals capable of acting and therefore capable of performing evil actions. World War I and II soldiers tended to see themselves as passive, as being acted upon by the war and by their societies. The anger that the soldier-writers of earlier wars turn upon their societies the Vietnam soldier-writers tend to turn upon themselves. Thus, Stan Platke writes in "And Then There Were None":

> Yea as I walk through the valley of death
> I shall fear no evil
> For the valleys are gone
> And only death awaits
> And I am the evil. (Rottman 101)

The differences between the literature of World War II and that of the Vietnam War suggest a relationship between each literature and the military culture that produced it. An analysis of this relationship provides a starting point from which to consider many of the literary aspects of the works which have been produced by Vietnam participants.

Specifically, a close study of the military circumstances will help us to isolate the specific ways in which this literature differs from the participant literature that emerged from earlier twentieth-century wars and also to isolate those themes and motifs which speak of a common experience. For example, the series of military decisions which caused the Vietnam War to be a much more solitary experience than earlier wars and the emphasis on causing death rather than capturing territory give us a line of departure from which to consider the deeply introspective nature of this literature and why the rage these men feel is turned inward upon themselves rather than back upon the society that sent them to war. Very little attention has been paid to these issues in the study of the voluminous literature produced by participants in the Vietnam War. We need to look more closely at the military cultures that inform participant war narratives in order to understand the differences between works by veterans of different wars.

WORKS CITED

Caputo, Philip. *A Rumor of War*. 1977. New York: Ballantine, 1978.

Cincinnatus. *Self-Destruction: The Disintegration and Decay of the United States Army during the Vietnam Era*. New York: Norton, 1981.

Gibson, James William. *The Perfect War: The War We Couldn't Lose and How We Did*. New York: Vintage, 1988.

Heinemann, Larry. *Close Quarters*. New York: Farrar, 1977.

Herr, Michael. *Dispatches*. New York: Knopf, 1977.

Keegan, John. *The Face of Battle: A Study of Agincourt, Waterloo and the Somme*. 1976. New York: Penguin, 1978.

Lifton, Robert Jay. *Home from the War: Vietnam Veterans, neither Victims nor Executioners*. New York: Simon, 1973.

MacDonald, Charles B. *Company Commander*. 1947. New York: Bantam, 1978.

Murphy, Audie. *To Hell and Back*. New York: Holt, 1949.

Rottman, Larry, Jan Barry, and Basil T. Pacquet, eds. *Winning Hearts and Minds: War Poems by Vietnam Veterans*. New York: McGraw-Hill, 1972.

Weigley, Russell F. *Eisenhower's Lieutenants: The Campaigns of France and Germany, 1944–1945*. Vol. 2. Bloomington: Indiana University Press, 1981.

Speaking the Language of Pain

Vietnam War Literature in

the Context of a Literature

of Trauma

O   O   O   O   O   O   O   O   O

Kali Tal

My intent here is to explore the traditional stance of critics writing about Vietnam War literature, to point out the failures and limitations of this stance, and to suggest a new way of interpretation based on a theory of literature of trauma. To posit a literature of trauma one must assume that the identity of the author as author is inseparable from the identity of author as trauma survivor. This means that literature written about the trauma of others is qualitatively different from literature by trauma survivors. Survivor narratives are linked across topic lines; narratives by those personally uninvolved with the trauma are not. This distinction connects literature by Vietnam veterans to Holocaust literature, A-bomb literature, the literature of combat veterans of other wars, rape literature, and incest literature. Literature of trauma, I will argue, is the product of three coincident factors: the experience of trauma, the urge to bear witness, and a sense of community. Trauma literature demonstrates the unbridgeable gap between writer and reader and thus defines itself by the impossibility of its task—the communication of the traumatic experience. This inherent contradiction within literature by Vietnam veterans has been ignored or misunderstood by all of the critics of Vietnam War literature.

Four important book-length studies on the literature of the Vietnam War have been written, all since 1982. Philip D. Beidler's *American Literature and the Experience of Vietnam* was published in 1982, the same year that James C. Wilson's *Vietnam in Prose and Film* appeared. John Hellmann's study *American Myth and the Legacy of Vietnam* followed in 1986, and Thomas Myers's *Walking Point: American Narratives of Vietnam* was issued in 1988. In order to understand the established methodological basis of critical evaluation of Vietnam War literature we must examine the strategies of these authors. As I shall demonstrate, all four of them have a similar—and ultimately inadequate—approach to the literature.

Beidler proposes a strong connection between classic American literature and the literature of the Vietnam War. Cooper, Conrad, Melville, and Twain created heroes who prefigured the heroes in Vietnam War novels. Beidler asserts:

> American writing about Vietnam, for all one's sense of the new and even unprecedented character of the experience it describes, often turns out to be very much in context . . . with regard to our national traditions of literature and popular myth-making at large. . . . [It] seems almost as if our classic inheritance of native expression has prophesied much of what we now know of Vietnam, made it by self-engendering symbolic fiat part of our collective mythology long before it existed in fact. (19)

Our classic literature embodies cultural myths which then have an effect upon our understandings of current events, influencing the course of history.

For Beidler, myth and actual events seem to be equally involved in generating history, a strangely retroactive process in which we revise our interpretations of the past as new cultural myths are generated that affect our future decisions and actions. This trend is reflected in

Vietnam War literature, he says, in the emergence of "a certain iden-tifiable centrality of vision." This centrality is rooted in the "under-standing that just as the 'real' war itself so often proved a hopeless tangle of experiential fact and projected common myth, so a 'true' lit-erary comprehending of it would come only as a function of experien-tial remembrance and imaginative invention considered in some rela-tionship to near-absolute reflexiveness" (195). By weighing equally real experience and mythic construction, Beidler collapses time and space, giving Cooper's Deerslayer the same authority as Philip Ca-puto, veteran and writer of Vietnam narratives.[1] Beidler conflates the fictional characters of classic American writers and the memoirs of Vietnam veterans. Beidler's goal seems to be to reduce the war to sign—to see Vietnam War literature as part of a continuing process of signification. The telling and retelling of the war inscribe it upon the nation's consciousness until "we have learned at what cost it was waged for everyone it touched then and now and beyond." When the signification is complete the war will be over: "Then we can say good-bye to it" (202). There is an urge to closure in Beidler's analysis. When the war becomes sign (and therefore not war) we won't have to think about it anymore.

James Wilson's perspective is more political than literary:

> I am not concerned with a purely formalist analysis here; rather I am interested in this body of literature and film for what it tells us about ourselves and our culture. For these works reflect the difficulties we have in comprehending the war; our evasions, our distortions, our denials. And yet, at the same time, they reflect our limited successes too. The best of the Vietnam books and films provide an invaluable record of the initial steps we have taken toward facing the unpleasant truth of an unpleasant war. (7)

He thinks it unimportant to connect Vietnam War literature to main-stream American literature, preferring to point out the special fea-tures of the literature:

> Almost all Vietnam writers and directors share an apocalyptic vi-sion of the war's end. . . . The world born in Vietnam becomes a monstrosity of senseless violence and random destruction. . . .

Out of this collective vision comes a literature and a cinema of despair laced with death. . . . The end, then, is physical annihilation, purely and simply. (100–101)

An important feature of the literature is that "the Vietnam writers and directors imply the destruction of human values and human morality" (101). To Wilson, this portrayal of annihilation and the destruction of values and morality is a metaphor for the current American cultural crisis, taking "to an extreme the unreality, the discontinuity, and the loss of values that may characterize much of our experience in America today . . ." (101). The answer to this crisis is to listen to the words of the Vietnam veterans rather than to the politicians. We must confront the reality of the war in Southeast Asia and take responsibility for the crimes our nation committed rather than succumb to the rationalizations provided by politicians who describe Vietnam as a noble cause.

Wilson is looking for reality while Beidler denies the existence of the real war. Vietnam War literature is a useful tool, a warning for Americans: "If we try, we can save the next generation from being crucified a decade from now in distant lands whose names we barely recognize now. We can prevent another misbegotten war" (102). Wilson demands political awareness from both his writers and readers: we read Vietnam War literature in order to learn what not to do next time.

Hellmann's work seems to be closer to the spirit of Beidler's analysis than to Wilson's. Also concerned with the question of the continuity of classical American cultural myths, he claims that Vietnam War literature reflects a national disillusionment with the frontier myth upon which we based our involvement in Vietnam and that veterans "have presented a Southeast Asian landscape that overturns the meaning of the previously known landscapes of American myth" (207).

The American mythic landscape is a place fixed between savagery and civilization, a middle landscape where the hero sheds the unnecessary refinements of the latter without entering into the darkness of the former. Ever-receding, this frontier gains its validation as a setting for the mythic hero because his killing makes way for the progress of the civilization advancing behind him. In the memoirs of the Vietnam War, however, the American hero has

somehow entered a nightmarish wilderness where he is allowed
no linear direction nor clear spreading of civilization, where neither his inner restraints nor the external ones of his civilization
are operating. (135)

This disruption may, Hellmann suggests, enable us to stretch our cultural perceptions enough to include the reality of the Vietnam experience.

Hellmann charges artists with the mission of taking the American
people "on their second journey through Vietnam. In the best of their
works, that meant finally moving back toward the realm of fantasy—of
symbolic imagining—to discover the continuing dimensions of Vietnam as a terrain of the American psyche. Having entered Vietnam as
a symbolic landscape, Americans would through highly imaginative
narrative art have to find their way back out to American myth, enabling them to journey again forward into history" (137). The contradictions contained within this argument are stunning: in order to understand the reality of the Vietnam War we must first properly
fantasize it—reduce it to a "symbolic landscape." The function of the
real event is the re-creation of a symbolic event (myth) which through
some mystical turnabout helps us to understand reality. Only then,
says Hellmann, will we be able "to journey again forward into history."

Hellmann asserts that "no nation can survive without a myth," and
that the best myths lie somewhere between "a cynical 'realism' " and a
"self-deluding fantasy" (222). He envisions a myth for America that
embraces our uniqueness and allows us to see ourselves as more than
an "ordinary country":

The United States certainly has had reason to feel a special obligation to the rest of the world. Its geography . . . allowed the
modern world's first republic to settle its major issues, develop its
institutions, and form its character without interference. In the
process, America became a nation identified, at its best, with possibility and freedom and progress. . . . We can see that the deeply
flawed past, from which the nation began by declaring its independence, is truly our father. But we can also see that only a second
failure, of nerve, would cause us then to draw back from the
American frontier, from our own better dreams. . . . Perhaps

from the landscape of our Vietnam failure, we can find a new determination to brave the opening expanse. (223–224)

In Hellmann's eyes the best Vietnam literature and the best new American literature help us reformulate a myth we can live with. Each element of Hellmann's myth is, of course, historically inaccurate (as are all generalizations), but what is important in his mythmaking effort is the assertion that as a nation we can continue on the road to progress: the journey forward into history. The Vietnam War, then, becomes a trial on the American path to progress—an episode in the development of the American character. Predicated on this artificial notion of progress the search for meaning becomes compromised: the assumption of the progressive "fact" becomes grounds for the disqualification of all Vietnam War (and all American) literature that does not support his thesis.

Thomas Myers borrows much from the arguments of Beidler and Hellman in his 1988 study, *Walking Point*. Fascinated by the interplay of history and myth in the generation of war narratives, he insists that it is in this literary genre that "the leviathan of the national cultural paradigm" can "sound and surface." War narrative can serve as both a record of history and a cultural document "as it responds to the rending and reconstituting of national mythos" (10–11). The war novel illustrates three crises: historical, cultural, aesthetic. Myers believes that historical and aesthetic changes occur simultaneously and that the proper response of the author to the uselessness of older American myths is to "light out for new aesthetic territory and begin anew" (13), basing new mythical constructions on the ruins of the earlier myths. Vietnam veteran writers resurrect the "secret history" of the war and serve as conduits for the experience of the soldier: the metamorphosis of the raw recruit into the hardened warrior serves as metaphor for the process which deforms and then reshapes the American self-image.

Unlike previous critics of Vietnam War literature, Myers admits that he has come face to face with a phenomenon that he does not fully understand: "With all its aesthetic restructurings, behind its many necessary transformations of the conventions of a specific literary tradition, there is in even the most powerful writing something that language cannot reach or explicate, an experience that words point toward but that only the reader's own creative energies can begin to trace" (31–32). But this observation is quickly abandoned as he takes up the task of the critic, examining various works and generating prescriptions for the writing and reading of Vietnam War literature:

> The writers who have produced what are likely to be the most lasting documents of the war are those who have assessed and incorporated into their works the battle of words and images that transformed the war into something as much symbolic as real. To do battle in compensatory history with the [war] managers' capacity for illusion and euphemism, the writer is required to first retrieve and then re-create the feelings, rhythms, and specific images that remained largely sequestered behind conveniently reconciled history and to place those components in opposition to the dominant text: in effect, both to reconstruct and to invent a historical debate. The failure of the managers to supply validation for human sacrifice is the true American defeat in Vietnam, one that placed the responsibility for the retrieval of meaning firmly on the shoulders of each soldier, citizen, journalist, and artist. (142)

Myers, like Wilson, has an explicit political agenda. Like Hellmann, he regards the mythmaking process as a crucial political tool (though his political ends seem closer to Wilson's than to Hellmann's). Like Beidler and Hellmann, Myers believes that the Vietnam War was "as much symbolic as real" (142). Like Beidler, he asserts that the war is not over until it is properly signified. The common assumptions of these four authors guarantee that they will come to similar conclusions which are seriously flawed.

The incapacity of traditional critics to deal with the literature of the Vietnam War is exemplified in their inevitable and total reduction of the war to metaphor. Because their critical strategies cannot encompass the actual events of the war, they must ignore these events and concentrate on symbol and image. Wilson's assertion that the war was an "illustration" of the destruction of American values (101–102) is the mildest of these offenses against the memory of those individuals who actually suffered and died in Vietnam. More disturbing are Hellmann's statement that "the enduring trauma of Vietnam has been the disruption of the American story" (221); Beidler's remark that "the 'real' war so often proved a hopeless tangle of experiential fact and projected common myth" (195); and Myers's incredible claim that "the most perceptive observers knew that the real battle was being waged not in the new geographical landscape of men and machines, but within the terrain of collective imagination, an area where the surface images of the war became a mere light show that dissolved in the stronger illumination of persistent cultural realities" (147).

The unfortunate truth is that the Vietnam War was the work of no one's imagination; it was, rather, a devastating reality—a series of events taking place on a physical rather than symbolic level. Only in memory or in narrative can war be elevated to the level of symbol; narratives are generated in retrospect in order to explain, rationalize, and define events. The symbols that narrators create to represent their wartime experiences are generated out of the war's traumatic events. They are frequently symbols for which the untraumatized have no parallels and thus are in no position to interpret correctly if they have not paid careful attention to the events upon which these symbols are based. The problem with traditional literary interpretation is that it assumes that all symbols are accessible to all readers—that the author and the reader speak a common language when in fact they do not. Their inability to see the inaccessibility of the symbolic universe of the survivor leads critics to dismiss the real war and its devastating effect on the individual author and to replace it with a set of symbols which describe the internal crisis of the American character. This problem is rooted in the conflation of two very different but constantly intersecting kinds of myth: national myth and personal myth.

National (collective) myth is propagated in such places as textbooks, official histories, popular-culture documents, and public schools. This myth belongs to no one individual, though individuals borrow from it and buy into it in varying degrees. Beidler's "cultural myths" and Hellmann's and Myers's "American myths" are collective myths which comprise our concepts of what America and the American character are. National myth, as these writers suggest, can be gradually revised as new elements are introduced into the public discourse and old ideas become outmoded. A major upheaval can introduce new ideas and images which are adopted into the popular consciousness. For example, the replacement of the horse by the automobile gradually made the traditional cowboy hero obsolete (now a beloved though outdated relic of the American past) and spurred the development of new heroes who drove cars. The hardboiled detectives who became popular heroes in the twenties and thirties have their roots in the lone cowboy hero of earlier years.

Personal myth is the particular set of explanations and expectations generated by an individual to account for his or her circumstances and actions. Psychologist Daniel Goleman suggests that personal myths take the form of schemas—unconscious assumptions about experience and the way the world works. The schemas operating in a particular situation determine the actual information an individual absorbs and interprets. Such operations inevitably skew perceptions of events; in fact, that is their purpose. The misinterpretation of what goes on around us is frequently useful as a coping strategy if a properly inter-preted event threatens important, foundational schemas. This process results in the "trade-off of a distorted awareness for a sense of secu-rity," and Goleman believes that this is an organizing principle of hu-man existence (21). Grand revision of a personal myth must always spring from a traumatic experience, for the mechanism which main-tains those foundational schemas will automatically distort or revise all but the most shattering revelations. Chaim Shatan, a psychiatrist who works with Vietnam combat veterans and other survivors of trauma, describes this drastic uprooting of belief as the "basic wound" which creates a new, permanent, and adaptive life-style (179).

The conflation of national and personal myth by traditional critics of Vietnam War literature is supported by their failure to distinguish be-tween works by combat veterans and those by nonveterans. Though a nod is always given to the value of veterans' writing (which gives us the "real" flavor of the war as it reveals the "secret history"), the uni-versal tendency of these critics ultimately is to compare on the same terms Graham Greene's *The Quiet American*, Lederer and Burdick's *The Ugly American*, and Norman Mailer's *Why Are We in Vietnam?* with Philip Caputo's *A Rumor of War*, O'Brien's *Cacciato*, and Herr's *Dispatches*. Whether, like Beidler, the critics believe that most Viet-nam War literature is written by veterans or, like Hellmann, that vet-erans play only a small role in the process of revising American myth, they never consider the possibility that *literatures* (rather than a lit-erature) of the Vietnam War might exist.

War literature by nonveterans can be critiqued in the same manner as other genre literatures. These works are the products of the authors' urge to tell a story, make a point, create an aesthetic experience, or move people in a particular way. Nonveteran literature is, in short, the product of a literary decision. To nonveteran writers, the war is simply a metaphor, a vehicle for their message—just as the war is a metaphor in the eyes of literary critics such as Wilson, Beidler, Hellmann, and Myers. The "real war" about which they write is the war of symbols and images.

For combat veterans, however, the personal investment of the author is immense. Retelling the war in a memoir or describing it in a novel involves not merely the development of alternative national myths through the manipulation of plot and literary techniques, but also the necessary rebuilding of shattered personal myths. To understand the literature of these veterans we must embrace critical strategies from various disciplines which acknowledge the peculiar position of the survivor-author.

Eric J. Leed's *No Man's Land: Combat and Identity in World War I* suggests a new subject for interdisciplinary study—"the transformation of personality in war"—and provides scholars with a new methodological approach. Stating first that his book is neither military history, literary analysis, nor psychohistory, Leed proposes a theory of transformation which incorporates both psychological examination of human response in wartime and the examination of the effect of cultural myth upon human reaction to war. Borrowing concepts from psychiatry, anthropology, history, and literary criticism, Leed discusses World War I as a "modernizing experience":

> World War I fundamentally altered traditional sources of identity, age-old images of war and men of war. The Great War was a nodal point in the history of industrial civilization because it brought together material realities and "traditional" mentalities in an unexpectedly disillusioning way. . . . The disillusioning realization of the inherent similitude of industrial societies and the wars they wage . . . eviscerated, drained, and confounded the logic upon which the moral significance of war and the figure of the warrior had been based. (193–194)

Leed makes good use of Arnold Van Gennep's anthropological theory which "divided rites of passage into three phases: rites of separation, which remove an individual or group of individuals from his or their accustomed place; liminal rites, which symbolically fix the character of the 'passenger' as one who is between states, places, or conditions; and finally rites of incorporation (postliminal rites), which welcome the individual back into the group" (14). Leed claims that liminality was the condition of the soldier at the front in World War I, and that rather than passing into the postliminal phase upon his return, the veteran continued to be a "liminal type": "He derives all of his features from the fact that he has crossed the boundaries of disjunctive social worlds, from peace to war, and back. He has been reshaped by his voyage along the margins of civilization, a voyage in which he has been presented with wonders, curiosities, and monsters—things that can only be guessed at by those who remained at home" (194). The theory of liminality describes a process of symbolic production based on the traumatic experiences of those entering the transitional or liminal state. But the symbols generated by liminality are readable only to those familiar with the alphabet of trauma; what they represent is not common knowledge, and, in fact, symbols that commonly represent a particular idea may be drastically transformed within the mind of the liminal type. For example, the symbolism in the Holocaust survivor's description of a bread oven is entirely different from the same invocation by a nontraumatized author.

Calling World War I "the first holocaust," Leed asserts that it was destined to lead to World War II: "Those who had internalized the war, its peculiar relationship between victims and victimizers, the liminality that it imposed upon combatants, were destined to play a significant part in this repetition. For many could not resolve the ambiguities that defined their identities in war and resume their place in civilian society without acknowledging their status as victims" (213). World War I provided a crushing blow to the fictions by which they lived their lives.

Gerald F. Linderman advances a similar argument in *Embattled Courage: The Experience of Combat in the American Civil War*, emphasizing the internal changes undergone by those who experienced combat. He rarely distinguishes between Union and Confederate soldiers, insisting that the psychological and sociological effects of combat were roughly equivalent in both groups. Linderman divides his book into two sections. The first describes the expectations and ideals of the men who joined the Union and Confederate armies; the second section deals with the increasing disillusionment and anger of these soldiers when they found the war was not at all like what they had imagined. Though he does not use the same terminology as Leed does, his characterization of veterans' liminality is quite similar.

After the Civil War, combat veterans returned to a society that still held those notions about war which soldiers knew from hard experience to be outdated (if indeed they ever had any validity). But the new truths that soldiers had discovered were out of place at home: "Killing once again became homicide; foraging was again theft, and incendiarism arson. Even language was a problem: Camp talk had to be cleaned up" (267). In order to cope with the demands of everyday life, soldiers had to rewrite their war experiences, smoothing over the difficult parts and revising the unpleasantness:

> While forgetfulness worked to efface painful experience, soldiers construed bad memories in a way that smoothed their departure. When they were able to discuss the problem among themselves, soldiers ordinarily did so under a rubric—"Time heals all wounds"—revelatory of their assumptions. Disturbing memories were to be kept to oneself, not to be aired publicly to relieve the sufferer and certainly not to correct public misapprehension of the nature of combat. (268)

Like Leed, Linderman believes that soldiers who remembered correctly would be forced to acknowledge their role as victims. Linderman and Leed also agree that veterans had a strong role in supporting and encouraging American involvement in a subsequent war. Participating gratefully in commemoration efforts, Civil War veterans benefited from and supported the revival of American interest in martial matters. "Although they remained 'men set apart,' their separation had been granted public recognition and their estrangement elevated to civic virtue" (280). Even veterans who had earlier been antiwar and alienated began to take part and encourage this martial spirit. This revision was so complete that by 1898 the nation enthusiastically applauded the start of the Spanish-American War. The old values were reestablished: "Civil War veterans had become symbols of changelessness—but only by obliterating or amending an experience of combat so convulsive of their values that it had for a time cut the cord of experience" (297).

These two important studies point us in a new direction, urging us toward an understanding of the personal revision process and its interaction with historical myth. Though they confine their discussion to the experience of the combat soldier, both authors describe a reaction to trauma that is not limited to men at war. Recent work in psychiatry suggests that we can make a connection between the trauma of soldiers and the trauma of other persons subjected to severe stress. Studies on posttraumatic stress disorder have shown that symptoms may be found in large percentages of traumatized populations, including Holocaust, A-bomb, rape, incest, prison camp, refugee camp, and natural disaster survivors.[2] Trauma is a transforming experience, and those who are transformed can never entirely return to a state of innocence. According to Lawrence L. Langer, "The survivor does not travel a road from the normal to the bizarre back to the normal, but from the normal to the bizarre back to a normalcy so permeated by the bizarre encounter with atrocity that it can never be purified again. The two worlds haunt each other . . ." (88). "After Auschwitz," writes Elie Wiesel, "everything brings us back to Auschwitz" (205). A careful study of the literature produced by trauma survivors points to a certain uniformity of experience and unanimity of intention which transcend the particular incidents described.

One of the strongest themes in the literature of trauma is the urge to bear witness, to carry the tale of horror back to the halls of normalcy and to testify to the truth of the experience. "In one sense, all writing about the Holocaust represents a retrospective effort to give meaningless history a context of meaning, to furnish the mind with a framework for insight without diminishing the sorrow of the event itself. Knowledge of the past cannot be exorcised . . ." (Langer 185). To be a survivor is to be bound to the dead, to impose upon oneself what Robert Jay Lifton calls "an impossible standard of literal recreation of 'how things were,' a kind of sacred historical truth, which leads to what might be called the documentary fallacy; or else a need to glorify the dead and deny them the dignity of their limitations" (*History* 206).

This universal drive to testify is articulated by trauma victims across traditional genre lines. Wiesel asserts, "I never intended to be a philosopher or a theologian. The only role I sought was witness. I believed that, having survived by chance, I was duty-bound to give meaning to my survival, to justify each moment of my life. I knew the story had to be told. Not to transmit an experience is to betray it . . ." (200–201). He is echoed by Vietnam veteran Larry Lee Rottman, who stated at the Winter Soldier investigations:

> There is a question in many people's minds here. They say, "Well, why do you talk now? Why do you come here and tell us these things that happened two, three, maybe four, five years ago? I'm here, speaking personally, because I can't not be here. I'm here because, like, I have nightmares about things that happened to me and my friends. I'm here because my conscience will not let me forget what I want to forget.
>
> I didn't want to talk about it when I first got back, you know, I didn't want to talk about it at all. But it gets to the point where you have to talk to somebody, and when I tried to talk to somebody, even my parents, they didn't want to know. And that made me realize that no matter how painful it was for me, I had to tell them. I mean, they had to know. The fact that they didn't want to know, told me they had to know. (Vietnam Veterans, *The Winter Soldier* 163–164)[3]

Jill Morgan, a victim of childhood sexual abuse, explains her desire to speak out in similar terms:

> A close personal friend (male) has asked me repeatedly, "Why do you have to rehash it? It happened. It's over. Now forget it and go on." Only by owning myself and my past, by affirming and confirming my innocence in the whole, sordid drama can I rest and feel comfortable with myself.
>
> If my survival is to be meaningful at all to me, it must be because it gave me the strength to fight, the will to survive and the empathy to reach out to other women. (Thornton 20)

Each of these authors articulates the belief that he or she is a storyteller with a mission; their responsibility as survivors is to bear the tale. Each also affirms the process of storytelling as a personally reconstitutive act and expresses the hope that it will also be a socially

reconstitutive act—changing the order of things as they are and working to prevent the enactment of similar horrors in the future.

But the task of the trauma author is an impossible one. For if the
goal is to convey the traumatic experience, no secondhand rendering
of it is adequate. The horrific events which have reshaped the author's
construction of reality can only be described, not re-created. The com-
bination of the drive to testify and the impossibility of re-creating the
event is one of the defining characteristics of trauma literature: "Could
it be surmounted? Could the reader be brought to the other side? I
knew the answer to be negative, and yet I also knew that 'no' had to
become 'yes'. . . . One had to break the shell enclosing the dark truth,
and give it a name. One had to force man to look" (Wiesel 201).

Caught forever in this liminal state, the survivor comes to represent
the shattering of our national myths without ever coming close to
shattering the reader's individual personal myths—the very myths
that support and uphold the most widely accepted national myths. No
grand restructuring of national myths can actually be accomplished
without a concurrent destruction of the personal myths which words
simply cannot reach. In a pioneer study, Terrance Des Pres describes
the survivor as "a disturber of the peace": "He is a runner of the
blockade men erect against knowledge of 'unspeakable' things. About
these he aims to speak, and in so doing he undermines, without in-
tending to, the validity of existing norms" (42). But the impact of the
survivor's strongest message—that his or her traumatic suffering
was seemingly without purpose, arbitrary, outside the framework of
meaning—simply cannot be absorbed by the reader, whose framework
of meaning remains essentially intact. It is this paradox which leads
John Hellmann to say:

> "Getting used to" moving through the perils of time without the
> assurance of luck, without the conviction of a special grace con-
> ferred by a special geography, is precisely the function of the lit-
> erary and cinematic narratives which American artists have pro-
> duced in response to the Vietnam experience. The stories through
> which we have retaken the Vietnam journey have presented a
> Southeast Asian landscape that overturns the meaning of the pre-
> viously known landscapes of American myth. These narratives

purge us, forcing the reader or viewer to reexperience, this time self-consciously, the tragic shattering of our old myths. This process may prepare the culture to accept a significant alteration of our view of ourselves and of our world, a new mythic interpretation of our historical experience that will intelligibly include the experience of Vietnam. (206–207)

Survivors never get used to losing their sense of meaning; they are forever changed by it. Many are transformed into liminal figures who must remain, like ghostly Cassandras, on the fringes of society. Some manage to become postliminal by repressing or revising their experiences, though this is seldom a completely successful tactic since the revelatory nature of their experiences has shown them the inadequacy of "normal" concepts of meaning in the world. Expression, in the form of narration, is frequently a step on the journey toward becoming postliminal, toward rewriting the traumatic events which severed their connections to the rest of society. The journey back is a journey based on rejection of experience. Untraumatized readers and viewers cannot retake a journey through a Vietnam they never actually visited and thus cannot reexperience a "tragic shattering" of old myths. I cannot emphasize too strongly the fact that the personal myths of the reader are never tragically shattered by reading. Only trauma can accomplish that kind of destruction. The revision of national myth occurs only as far as the changes made do not interfere with untraumatized persons' basic conceptions of themselves.

The inability to communicate trauma is evident in the preoccupation of trauma authors with the limitations of language. Once again, this preoccupation is evident across genre lines:

> We all knew that we could never, never say what had to be said, that we could never express in words, coherent, intelligible words, our experience of madness on an absolute scale. . . . The language of night was not human; it was primitive, almost animal. . . . A brute striking wildly, a body falling; an officer raises his arm and a whole community walks toward a common grave. . . . This is the concentration camp language. It negated all other language and took its place. Rather than link, it became wall. (Wiesel 201)

In his first novel, *Close Quarters*, Vietnam combat veteran Larry Heinemann inscribes his protagonist's deep sense of alienation, a barrier that language cannot surmount:

> I have travelled to a place where the dead lie above the ground in rows and bunches. Time has gone somewhere without me. This is not my country, not my time. My skin is drawn tight around my eyes. My clothes smell of blood. I bleed inside. I am water. I am stone. I have not come home, Ma. I have gone ahead, gone back. There is glass between us, we cannot speak. (289)

For at least twenty years the subject of language as a limitation on the expression of women's thought has been discussed in feminist circles.[4] It may be that a partial explanation for the silence of women is that such a large percentage of us have survived the trauma of rape, incest, or battering. Our stories may not be incoherent or inarticulately told but simply inconceivable—as the stories of other liminal types are inconceivable. A continuing history of gynocidal persecution may well have resulted in the current perception that male language cannot encompass our experience:

> We know only the language of these folks who enter and occupy us: they keep telling us that we are different from them; yet we speak only their language and have none, or none that we remember, of our own; and we do not dare, it seems invent one, even in signs and gestures. Our bodies speak their language. Our minds think in it. The men are inside us through and through. We hear something, a dim whisper, barely audible, somewhere at the back of the brain; there is some other word, and we think, some of us, sometimes, that once it belonged to us. (Dworkin 134–135)

Andrea Dworkin's assertion is strikingly similar to Sidra Ezrahi's observation about the transformation of the German language by the Nazi system, "whose syntax, style, and symbolic associations were profoundly and abidingly violated by what came to be known as 'Nazi-Deutsch,' the perverse rhetoric that signified the collective actions of the National Socialists" (11). Ezrahi argues that the ideology of Nazism extended into "every area of cultural expression," literally taking over the language. Preoccupied with maintaining written records yet determined to conceal the actions of the state from the outside world, the Nazis "created a complex of verbal acrobatics which subsequent generations of linguists would strive painstakingly to sort out" (11). Much German postwar writing, she claims, is "an attempt to purge, through subtle parodies, and ironic reversals of traditional literary modes and forms of speech, the language and the literature of their implication in the crimes of Nazism" (11).

Des Pres says that "extremity makes bad art because events are too obviously 'symbolic'" (176). Reality so violates personal mythologies during traumatic events that symbol seems to transcend itself and take physical form. Des Pres devotes an entire chapter of *The Survivor* to this process, which he refers to as "excremental assault," using as his example the literal immersion of concentration camp victims in shit. The physical experience of being forced to wear, eat, or swim in excrement, he argues, is not nearly as devastating as the violation of psychological and social boundaries which have been constructed around the biological processes of elimination. These violations strike at the very core of the victim's conception of self in the world, forcing the most radical restructuring of personal myth which must be revised to include the previously unthinkable.

Immersion in shit is still, for the reader, a metaphor. No violation of personal mythology is entailed in reading about excremental assault on other people. The social and psychological boundaries are still intact. Other examples of the reader's inherent inability to encompass such violations of personal myth abound. The most common is the description of the burning of corpses in the ovens of Auschwitz, tens of thousands of individuals literally becoming the rising smoke—a strong image but not a metaphorical one. Yet in the reader's mind the rising smoke must become symbol once again:

> The concentration camps have done what art always does: they have brought us face to face with archetypes, they have invested body with mind and mind with body, they have given visible embodiment to man's spiritual universe, so that the primary states of good and evil are resident in the look and sound and smell of things. The essence of survival is passage through death; this way of speaking may be metaphorical for us, but not for survivors. . . .

The survivor is not a metaphor, not an emblem, but *an example*.
(Des Pres 176)

A crucial question, and one which is rarely explored in studies of either Holocaust or war literature, is, To whom does the survivor bear witness? To begin to answer this question we must examine carefully the trauma victim's notion of self and community.

Each of the traumas I have discussed has as its victims a group of persons definable by characteristics of race, sex, religion, or geographical location. If the members of a persecuted group define themselves as a community bonded by their common misfortune and see their individual sufferings as part of a common plight, then and only then will the urge to bear witness be present. A trauma victim who perceives himself or herself as suffering alone, who has no sense of belonging to a community of victims, will remain silent, imagining that his or her pain has no relevance to the larger society. Such victims will likely come to believe that they have, in some way, brought their suffering upon themselves. Internalizing blame for the evils which befall one is difficult to escape even when the notion of community exists;[5] it is all but impossible to avoid when one feels no connection with a community of victims. The community of Holocaust victims, the community of combat survivors, and the community of rape and incest survivors are very different in composition, and thus the work of bearing witness is quite different within each of them.

Holocaust survivors see themselves most clearly as members of a community of victims:

Firsthand accounts of life in the concentration camps almost never focus on the trials of the writer apart from his or her comrades, apart from the thousands of identical others whose names were never known. Books by survivors are invariably group portraits, in which the writer's personal experience is representative and used to provide a perspective on the common plight. Survival is a collective act, and so is bearing witness. Both are rooted in compassion and care, and both expose the illusion of separateness. It is not an exaggeration, nor merely a metaphor, to say that the survivor's identity includes the dead. (Des Pres 38)

Des Pres claims that the task of survivors is to wake the conscience of the greater community and that the testimony of survivors bears witness to "objective conditions of evil" which will naturally arouse the sympathies of ordinary people. "Conscience," writes Des Pres, "is a social achievement" (46). He assumes that the terror and mass murder visited upon the community of victims is irregular and distinguishably evil, that all good people everywhere would object to such acts if only they were aware of their commission. Holocaust victims are a part of both the community of victims and the greater community of good people to whom they can appeal.

Survival literature tends to appear at least a decade after the traumatic experience in question.[6] As the immediacy of the event fades into memory, the natural process of revision begins to occur in the mind of the survivor. The dislocation of trauma, which removed meaning from the world, is gradually replaced by new stories about the past which can support a rewritten personal myth. The survivor's perception of community is a crucial element in the shaping of the new myth. To Jews with strong feelings of community with other Jews, testimony becomes a rallying cry, leading to the pledge, "Never again!" Previously assimilated Jews with little sense of belonging to the Jewish community[7] may identify with the greater community of "good people" whom Des Pres describes and tell their stories to appeal to the conscience of the world. The Holocaust can serve as a justification for the creation of the state of Israel and thus take its place in the greater story of Jewish history. Survivors can make sense of their sufferings by creating a historical context.

Without a sense of community power testimony is useless, for testimonials have as their premise sympathetic listeners with the power to prevent the re-creation of such traumatic experiences in the future. Natalie Shainess makes connections across traumas when she ties the silence of the abused child to the silence of the Jews in Nazi Germany: "Why doesn't she tell her mother? Why doesn't she run away? Why doesn't she go to the police? It calls to mind the problem of Jews in Nazi Germany: how many Germans would go against their own interests to help? What hope was there? Who would listen, who would believe?" (vi).

The need for a powerful community within which and to which one can testify is evident in the scarcity of testimony by victims of rape, incest, and other forms of sexual abuse. Less than 10 percent of the rapes in America are reported; abused women know that their stories will not be listened to. Though generally acknowledged by the psychiatric establishment as victims of severe trauma and suffering in numbers that would seem to indicate a distinct pattern of abuse, women who have been raped rarely testify publicly to their experiences. This is due in large part to the special context of women's trauma. For almost all other trauma victims there exists a "time before" and a "time after": a greater social structure in which the commission of crimes against the community is considered improper. Atrocities against women are grounded in a system that supports and even encourages crimes against women:

> In the traditional professional approach to dealing with violence, the legal system and the police in effect aided and abetted the woman-beater. Moreover, medical and social services were powerless, in fact, to provide even short-term or intermediate solutions to the problem of spousal violence. . . . A woman either was sent back home or went to stay with relatives. Whichever she chose, she remained vulnerable, easy to find, and thus a defence-less target for pressure and attack by her aggressor. The result was that she was forced to withdraw legal charges, resume her role as wife and mother and try to swallow her anger and bury her fear. (Beaudry 19)

Louise Wisechild, who testifies to incest, insists:

> Incest is not separate from other abusive messages in our social culture. I couldn't write about incest apart from what I was told as a girl-child growing up in the 50s and 60s. The religious attitudes of my childhood, the myths surrounding the "normal" family and my experience at school helped keep the incest a secret. These messages reinforced the self-hating images I saw in my internal mirror. In addition, each member of my family had a role in the dynamic of secrecy. (iv)

The victim of violence against women has no preatrocity conscious-ness, and interpretation of the event occurs in a mind which, at some level, expects atrocity and has been prepared for it since birth. Internalizing blame is a natural consequence of growing up in a dehumanizing system. We know that it is common for the victim of even unexpected trauma to feel responsibility for the event (for example, Lifton's comment about Hiroshima victims). How much easier it is to accept responsibility for an event when one has been raised listening to the insistent repetition of the phrase, "If it happens, it's your fault; you were looking for it."

Those few women who do testify about atrocities have a strong sense of community, chiefly with other women whom they see as potentially powerful enough to have an effect on the social, political, and economic structures that support sexual abuse. Louise Thornton believes that the testimony of a few abused women will reach other such women, unlocking "the power of the spoken or written word for the thousands of additional women who never told anyone" (22). Ellen Bass, writing in the introduction to the same anthology, claims:

> In this book, survivors of childhood sexual abuse use the power of speech to transform, to fuse secret shame, pain, and anger into a sharp useful tool, common as a kitchen knife, for cutting away lies and deception like rotten fruit, leaving the clean hard pit, that kernel of truth: these insults were inflicted, are inflicted, now, every day. The repercussions are deep and lasting. The will to survive is strong, the tenacity and beauty of survival inspiring. We are not alone. We are not to blame. We are innocent, innocent and powerful, worthy of our healing fury, self-love, and love for each other. (59)

The most important factor in a woman's decision to testify to atrocity is the feeling of sisterhood and the hope that the community of women will be strong enough to prevent the commission of atrocities in the future.

Unlike women and Holocaust victims, combat soldiers are physically removed from the civilian communities with which they identify; they are relocated to a new and foreign environment where previous notions of self are rendered useless and the development of a new set of personal myths is required. Basic training is designed to traumatize recruits, to systematically strip them of their civilian identity:

The recruit brings with him to Basic Training a set of values, beliefs, and expectations about his rights as an individual member of society. He has taken for granted a whole framework of supporting cultural factors, a conception of himself and his achievements which reflects the status he has been accorded in his past social environment, and a set of defensive maneuvers which have served him well in dealing with conflicts, failures, and other personal adversity. The early weeks of training are characterized by physical and verbal abuse, humiliation, and a constant discounting and discrediting of everything in which the recruit believes and everything which serves to characterize him as an individual. (Bourne 463–464)

According to Peter Bourne, the three goals of basic training are to destroy the recruits' civilian identities, to force them to acknowledge and accept discipline from the military, and to convince them of the validity and justice of the military system. Armed with this revised perspective on life, the soldiers are sent off to battle, believing that they have earned the right to join the ranks of the warrior. Once in combat, however, disillusion sets in, beginning the process of alienation so eloquently described by Leed and Linderman. Ideas of valor and heroism are undermined by the randomness of death in combat. The failure of the social myths upon which soldiers' personal myths are based occurs as the result of immediate and traumatic experience. Soldiers enter the liminal state and have no community outside of the war; like the Holocaust survivors, they have gone beyond metaphor: "Once there is a wedding of the symbolic world of language and the nonsymbolic world of physical experience, the realities of the war become 'things to think with,' to fantasize with, to apply in action within political and social contexts" (Leed 78).

The acts that soldiers commit in battle are comprehensible only in a world defined by war: the killing of human beings, the burning of homes, the defoliation of land. In "Beyond Atrocity," Robert Jay Lifton argues that much violence can be done by those desperate to define their world in a coherent manner. He calls atrocity "a perverse quest for meaning, the end result of a spurious sense of mission, the product of false witness" (23). At My Lai, for example, soldiers fired upon men, women, and children because they equated them with the enemy: "They were finally involved in a genuine 'military action,' their elusive adversaries had finally been located, made to stand still, and annihilated—an illustration, in other words, that they had finally put their world back in order" (Lifton, "Victims" 422). But the order of war cannot be assimilated into the order of civilian life, and combat soldiers returning home cannot recall their wartime experiences without negating the national myth. Soldiers who desire to bear witness against their own crimes in war and against the crimes of their nation speak to a community that does not wish to hear their story. Additionally, they know that to speak is to condemn themselves, to confess to crimes for which they would be punished under civilian law.

Langer tells of the SS doctor at Auschwitz who protested Nazi policies of selection for the gas chamber and refused to participate in the process. The infamous Dr. Mengele explained that the death sentence had already been passed on all Jews and that the process merely determined who would live for a short time longer. The doctor was persuaded and cooperated. When the war was over and he was to be arrested, the doctor killed himself. Langer suggests that the reason for his suicide lay in his inability to face "a traditional world of justice" whose values he had "never entirely repudiated" (122–123). Combat soldiers, too, are faced with the reestablishment of the "traditional world of justice"; if they have committed crimes, they suspect that they must ultimately be judged according to the rules of the society to which they have returned.

The process of psychic numbing is frequently an effective coping or delay mechanism for those who are not ready to acknowledge the enormous gap between their society's expectations and the wartime realities they experienced as soldiers. Vietnam veteran Al Hubbard describes the process:

> sacrificing a portion of your
>   consciousness so *you* won't have
>   to deal with
>   Being there
>   and
>   building mental blocks

so *you* won't have to deal with
having been there. (Kerry 92)

But veterans who are incapable of successfully repressing their combat experiences will be disturbed by the intrusion of memories of wartime actions into civilian life. This double vision is troubling, intolerable for some, including Rottman and the ninety-nine other Winter
Soldiers who testified to war crimes in 1971.

Also in 1971, some one thousand Vietnam veterans gathered in
Washington, D.C., and hurled their medals over the White House
fence, protesting U.S. involvement in Vietnam and the needless
deaths of tens of thousands of Vietnamese and Americans. The testimony of these men was given at tremendous personal cost: their con-
demnation of the American policy in Vietnam contained an implicit
criticism of their own complicity in acts of brutality and atrocity.
"There's not so much charm in war stories, you know," said Christo-
pher Soares, "but at times you have to tell war stories because what
happened to you in Vietnam is always on your conscience. There is so
much you have to get rid of in your mind. Sometimes I just stay up
half the night and cannot go to sleep because my mind bleeds from hell
when it goes back to Vietnam" (Kerry 116). At the same time, testi-
fying to crimes can be a purging experience—the confession which
purifies the soul and prepares it for readmission into the house of God.
By evaluating their acts in light of reestablished social and moral
norms, soldiers can put their experiences into context: "I was bad
then, but I'm good again now." Once they repent their crimes and suffer punishment they are free to rejoin contemporary society, sadder
but wiser. As veteran Bestor Cramm concluded:

The new American soldier, as I see it, is a person who has come
to a point in his life where he's rejected violence—he's seen too
much of it. He's been so much a part of it. He's learned about how
and to what extent human beings can really torture one another.
So now, he's thinking about the future, about his own kids, about
the other people who haven't been born yet, and how the last thing
in the world he could wish for would be for them to go through
what he's been through. He's got eyes that are set really deep,
because he's cried a lot. I think he's cried a lot in shame, for the

year, maybe two years of his life in which he killed, in which he raped the countryside, and I think that's a shame he's going to live with for his whole life. And that's a really incredibly hard road, I think, for the new American soldier because he has to accept the fact that he spent a portion of his life doing these things. (Kerry 152)

When Sgt. Jim Weber went to Vietnam he was a good soldier, trained to fight and kill. He believed in the American cause. But his attitude changed immediately when he witnessed the beatings of Vietnamese children: "And from there on, it was all downhill and, man, like I was a great American, and I think I still am a great American, you know" (Kerry 38). Obviously, Weber's notion of what makes a great American has undergone some drastic restructuring. This restructuring places Weber's definition of the great American in conflict with the tenets of national mythology: national mythology supports a war that Weber's great American would oppose.

If Weber were a lone voice, a man without a community, he would soon be drowned out by the multitude and his new mythology would go unnoticed. However, there is a community of combat survivors; or rather, there are multiple communities. One kind of community is composed of those who have rejected, repressed, and revised most of their war experiences until the parts that they can recall seem to be consonant with the greater body of national myth—these people belong to the VFW or the American Legion, support traditional patriotic ventures, and back U.S. policy in Central America. They mirror, in short, the community of Civil War veterans Linderman describes in *Embattled Courage*, veterans such as Oliver Wendell Holmes, Jr.:

In combat, twenty years earlier, he had undergone severe disillusionment. He had grown weary of such words as "cowardice," "gallantry," and "chivalry." In May 1863 he had prayed that he might lose a foot in order to escape a return to combat, and a year later he had feared that battle's "terrible pressure on mind and body" was pushing him toward insanity. He finally resigned his commission, prior to the end of the war, because he no longer thought it a duty to serve. By 1885, however, the war of 1864–65 had largely departed from his consciousness. . . . He installed his sword and regimental colors above the mantel in his study. In public addresses he exalted unquestioning faith and obedience to command as the hallmarks of the true soldier. . . . "War, when you are at it, is horrible and dull," he told the Harvard graduating class of 1895. "It is only when time has passed that you see that its message was divine. . . . For high and dangerous action teaches us to believe as right beyond dispute things for which our doubting minds are slow to find words of proof. Out of heroism grows faith in the worth of heroism." (281–282)

Another sort of veterans' community does not seek to valorize their deeds in war or to rewrite the history of the war so as to make their presence there more honorable. These combat veterans attempt to come to terms with their experiences by undertaking the task of rewriting national mythology so that it conforms to the basic tenets of their revised personal myths. Gathering in groups as diverse as Vietnam Veterans Against the War, Vietnam Veterans Against the War (Anti-Imperialist),[8] Veterans for Peace, Vietnam Veterans Foreign Policy Watch, the Smedley Butler Brigade (a group of veterans who attempted to bring food and medical supplies to Nicaragua), and the renegade VFW post in Santa Cruz, California, these men and women work toward changing our conception of the American character. They believe, like writers of trauma literature (which many of them are), that if they can only make us see what they have seen we too will be changed: we too will see as they see.

Those who have experienced trauma see it as connected across history to other atrocities. The strongest image of atrocity is, of course, the Holocaust, and survivors of most other traumas naturally relate their own experiences to that event. In the late sixties and early seventies the comparison was made repeatedly between American soldiers committing atrocities in Vietnam and German soldiers committing atrocities during the Nazi regime. "Most American soldiers in Viet-Nam do not question the orders that lead them to raze villages and wipe out men, women and children for the 'crime' of living in Viet Cong-controlled or infiltrated areas," writes Eric Norden. "To many critics of the war this 'new breed of Americans' bears a disquieting resemblance to an old breed of Germans" (278). Jean-Paul Sartre firmly maintained that the Vietnam War met all of Hitler's criteria: "Hitler killed the Jews because they were Jews. The armed forces of the United States torture and kill men, women, and children in Vietnam merely because they are Vietnamese. Whatever lies or euphemisms the government may think up, the spirit of genocide is in the minds of the soldiers" (547). Satirist Art Hoppe makes the same connection in a cartoon depicting a German psychiatrist counseling his patient—a participant in the My Lai massacre—to repeat three times a day: "I didn't know what was going on. These things happen in war. I was only following orders as a good American. Our soldiers are good American boys. The war is to save the world from Communism. Our leaders were wrong. The unfortunate victims were members of an inferior race" (Opton 441).

Though this comparison may sound shocking today (in light of the rehabilitation of Vietnam veterans, and our current tendency to accept them as victims, rather than executioners) it is worth paying attention to especially since that comparison was frequently made by the GIs themselves:

> They wanted to call us heroes for serving the country. They offer us recognition and honor, even a national monument. Heroes for serving a country that burned down villages and shot anything that moved. Recognition for being the pawns and agents of a ruthless death machine. . . . Should we pin medals on the chests of the guards at Auschwitz! Should there be a cheering ticker-tape parade for the flight crews that dropped atomic death on Hiroshima and Nagasaki or fire-bombed Dresden! Perhaps we should build a monument to the nun-murdering troops of the Salvadoran National Guard or to the National Guard at Kent State. (Vietnam Veterans, "Statement" 1)[9]

Rape victims and incest victims also connect their trauma to the trauma of the Holocaust, as Natalie Shainess clearly illustrates. Even more interesting is the observation that they also connect their sufferings to the same institutional structures which send soldiers to war. A statement from the Arlington jail by 43 women who were arrested at a peace protest while 3,500 others blocked entrances to the Pentagon put forward this analysis: "We came to this action as women and feminists, connecting crimes against us in our daily lives with the world-wide violence of the military machine. . . . We acted because we fear for our own lives and because we oppose the military mentality. . . . We see this military mentality as intimately tied to the oppression and fears we women live with every day—the fear of rape, the oppression of having our reproductive choices taken from us, the coercion of compulsory heterosexuality . . ." (Griffin 133). As Louise Wisechild says, "It is hard to imagine power without thinking of war. . . . It's never been connected to being a woman" (15–16). Male critics, too, sometimes make this comparison: "The masculine game resorts habitually to violence in its battles on the field of sexual politics. It provides psychological support for the military state and is in its turn stimulated by it" (Kokopeli and Lakey 1).

The structures that generate atrocities in each of these cases are perceived as interconnected; each can serve as an analogy for the other. This is not because each situation is equivalent but because the result—trauma on a massive scale—is the same. Dworkin draws this parallel most strongly:

> In the normal but hidden world of everyday, regular sexual exploitation of women as inferiors, the dirty women are sadistically abused because sex itself is used sadistically; intercourse becomes a form of explicit sadism against women. In the heinous, abnormal world of prison and concentration camps, dirt, death and sadism go wild, there being no limits on what men do to women; yet the elements of sadism, so extreme, so incomprehensible we insist with bland and committed innocence, are not really unrecognizable. They mimic with stunning cogency the norms of disparagement and cruelty that constitute fucking male-to-female. The intensely cruel and ugly acts are not genuinely alien from ordinary practices and meanings. (189)

The effect of trauma on a community of victims and potential victims is profound; it is a force that acts to drastically revise personal and communal myths. The truth of this assertion can be seen in even a cursory examination of any of the following: the literary and oral tradition of Jewish culture, American women's literature and tradition, the underground literature and whispered tales of Soviet citizenry under Stalin, and Japanese literature after World War II. These myths are generated to explain the infliction of suffering and reflect the tense atmosphere of a society where violence might be inflicted on any member of the community at any time. Frequently the community of victims is, however, on the margins of the greater community, and the presence of institutionally supported atrocity in marginal communities has only minor effect on national myths. National myths are unaffected by the exposure of these atrocities because the pain of marginal people is not *American* pain; the American character is male, white, able-bodied, and over twenty-one (and not a Vietnam combat veteran). National myth does not have to encompass atrocities against marginal communities, it can simply ignore them.

To those outside of the marginal, traumatized community trauma is a curiosity, or it is indicative of a problem, or it is a useful example. At this point I would like to introduce a new term—Other People's Trauma (OPT). Much pleasanter than trauma of your own (in the same way that other people's money is more enjoyable to risk when you are looking for that big payoff), OPT is, by definition, always metaphoric. It is never a personally shattering experience. There are several rhetorical strategies that utilize OPT, appropriating the writings of trauma survivors to support particular versions of national myth. OPT can easily serve as a tool in the hands of those who are interested in shaping public perceptions about particular issues.

Appropriation of OPT can take several forms: the Object Lesson (if you let the Communists take over, then we'll all wind up in gulags); the Great Rationalization (we restrict your civil liberties to prevent the Communists from taking over and putting you all in Gulags); the Punishment for Transgression of Social Rules Supporting the Current Power Structure (if you hadn't gone walking around by yourself at night, then you would never have gotten raped); and the Proof Positive of the Superiority of Our System (because we are a democratic society we could never have gulags in this country). All of these examples use OPT as an implicit warning; they do not deal with the conditions that produce trauma or the effects of trauma on an individual—the two important foci in trauma literature.

It should by now be obvious that an author's status as trauma survivor has a profound effect on both the motivation to write and the actual story told. The differences in intent and in content of trauma literature and literature of Other People's Trauma should be quite clear.

The imperative of trauma critics is to define their position as outside readers and to recognize that however empathetic, the trauma of the author becomes merely metaphor. The shattering of individual myth and the transformation of the protagonist cannot happen to the reader; it can only be described and studied from without. Crucial, then, is the ability to consider the author as survivor, to bring to bear the tools of sociology, psychology, and psychiatry—an understanding of *trauma*—to the task of reading the literature of survivors. If we begin here we can start to examine the process of writing as an act of personal revision and then ask the important questions: What fundamental changes in the author's personal myths have occurred? How do these affect the author's conception of national myth? How is this public revision of personal myth perceived or utilized outside of the marginal community which supports it? How does it change the national myth? This last question suggests a whole new field of critical inquiry: the study of the response of the outside reader. When trauma is written as text it transcends the bounds of the personal, becoming metaphor; yet, when such texts are read they are once again personalized, assimilated somehow by the reader. How do readers interact with texts of trauma? How are these texts revised and adapted so that we can incorporate them into personal myth systems that do not include traumatic experience? These questions, and others like them, should point students of Vietnam War literature in a new direction.

NOTES

1. The words 'real' and 'reality' are extremely troublesome in this context. I assume that a certain set of events actually took place, which was the war, and that these events are the "real" ones. But it seems important to point out that acknowledging the existence of the reality of the Vietnam War is not the same thing as claiming to know what really happened.

2. See, for example, Veterans Administration, *Selected Bibliography*.

3. The Winter Soldier investigations were convened in Detroit on January 31 and February 1 and 2, 1971, by Vietnam Veterans Against the War to pro-

vide a forum for soldiers who wanted to testify to having committed or witnessed war crimes in Vietnam.

4. French feminists such as Monique Wittig, Luce Irigary, and Hélène Cixous and American feminists such as Elizabeth Meese, Alice Jardine, and Barbara Johnson have dealt with the subject.

5. "I encountered among Hiroshima survivors a frequent sense of being 'as-if dead', or what I called an 'identity of the dead', which took the following inner sequence: I almost died; I should have died; I did die or at least am not really alive; or if I am alive, it is impure of me to be so and anything I do which affirms life is also impure and an insult to the dead, who alone are pure. An expression of this sense of themselves can be found in the life-style of many survivors, one of marked constriction and self-abnegation, based upon the feeling that any show of vitality is in some way inappropriate for them, not inwardly permissible. They retain a sense of infinite culpability, and even, ironically enough, of guilt and responsibility for the catastrophe itself, despite being victims rather than perpetrators of that catastrophe" (Lifton, *Boundaries* 13).

6. Most of the literature of the Holocaust actually appeared almost twenty years after the end of the war (see Ezrahi 67–68). A quick check of the publication dates of most World War I, World War II, and Vietnam War literature will support the claim of the lapse of over a decade before the publication of most works. I have not yet come across a piece of rape or incest literature that was not published at least ten years after the event.

7. A number of Jews who had not, before their persecution, identified very strongly with the Jewish community changed their minds in the camps or after. Being persecuted as a Jew had the effect of making some victims see themselves for the first time as belonging to the Jewish community. Becoming what one is named is a common coping mechanism for those who are persecuted and abused; bearing unavoidable punishment is simpler if one thinks that somehow one deserves it.

8. A radical antiwar veterans group composed of some of the members of Vietnam Veterans Against the War after that organization splintered in the 1970s, they feel that American imperialism is responsible for the prosecution of unjust wars against forces of national liberation throughout the world.

9. For another comparison of American soldiers in Vietnam to Nazi soldiers, see Robert Jay Lifton's "Beyond Atrocity" in *Crimes of War*.

WORKS CITED

Bass, Ellen. Introduction. *I Never Told Anyone: Writings by Women Survivors of Child Sexual Abuse.* Ed. Ellen Bass and Louise Thornton. New York: Harper, 1983.

Beaudry, Micheline. *Battered Women.* Trans. Lorne Huston and Margaret Heap. Montreal: Black Rose, 1985.

Beidler, Philip D. *American Literature and the Experience of Vietnam.* Athens: University of Georgia Press, 1982.

Bourne, Peter G. "From Boot Camp to My Lai." *Crimes of War: A Legal, Political-Documentary, and Psychological Inquiry into the Responsibility of Leaders, Citizens, and Soldiers for Criminal Acts in War.* Ed. Richard A. Falk, Gabriel Kolko, and Robert Jay Lifton. New York: Random, 1971.

Des Pres, Terrance. *The Survivor: An Anatomy of Life in the Death Camps.* New York: Oxford University Press, 1976.

Dworkin, Andrea. *Intercourse.* New York: Free Press, 1987.

Ezrahi, Sidra DeKoven. *By Words Alone: The Holocaust in Literature.* Chicago: University of Chicago Press, 1980.

Goleman, Daniel. *Vital Lies, Simple Truths: The Psychology of Self-Deception and Shared Illusions.* New York: Simon, 1985.

Griffin, Susan. *Race: The Politics of Consciousness.* 3d ed. rev. San Francisco: Harper, 1986.

Heinemann, Larry. *Close Quarters.* New York: Farrar, 1977.

Hellmann, John. *American Myth and the Legacy of Vietnam.* New York: Columbia University Press, 1986.

Kerry, John, and Vietnam Veterans Against the War. *The New Soldier.* Ed. David Thorne and George Butler. New York: Macmillan, 1971.

Kokopeli, Bruce, and George Lakey. "Masculinity and Violence." *Reweaving the Web of Life: Feminism and Nonviolence.* Ed. Pam McAllister. Philadelphia: New Society, 1982.

Langer, Lawrence L. *Versions of Survival: The Holocaust and the Human Spirit.* Albany: State University of New York Press, 1982.

Leed, Eric J. *No Man's Land: Combat and Identity in World War I.* Cambridge, England: Cambridge University Press, 1979.

Lifton, Robert Jay. "Beyond Atrocity." In *Crimes of War.*

———. *Boundaries.* New York: Random, 1969.

———. *History and Human Survival.* New York: Random, 1970.

———. "Victims and Executioners." In *Crimes of War.*

Linderman, Gerald F. *Embattled Courage: The Experience of Combat in the American Civil War.* New York: Free Press, 1987.

Myers, Thomas. *Walking Point: American Narratives of Vietnam.* New York: Oxford University Press, 1988.

Norden, Eric. "American Atrocities in Vietnam." In *Crimes of War.*

Opton, Edward M., and Robert Duckles. "It Didn't Happen and Besides, They Deserved It." In *Crimes of War.*

Sartre, Jean-Paul, "On Genocide." In *Crimes of War.*

Shainess, Natalie. Foreword. *The Family Secret: A Personal Account of Incest.* Eleanore Hill. 1985. New York: Laurel-Dell, 1987.

Shatan, Chaim. Afterword. *The Vietnam Veterans Redefined: Fact and Fiction.* Ed. Ghislaine Boulanger and Charles Kadushin. Hillsdale, N.J.: L. Erlbaum, 1986.

Thornton, Louise. Preface. In *I Never Told Anyone.*

Veterans Administration. *Selected Bibliography 2: Post Traumatic Stress Disorder with Special Attention to Vietnam Veterans.* Revision 25. Phoenix: VA Medical Center, January 16, 1986.

Vietnam Veterans Against the War. *The Winter Soldier Investigation: An Inquiry into American War Crimes.* Boston: Beacon, 1972.

Vietnam Veterans Against the War (Anti-Imperialist). "Statement from Vietnam Era Veterans." *About Face* (Nov. 1982): 1.

Wiesel, Elie. "Why I Write." *Confronting the Holocaust: The Impact of Elie Wiesel.* Ed. Alvin H. Rosenfeld and Irving Greenberg. Bloomington: Indiana University Press, 1978.

Wilson, James C. *Vietnam in Prose and Film.* Jefferson, N.C.: McFarland, 1982.

Wisechild, Louise. *The Obsidian Mirror: An Adult Healing from Incest.* Seattle: Seal, 1988.

1580